Writing Program Administration

Journal of the
Council of Writing Program Administrators

Managing Editor
Alice Horning .... Oakland University

Co-Editors
Debra Frank Dew .... University of Colorado at Colorado Springs
Glenn Blalock .... Our Lady of the Lake College

Assistant Editors
Gregory Giberson .... Oakland University
Jim Nugent .... Oakland University
Lori Ostergaard .... Oakland University

Book Review Editor
Edward M. White .... University of Arizona

Editorial Assistants
Donna Scheidt ....University of Michigan
Jason Carabelli .... Oakland University

Editorial Board
Anne Beaufort ....University of Washington, Tacoma
Russel K. Durst ....University of Cincinnati
Norbert Elliot .... New Jersey Institute of Technology
Patricia Freitag Ericsson .... Washington State University
Gregory R. Glau .... Northern Arizona University
Eli Goldblatt.. Temple University
Richard H. Haswell................. Texas A & M University, Corpus Christi
Brian Huot.. Kent State University
Asao B. Inoue................................... California State University, Fresno
Paul Kei Matsuda ....Arizona State University
Rita Malenczyk ....Eastern Connecticut University
Mark McBeth .... John Jay College of Criminal Justice / CUNY
Peggy O'Neill..................................... Loyola University, Maryland
Charles Paine .... University of New Mexico
E. Shelley Reid.. George Mason University
Rochelle (Shelley) Rodrigo .... Mesa Community College
Duane Roen...Arizona State University
Shirley K Rose..Arizona State University
Ellen Schendel ....Grand Valley State University
Martha A. Townsend...University of Missouri
Elizabeth Vander Lei .... Calvin College
Scott Warnock .... Drexel University

WPA: Writing Program Administration is published twice per year—fall/
winter and spring—by the Council of Writing Program Administrators.

Council of Writing Program Administrators

Executive Board

The Council of Writing Program Administrators is a national association of college and university faculty who serve or have served as directors of first-year composition or writing programs, coordinators of writing centers and writing workshops, chairpersons and members of writing-program-related committees, or in similar administrative capacities. The Council of Writing Program Administrators is an affiliate of the Association of American Colleges and the Modern Language Association.

President
Linda Adler-Kassner .... University of California, Santa Barbara

Vice President
Duane Roen .... Arizona State University

Secretary
Keith Rhodes .... Grand Valley State University

Treasurer
Charles Lowe .... Grand Valley State University

Past President
Joe Janangelo .... Loyola University (Chicago)

Executive Committee
Darsie Bowden .... DePaul University
Doug Downs .... Montana State University
Eileen Ferretti .... Kingsborough Community College
Brian Huot .... Kent State University
Melissa Ianetta .... University of Delaware
Barbara Lutz .... University of Delaware
Chuck Paine .... University of New Mexico
E. Shelley Reid .... George Mason University
Susan Thomas .... University of Sydney

Journal Editors
Alice Horning .... Oakland University
Debra Frank Dew .... University of Colorado at Colorado Springs
Glenn Blalock .... Our Lady of the Lake College

Web Developer
Charles Lowe .... Grand Valley State University

Consultant Evaluator Service Director
Charles Schuster .... University of Wisconsin-Milwaukee

Authors' Guide

WPA: Writing Program Administration publishes articles and essays concerning the organization, administration, practices, and aims of college and university writing programs. Possible topics include

- Writing Faculty Education, Training, and Professional Development
- Writing Program Creation and Design
- The Development of Rhetoric and Writing Curricula
- Writing Assessment within Programmatic Contexts
- Advocacy and Institutional Critique and Change
- Writing Programs and Their Extra-Institutional Relationships with Writing's Publics
- Technology and the Delivery of Writing Instruction within Programmatic Contexts
- WPA and Writing Program Histories and Contexts
- WAC / ECAC / WID and Their Intersections with Writing Programs
- The Theory and Philosophy of Writing Program Administration
- Issues of Professional Advancement and WPA Work
- Projects that Enhance WPA Work with Diverse Stakeholders

This list is meant to be suggestive, not exhaustive, but contributions must be appropriate to the interests and concerns of those who administer writing programs. The editors welcome empirical research (quantitative as well as qualitative), historical research, and theoretical, essayistic, or reflective pieces.

Submission Guidelines

Submissions should be approximately 4,000–7,000 words, though occasionally longer articles will be accepted if the subject warrants.

For complete submission guidelines, please see the information at the journal's website <http://wpacouncil.org/info-for-authors>. Editors will acknowledge receipt of articles.

Reviews

WPA publishes reviews of books related to writing programs and their administration. Publishers are invited to send appropriate professional books to Ed White, 3045 W. Brenda Loop, Flagstaff, AZ 86001, who assigns reviews.

Announcements and Calls

Relevant announcements and calls for papers will be published as space permits. Announcements should not exceed 500 words, and calls for proposals/participation should not exceed 1,000 words. Please include contact information and/or links for further information. Submission deadlines in calls should be no sooner than January 1 for the fall/winter issue and June 1 for the spring issue. Please e-mail your calls and announcements to journal@wpacouncil.org and include the text in both the body of the message and as an MS Word or RTF attachment.

Addresses

Address articles and editorial correspondence to Alice Horning, Editor, WPA, Department of Writing and Rhetoric, 378 O'Dowd Hall, Oakland University, Rochester, MI 48309. Email: journal@wpacouncil.org. Address advertising and production questions to journal@wpacouncil.org. Address book reviews to Ed White, emwhite@u.arizona.edu.

Subscriptions

WPA: Writing Program Administration is published twice per year—fall/winter and spring—by the Council of Writing Program Administrators.

Members of the Council of Writing Program Administrators receive subscription to the journal as a part of their membership. Join here: <http://wpacouncil.org/join-renew>. Active members have access to online versions of current and past issues through the WPA website: <http://wpacouncil.org/journalarchives>. Also see information about Library Subscriptions: <http://wpacouncil.org/library-membership>.

Writing Program Administration

Journal of the
Council of Writing Program Administrators
Volume 34.2 (Spring 2011)

Contents

Review Essays

From the Editors

Although we do not intentionally assemble issues with a particular theme or focus in (our collective) mind, the four articles and three Symposium responses in this issue seem to share a common focus. They might be seen as diverse responses to the question of "Why and how and with whom do we create, maintain, sustain productive relationships?"

As journal editors, we grapple with this question about relationships regularly, often unconsciously: about the relationship(s) among members of our editorial team, between us and the many authors who submit their work to the journal, between the journal and its readers, between the journal and CWPA, between the journal and our "profession." Unlike active WPAs and their local colleagues and connections, though, journal editors don't experience the daily interactions with all those with whom the journal is in relation. We hope readers know that our "door" is open. We welcome comments, questions, and / or conversations that might help us all—editors and contributors—make this journal and our collective work more meaningful and useful.

ARTICLES IN THIS ISSUE

In "Addressing Instructor Ambivalence about Peer Review and Self-Assessment," Pamela Bedore and Brian O'Sullivan report on a small study of ways in which WPAs can help instructors to use these approaches. They conclude that WPAs who believe in collaborative assessment models of writing feedback should engage instructors in ongoing conversations about peer-review and self-assessment that include discussions of their own experiences as students giving and receiving feedback to peers and assessing their own writing. They offer nine key themes arising from their data that might be points of focus for such discussions.

In "Troubling the Boundaries: (De)Constructing WPA Identities at the Intersections of Race and Gender," Collin Craig and Staci Maree Perryman-Clark theorize their professional experiences as Research Assistants to their local WPA and as African American WPAs entering the racialized and gendered spaces of the institution and the CWPA conference.

Brad Peters shares the results of an exploratory, multi-year project in "Lessons about Writing to Learn from a University-High School Partnership." One result "suggests that such partnerships can provide the training and follow-up necessary for cross-curricular faculty to produce statistically significant student learning outcomes through the implementation of writing to learn." Another result, perhaps as important, "suggests the efficacy of specific practices in writing to learn, even in difficult learning environments, contributing to a more 'pedagogically useful theory' for implementing writing to learn in secondary and post-secondary settings."

In "Program Transitions and TA Training: What TAs Say Makes the Difference," Amy Rupiper Taggart and Margaret Lowry offer a cross-institutional, TA survey assessment study with the dual aims of mediating local WPA transitions and improving the graduate TA practicum.

Responses to the "Symposium on Fostering Teacher Quality"

Three respondents challenge us to extend and emphasize further the challenging themes presented in the Symposium.

Sue Doe believes the essays ask us to "commit to professionalism," but more important, recognize "what can happen when we take hold of the potential of our writing programs in their current forms[,] embrac[ing] what is over some eidolon of what was or what ought to be."

Claire Lamonica expands the purpose of the Symposium essay, calling for a "culture of professionalism in our work to improve teacher quality and improve student learning, . . . creating a community of caring professionals who share high standards for themselves and their students', work collaboratively to help each other reach those standards, and continually evaluate and re-evaluate their own progress as developing professionals in light of those standards."

Mike Palmquist foregrounds "our increasing reliance on instructors who work in contingent positions," and emphasizes that our "[p]rofessional development initiatives must begin with an understanding of the places in which so many members of our discipline find themselves and of the places where we hope to go, together, as a profession."

Book Reviews

In "What is Real College Writing? Let the Disagreement Never End," Peter Elbow follows his classic book *What is English?* with his review essay on the first and second editions of *What is College-Level Writing?* (2006, 2010).

While he finds much to praise in these books, he focuses on his frustration with levels and standards: "My goal is real excellence . . . . We seldom get it unless some standards or criteria are not met. Really excellent writing often has some genuine faults or problems." Thus he argues for "the deep tradition of permeability or even chaotic non-standards across US higher education."

"Reinventing Writing Assessment: How the Conversation is Shifting" is William Condon's encyclopedic review essay about—but not entirely restricted to—twelve new books on writing assessment. Condon sees the central thread of this work as not only "the entry of the writing classroom into the writing assessment arena, but . . . the engagement of writing assessment within the writing classroom." This overview is essential reading for every WPA encountering assessment issues, which is to say, for every WPA.

SPECIAL FEATURE

Anticipating this summer's CWPA Conference in Baton Rouge, Louisiana, Shirley Rose interviewed Irv Peckham and Jim McDonald, the two local hosts of the conference. She shares those conversations in "Crabgrass and Gumbo: Interviews with 2011 WPA Conference Local Hosts about the Place of Writing Programs at their Home Institutions," inviting readers (and conference attendees) to learn more about the unique culture and context of southeastern Louisiana and how it affects two local writing programs.

Extending an invitation to join the

Council of

Writing Program Administrators

The Council of Writing Program Administrators offers a national network of scholarship and support for leaders of college and university writing programs.

Membership benefits include the following:

- A subscription to *WPA: Writing Program Administration*, a semi-annual refereed journal
- Invitations to the annual WPA Summer Workshops and Conferences
- Invitations to submit papers for sessions that WPA sponsors at MLA and CCCC
- Participation in the WPA Research Grant Program, which distributes several awards, ranging from $1000 to $2000
- Invitations to the annual WPA breakfast at CCCC and the annual WPA party at MLA
- Information about the WPA Consultant-Evaluator program

ANNUAL DUES
Members: $30
Graduate Students: $10
Libraries: $40

TO JOIN
Visit us online at http://wpacouncil.org/membership or send your name, address, email address, institutional affiliation, and dues to

Charlie Lowe, WPA Treasurer
341 Lake Ontario Hall
Grand Valley State University
Allendale, MI 49401
lowech@gvsu.edu

Addressing Instructor Ambivalence about Peer Review and Self-Assessment

Pamela Bedore and Brian O'Sullivan

ABSTRACT

This paper reports on survey and focus group data about instructor perceptions of peer review and self-assessment in first-year writing classrooms. We find that the concerns of graduate-student instructors, which have sometimes been characterized as resistance, might more productively be understood as thoughtful and considered ambivalence. Our participants acknowledge that peer review and self-assessment promote a democratic classroom and a genuine attention to audience, but they also reasonably characterize these practices as difficult to teach as well as challenging to their authority as new instructors. We conclude that WPAs who believe in collaborative assessment models of writing feedback, as we do, should engage instructors in ongoing conversations about peer-review and self-assessment that include discussions of their own experiences as students giving and receiving feedback to peers and assessing their own writing. We provide several suggestions for making such faculty development conversations effective.

> I think we all struggle. This is something we talk about around the water cooler or the coffee machine at the Writing Center. Which is, how do we teach peer review? How do we model it? How do we teach it? Not just, why it's useful, but how to actually do it. I mean, we've had so much trouble finding an effective way to teach it.
>
> —(Graduate-Student Writing Instructor)

INTRODUCTION

"Around the water cooler or the coffee machine," much of the talk about peer review and self-assessment at our writing program seemed tinged, if not saturated, with frustration. We heard about the peer who could only say "great job!," the student who felt "dissed" by fellow students, and the writer who self-castigated instead of self-critiquing. These disaffected figures seemed to be to a new generation what the bespectacled, red-pen-wielding instructor and enforcer of grammatical correctness was to the composition-ists of the sixties and seventies. As junior writing program administrators at a research-extensive university, and members (more or less) of our instruc-tors' generation, we sympathized with them—but we also wondered why there seemed to be such a disparity between their view and that of the com-position and rhetoric literature and lore that informed our program.

Like many first-year writing programs, ours had a deep commitment to peer review and self-assessment. We followed in the tradition of the Uni-versity of Minnesota Writing Workshops, where heavy stress was placed on modeling the professional peer review process. We also followed the same collaborative principles in assessing our program as a whole that we fol-lowed in assessing and developing student writing, so we sought feedback from the undergraduate students in the first-year writing class as well as the graduate-student instructors teaching the class. Our preliminary stud-ies—broadly distributed surveys—suggested that instructor concerns about peer review and self-assessment might run deeper than doubts harbored by students. We thus dug more deeply into instructor attitudes on teach-ing collaborative assessment by conducting focus groups of instructors and interviews of the program director and the Instructor Training Coordina-tors (ITCs) responsible for their pedagogical training.

This paper employs our findings about instructor attitudes towards collaborative assessment to argue that WPAs must more actively engage instructors of first-year writing in honestly expressing and addressing their own attitudes towards peer review and self-assessment. Our instructors and ITCs show an active and thoughtful ambivalence that results in part from an underestimation of the degree to which students and/or other instructors value collaborative assessment as a goal, and in part from legitimate con-cerns about the viability of these teaching practices. Finally, we provide dis-cussion of nine themes that can be productively deployed in faculty devel-opment to discuss instructor ambivalence about collaborative assessment.

This article is not about whether first-year writing programs should or should not utilize peer review and self-assessment. We assume that the learning goals of most such programs include the abilities to critique one's own writing productively as well as that of others. Whether we teach cri-tique of others' writing through an activity called "peer review" or though "collaborative writing," "writing groups," "workshops," or other methods, we ask students to review each other's work, and whether we call critiquing one's own writing "self-assessment," "reflective writing," an exercise in "self-efficacy," or simply an aspect of revision, we surely want students to do it. The authors, and in general their participants, do not doubt the necessity of these goals or activities. But we do believe that instructors' doubts about peer review as it is actually practiced in many classrooms are serious and worthy of careful consideration and dialogue.

Engaging these doubts must begin by teasing apart and defining peer review and self-assessment. In the program in which both of us worked, peer review and self-assessment, along with instructor feedback, were closely linked in what we came to think of as "collaborative assessment." We liked—and still like—this collaborative assessment model and the ways in which it embodied give and take between writers and readers. Yet our results suggest that instructors' concerns sometimes result from a hazy view of the distinctions between the responsibilities of a peer reviewer and those of a self-critical writer. Seemingly opposite but deeply similar problems of definition may face programs that teach peer review and self-assessment separately and do not link them to instructor feedback; students in such programs may not learn to define the roles of writer and different kinds of readers in relation to each other.

LITERATURE REVIEW

Collaborative assessment is based on the principle that dialogue produces better understanding and evaluation than a single perspective. Much of the literature on peer review and self-assessment values these practices for their potential to remove the instructor from the position of sole authority on student writing, an element our instructors warmly embraced in discussing their teaching philosophies. Since the 1960's, peer review and self-assessment have been major elements in efforts to foster "writing without teachers" (Elbow), to displace "teacher talk" and the morbidly ossified academic discourse dubbed "Engfish" (Moffett), and to introduce students to the "conversation of mankind" (Bruffee). Increasingly, theorists have argued for giving students a more substantial, consequential voice in writing assessment (see, for example, White, Huot and Inoue).

On the other hand, peer response has been critiqued by those who value maintaining the instructor's centrality. "A teacher's definition of 'better writers,'" as Brooke, Mirtz and Evans note, determines the relative importance of student and instructor feedback in meeting course goals. David Bartholomae, they observe, argues against peer response because he believes the function of composition is to make writers "better" by leading them towards greater mastery of the conventions of academic communities, and peers who are equally deficient in knowledge of these conventions cannot lead each other towards such a goal. For Brooke, Mirtz and Evans, on the other hand, "to be better writers means…to understand the ways in which writing can be useful in many areas of one's life, as well as to have experiences which adapt writing to any of those uses" (9). For these goals, small groups and peer response seem indispensable; they act as "invitations to a writer's life," allowing students to experience authentic communication with readers (12).

Constructions of students' individuality have concerned some scholars examining aspects of collaborative assessment. For instance, Candace Spigelman studies student responses to show how peer review in writing groups uncomfortably conflicts with the ideology of individual ownership, even though it is ultimately productive in challenging students to recognize the social dimension of writing. Similarly, Susan Latta and Janice Lauer ask whether the "selves" under review in formal self-assessment exercises may find themselves subjected to scrutiny that limits their expressive freedom and heightens their writing apprehension. Additionally, Peggy O'Neill argues that self-assessment, when required but not dialogically engaged by peers and the instructor, degenerates into what Michel Foucault would describe as "ritualistic discourse"—a rote confession, invoked as part of a regimen of evaluation, classification and discipline—not as an organic part of revision and learning. Consequently, O'Neill agrees with Glenda Conway that "required reflection is ethical only if it exists as an ongoing component of a course and if the teacher of that course openly discusses his or her reactions to reflections with students" (Conway 92). All these compositionists are concerned with the subjectivity of the student; none fully addresses the question of whether collaborative assessment undermines or conceals a teacher's authority—a very real question for many of the graduate-student instructors with whom we worked.

These concerns also resonate in Jane Bowerman Smith and Kathleen Blake Yancey's collection of essays, which attends to self-assessment on the part of both students and instructors. Thomas Hilgers, Edna Hussey and Monica Stitt-Bergh note that "teachers embrace the theoretical promise of self-assessment, although few devote much time to its practice" (9), marking a need to return attention to the now decentered instructor. While Hilgers et. al, along with several other authors in the collection, focus on students' assessments of their own writing, others focus on instructors' self-assessment of pedagogy. Sandra Mano, for example, recounts the story of her own need for self-assessment in the process of engaging with, and ultimately transforming, a culture of teaching assistants around pedagogical practices. Mano reports difficulty in compelling new graduate-student composition instructors to adopt a process-based collaborative pedagogy, including peer review; new instructors questioned her authority and expertise and clung to their own prejudices about how to teach. Mano's own self-assessment alters her approach to teaching the pedagogy of collaborative assessment when she realizes that student concerns about collaborative assessment must be met with a willingness to "share power with the graduate students" (164).

We agree with Mano that self-assessment is a critical element of pedagogical transformation, and in our study we invited instructors as well as students to collaborate in the program's self-assessment. Any study that draws on voices of students, instructors and administrators to assess an aspect of a writing program will inevitably be a study *in* collaborative assessment; by making it also a study *of* collaborative assessment in the classroom, we thematize the problem of collaboration rather than allowing it to be marginalized.

Our attention to instructor attitudes about collaborative assessment extends recent work in the field. In their study on attitudes towards peer review, for example, Charlotte Brammer and Mary Rees administered companion surveys asking faculty about their use of peer review in the classroom, and asking students about its effectiveness and their voluntary use of the practice outside the classroom. Although they report briefly on faculty responses, most of Brammer and Rees's analysis focuses on student attitudes as they make recommendations for ways in which faculty can provide more effective contexts for successful peer review. They acknowledge the importance of instructor attitudes, to be sure: "Students seem to take their cues from instructors. If we stress the importance of peer review, our students are more likely to do so, but if we just go through the motions, perhaps passing out recycled handouts, our students will pick up on our lack of dedication and act accordingly" (81). Their productive analysis of student attitudes sets the stage for an equally productive analysis of instructor attitudes. How can we explain the phenomenon of instructors just going through the motions? Why might instructors lack dedication to peer review? In Lynne Belcher's informal survey of 31 writing instructors regarding their practices and experiences with peer review, she provides more questions than she answers. Belcher finds that although 30 of her 31 respondents recommend peer review as a teaching strategy for new instructors, their responses to individual questions about specific aspects of teaching peer review were far less positive.

Methods

We conducted our study at a research-extensive university in which the first-year writing course was the only required course for all undergraduates. The course was supervised by a free-standing writing program and taught almost exclusively by graduate students, most from English and some from other departments. Instructors designed individual course topics and syllabi within broad program requirements that included instructor feedback in dialogue with peer review and self-assessment. Collaborative assessment was incorporated into all components of training, including the five-credit writing pedagogy course in the summer before instructors began teaching, the two-credit pedagogy workshop (in the form of small mentoring groups) in their first year of teaching, and several brown-bag pedagogy meetings open to all instructors. Instructors were free to choose from among existing models of peer review and self-assessment or to design their own.

In a survey, students rated self-assessment 2nd and peer review 14th out of fifteen writing skills targeted by the first-year writing course (see Appendix 1 for the relevant portion of the student survey). In terms of the value of the skills to their future writing, students ranked self-assessment 5th and peer review 15th. Since the program philosophy explicitly linked peer review and self-assessment, we found the disjunct in how students saw the two skills surprising, especially when we considered that the program had been emphasizing peer review longer than self-assessment. We had an anecdotal sense that not all instructors felt comfortable teaching these elements of writing, so we designed a companion survey that asked instructors to rank their ability to teach the fifteen skills and their perception of the value of these skills in students' future writing (see Appendix 2 for instructor survey). In ranking their own ability to teach the fifteen target skills, instructors ranked self-assessment 14th and peer review 15th. In terms of the value of the skills to students' future writing, instructors ranked self-assessment 9th and peer review 15th. In trying to understand why peer review was ranked so low across constituencies while self-assessment was ranked rather high by students but very low by instructors, we turned to student focus groups, where we heard relatively positive feedback about both peer review and self-assessment. We recognize, of course, that student responses may lack reliability, especially when students are speaking in person with a focus group leader who may be perceived as an authority figure. Nonetheless, it seems telling that in both student focus groups, students included peer review in response to the opening question, "What was most helpful about your writing class?" It seemed that students viewed self-assessment and, to a degree, peer review more positively than their instructors did, and we wanted to understand why.

We used selected quotations from student focus groups in designing focus group questions for instructors. The resulting questions were designed to elicit more detailed responses about collaborative assessment (see Appendix 3 for focus group questions). These focus groups were moderated by psychology graduate students with focus group experience who were not writing instructors but who worked at the Writing Center (as did some of the focus group participants). We also conducted interviews of the faculty member who directed the Writing Program and three Instructor Training Coordinators (ITCs) who had been advanced graduate students when they served in that role, although one was a professor at another institution by the time we interviewed her (see Appendix 4 for ITC interview questions). All study instruments had IRB approval, and participant names have been changed to preserve anonymity.

This paper provides a qualitative analysis of the focus groups and interviews, discussing the attitudes of a small number of people (nine participants in total: five instructors, three ITCs and one program director). We chose this approach over broader assessment tools like surveys because, like Eubanks and Abbott, we believe that focus groups allow us to "bridge the gap between potentially superficial quantitative methods and potentially subjective naturalistic methods" (33). Our results, based on intensive study of the comments of this small group of instructors and administrators, are deeper than they are wide, but from our perspectives as WPAs now working at different institutions, we are confident that the ambivalence reflected by this small group of participants at a single institution is hardly unique. After all, this institution has a deep commitment to collaborative assessment; this study itself results from that commitment. Doubts reflected within this program might be even more pronounced in other institutional contexts.

We did three separate strands of analysis to better understand our data. In our quantitative coding, we used the utterance as the basic unit. For the focus groups, all utterances were under 140 words, since participants interrupted each other often. For the interviews, we occasionally broke up the longest monologues (several were over three hundred words) into two or three utterances based on their content in order to count them more accurately. To determine significant utterances, we counted as trivial any utterance asking for clarification such as "could you repeat the question?" and any utterance that didn't specifically address elements of collaborative assessment, such as "I used to be a grant writer." In the focus groups, we also removed utterances that marked only agreement, i.e. comments whose entirety was "yes," "right," "I agree," etc. We found our focus group members to be highly supportive of each other's statements, with 20% of all utterances and 32% of non-trivial utterances marking simple agreement. Although the program director and the graduate-student ITCs were asked the same interview questions, we report on them separately since their responses tell quite different stories, perhaps unsurprisingly given their different institutional positions. We analyzed a total of 743 codeable utterances, 379 from instructors, 311 from ITCs, and 53 from the program director.

In processing the transcripts, the two investigators separately coded all utterances and then met to adjust to a single set of codes. This activity simultaneously allowed us to develop a useful set of robust quantitative data and to more deeply interrogate each of the utterances that had been made; in short, this tedious process made us extremely familiar with our transcripts. We report here on three sets of codes: a relatively simple identification of positive/negative attitudes in our participants, a count of adjectives referring to the attitudes of others, and a more nuanced identification of recurring themes. We coded utterances as "positive" or "negative" when they expressed commitment or skepticism, respectively, about either the process or the results of peer review, self-assessment, or instructor feedback that responded to peer review and self assessment. Thus, we coded as negative utterances such as "I find that students don't really engage with self-assessment" or "peer review always makes me feel bad." We coded statements neutral when they described collaborative assessment practices without value judgments or evaluation; for example, "I put my students in pairs for peer review," or "In my class, peer review is worth 5% of your grade." We coded as mixed those utterances that included both positive and negative attitudes towards collaborative assessment, such as "I think peer review is helpful to students, but it's very hard to teach."

In coding for respondents' own attitudes about peer review and self-assessment, we found that we had to separate their characterizations of the attitudes of others carefully. We found these characterizations interesting in their own right, so we coded for perceptions of undergraduate student attitudes on the part of instructors and ITCs, and of instructor attitudes on the part of ITCs and the program director. As an index of these attitudes, we compiled a list of the adjectives used to describe them. Finally, we identified recurring themes underlying our participants' discussions of peer review and self-assessment, and we coded for mentions of those themes.

RESULTS AND DISCUSSION

Our main finding is a deeply-rooted ambivalence about collaborative assessment in graduate-student instructors and administrators, in contrast to a much more serene commitment to this practice in the full-time faculty member directing the program. While we recognize the limitations of comparing the views of a single person to those of a small group, the director's views are representative of the predilection in favor of collaborative assessment common to many WPAs, as shown in our literature review. The contrast between the program director and the graduate-student ITCs and instructors can be seen quite starkly in Table 1.

Table 1. Positive/Negative Attitudes towards Collaborative Assessment by Group

	Positive	Negative	Mixed	Neutral
Program Director (1 participant, 53 utterances)	54.7% (29)	3.8% (2)	22.6% (12)	18.9% (10)
ITCs (3 participants, 311 utterances)	29.3% (91)	15.1% (47)	38.9% (121)	16.7% (52)
Instructors (5 participants, 379 utterances)	24.5% (93)	28.5% (108)	34.8% (132)	12.1% (46)

Note the significant difference between the director and the graduate students, especially in the fact that over half the program director's comments are based in positive attitudes towards collaborative assessment, while only about one quarter of utterances made by graduate students are positive. There are also differences between the graduate students who serve as administrators in the program and those whose duties are only instruction; most notably, almost 30% of instructor utterances about collaborative assessment reflective negative attitudes, nearly double the percentage of those made by the ITCs charged with teaching them. Note too that over one third of comments by graduate students—instructors and ITCs alike—reflect mixed attitudes. In many cases, the mixed label refers to a participant articulating a benefit of a practice in the same breath as an anxiety about teaching it. For example, in describing as effective her practice of modeling reader comments for her students, Ann immediately added, "I mean, assuming that I do it properly or well."

Separating our data by participant yielded one insight: the one male instructor in our sample had an attitude profile far closer to that of the program director than to his peers (his 25 utterances were 44.0% positive, 16.0% negative, 32.0% mixed and 8.0% neutral). Obviously, we cannot generalize based on such a small sample size, but the impact of gender on (graduate-student or other) instructor attitudes may be ripe for future research.

Further separating our data by element of collaborative assessment discussed (peer review, self-assessment, or both) showed similar attitudes towards each element. However, instructors were more likely to speak of peer review and self-assessment separately, with only 13.1% of their utterances addressing the two practices working in concert, while those responsible for their training more often linked the practices (28.9% of ITC utterances and 34.0% of program director utterances). This suggests that the theoretical links between peer review and self-assessment may not always translate fluidly into classroom practice.

In attempting to better understand the ambivalence of our participants, we counted the number of times they characterized the attitudes of others. Our transcripts revealed characterizations of student attitudes that resonated with conversations we've had with each other and with faculty at this and other institutions. We found 107 instances in which graduate students characterized undergraduate student attitudes, with 70 of these characterizations falling under negative valences, 33 under positive, and 4 under neutral. The most repeated terms are: hated (9 mentions), comfortable (6), resistant (6), disliked (5), critical (4), frustrated (4), not mean (4), and trusting (3).

These characterizations tell an interesting and somewhat contrapuntal story. The majority of terms were mentioned only once or twice, and so we grouped the terms based on their contexts in three categories: general attitudes towards collaborative assessment; dispositions towards collaborative assessment; and attitudes about the outcomes of collaborative assessment. Broad-strokes characterizations of students' general attitudes towards collaborative assessment are quite negative, with students described as "hating" or "disliking" collaborative assessment a total of 14 times, while they were described as "loving," "liking," or "enjoying" it only 4 times.

In terms of student disposition towards collaborative assessment, we find a less significant gap between negative and positive characterizations, although the negative terms chosen seem more charged than the positive ones. The 31 negative characterizations can be broken into three main categories: 11 mentions of aggression (which includes antagonistic, competitive, critical, harsh, mean, and uncivil); 10 of resistance (inattentive, lost, reluctant, resistant, and uninvested); and 10 of fear (anxious, dreading, fearful, hesitant, insecure, intimidated, nervous and touchy). The 25 positive characterizations can be broken into four main categories: 12 of comfort (comfortable, not in danger, safe and trusting); 9 of civility (civil, honest, nice, nonjudgmental, and not mean); 3 of willingness (cooperative, game and open-minded); and 1 of happiness ("students are happy to do peer reviews").

While instructors showed an active ambivalence about the value of collaborative assessment in the face of its difficulty, their perceptions of how students saw the outcomes of peer review and self-assessment were quite negative. Here we get 18 negative characterizations and only 5 positive ones. The negative descriptors can be divided into categories of injury (chastised, demoralized, devastated, exposed, horrified, hurt, sick, traumatized) and fatigue (annoyed, frustrated, hassled, overwhelmed, and "self-assessed-out"). While these negative adjectives tend towards the dramatic, those we categorized as positive represent an emotive range: excited, enlightened, appreciative, not offended, and surprised (that it worked).

The tendency of instructors to see student attitudes as largely negative may well be underestimating student buy-in of collaborative assessment. At this institution, after all, student surveys ranked self-assessment quite highly in terms of effectiveness of instruction and future usefulness, and despite lower survey rankings, peer review came up spontaneously as one of the most effective writing tools in student focus groups.

Similarly, those responsible for training writing instructors may also be underestimating instructor buy-in of collaborative assessment or interpreting ambivalence as resistance. We hope that this article, like Belcher's informal survey of instructors on peer review, will be useful to WPAs in understanding the complexity of attitudes instructors may be bringing to teaching collaborative assessment. The WPAs in our study characterized instructor attitudes more negatively than did the instructors they were working with. Their characterizations of instructor attitudes included 26 mentions of negative attitudes, 9 of positive attitudes, and 3 of neutral attitudes. The most common negative attitudes were resistant (9 mentions), overwhelmed (4), and skeptical (3). Negative attitudes were discussed in fairly strong language, including anxious, fearful, struggling, frustrated and hating. Only two of the positive attitudes were mentioned more than once: embracing and converted. Other positive attitudes were described in fairly weak language: accepting, good-hearted, hard-working, inspired, and surprised that it worked.

Faced with what they saw as resistant and skeptical cadres of new instructors, the director and ITCs were focused more on the problem of persuading these instructors of the benefits of proven pedagogical methods than on collaboratively reevaluating these methods. The positive characterizations suggest something about the trainers' goals; they wanted new instructors to good-naturedly accept the prescribed methods, and to be so pleased with the results that they would even "convert." Gretchen recalls her own "conversion experience" when she first taught in the program: "You know, I'd never worked with this model, and it took me a while. I was skeptical...I tried a couple of times, failed a couple of times. Eventually, one day it was a success, and I said, wow, this is great, this could work, and I was converted at the point." This missionary language was used lightly, not to elevate the ITC above the new instructors, but to identify with them. Helen, the incumbent ITC, recalled an exercise in which these concerns were addressed head-on in training. She and the director asked new instructor trainees to reflect on their best and worst experiences of receiving feedback on their writing. She shared her own most prominent memory of writing feedback, in which a faculty member had told her that, by summarizing too much and not critiquing enough, she was reducing herself to the state of a "mechanical tour guide." Recalling this sensitized her to students' anxieties about receiving each others' feedback—and to instructors' anxieties about requiring such feedback. By having instructors discuss their own experiences, she hoped to help them understand and perhaps transcend the personal origins of their own ambivalence about using collaborative assessment in their classrooms. At the same time, listening to the instructors' stories might inform the program's continuing efforts to reassess and readjust its approach to collaborative assessment.

The instructors' ambivalences are located, we found, in nine key issues, and we provide discussion and analysis of these themes so WPAs can use them as points of departure for discussions with instructors. While three themes were predominantly discussed as negative (difficult, superficial, deception) and three were almost always positive valenced (audience, democracy, transfer), the others were more complexly characterized. Table 2, which shows the number of times each group mentions a specific theme, reveals the depth of ambivalence our participants experienced in thinking about collaborative assessment.

Table 2. Mention of Themes, Ranked[1]

	Director (1 participant, 53 utterances)	ITCs (3 participants, 311 utterances)	Instructors (5 participants, 379 utterances)	Totals (743 utterances)	Rank
Difficult to teach	8	83	105	196 (26.4%)	1
Audience (CA helping students think about audience)	12	40	55	107 (14.4%)	2
Democratic classroom (CA distributing power)	4	38	65	107 (14.4%)	3
Transfer of skills to future writing contexts	3	23	39	65 (8.7%)	4
Superficiality of comments	0	24	36	60 (8.1%)	5
Instructor Negative Experience	1	9	37	47 (6.3%)	6
Instructor Positive Experience	0	7	33	40 (5.4%)	7
Grade	1	17	15	33 (4.4%)	8
Instructor Invisibility	2	14	13	29 (3.9%)	9
Deception (Instructor deceiving students)	0	5	11	16 (2.1%)	10

Theme 1: The Difficulty of Teaching Collaborative Assessment

As the most prevalent theme in our study, mentioned in over one-quarter of all utterances, the difficulty of assessing writing—whether one's own or a peer's—must be central to conversations about teaching collaborative assessment. As revealed by the literature and by studies such as Belcher's, collaborative assessment has many benefits. And yet, it is also very hard to teach, and instructors should be aware of that and should be encouraged to discuss the challenges it poses in the classroom without feeling that they have failed. Our participants identified several specific sites of challenge: the difficulty for students to take on another person's perspective, the overwhelming nature of the material generated by collaborative assessment, its interconnectedness with other portions of the course, and ambiguity about the instructor's role.

In one of the focus groups, Carla articulated a difficulty students often face when receiving peer feedback: "And you have to put yourself now in that person's [the peer's] perspective, kind of outside, and try to understand what they don't understand." Ann agreed, noting that students sometimes find it harder to respond to a good peer review than to produce one: finding a problem is the easy part, but then the writer must ask, "'how do I revise, if I just found out that my paragraphs just don't make sense, how do I actually make it operational?'" The challenge of getting students to respond effectively to feedback is often equally present when students receive instructor feedback, and having students consider multiple readers—the instructor, the peer, and the self, at minimum—we hope prompts student writers to develop broader perspectives on the quality and presentation of their own arguments.

These multiple perspectives were, as ITC Fiona said, both "great" and "overwhelming;" they complicated the writing process even as they enriched it. The only way to resolve the complexities introduced by one round of self-assessment or peer review seemed to be another round of self-assessment and peer review, ad infinitum. "But," Ann said, "I'm not advocating a third synthesis of each paper. And the second peer review. And having peers read everything." To which Carla responded, "But ideally, that's what needs to happens." Ann and Danielle agreed; to teach collaborative assessment well seemed to require teaching it forever.

And it also seemed to require teaching peer review and self-assessment constantly and integrating it into every part of a course. As Carla said, peer review involves "all of those things that have to do with what we think of as reasoning and writing." To which Ann replied, "Gosh, and we throw it in in, like, week two or three." The conversation went on to consider whether peer review should be taught only later in the semester, with instructors coming to the consensus that although peer review may call upon more skills than students have early in the semester, it is also essential in helping them build those skills.

Despite this commitment to collaborative assessment, though, instructors sometimes faced anxiety in defining their own role, as Fiona articulated: "is it [the instructor's role] just to facilitate the comments that come from the writer him or herself and the peer reviewer, or actually serve as an arbiter of who's right and who's wrong?" This challenge is one of the instructor not only defining her own role, but also maintaining a careful balance where student input on their own or each others' writing is respected but also "corrected" as such corrections help students improve writing.

THEME 2: ATTENTION TO AUDIENCE

The most frequently mentioned positive characterization of collaborative assessment, unsurprisingly, celebrated its ability to help students engage with audiences, real and imagined, in their writing. In thinking about audience, one instructor cited Linda Flower's work on moving from writer-based to reader-based prose, a philosophy consonant with that of the program director, who recommended an approach where reader-based prose could be achieved through peer review, self-assessment and instructor feedback all working together to create a complex sense of audience for students. Multiple perspectives, the program director said, "help them see that there are different minds out there, and get to the heart of an important communication principle, which is that each mind is unique, and that our goal as a writer is to do our best to communicate as clearly as possible our text to whatever intended audience we might have."

THEME 3: DEMOCRATIC CLASSROOM

Our participants were attracted to using collaborative assessment to build a democratic classroom, but also saw in it some inherent tensions. For example, in explaining the potential of collaborative assessment to empower students in the classroom, Carla referred to a teaching philosophy she had recently composed: "...writing about how my students always had more interesting things to say than I do, in every class period, and how I think that's the goal of this kind of community that you create, with a student-centered work, that you [the instructor] would start to become less and less the voice, and how there are all these other voices that are equally valid." A confident instructor might be comfortable with admitting that students provide feedback superior to the instructor's, but this position might be difficult for a newer instructor whose authority still feels tenuous. And creating the kind of community Carla espouses, which means deconstructing the hierarchy students expect, is what she sees as "the hardest part of teaching peer review." Danielle agreed with Carla's assessment of both the difficulty and importance of getting students beyond a hierarchical model of writing in which only the instructor's assessment is valued, characterizing the process of getting students "dependent on their own instincts in terms of giving and receiving feedback" as "weaning" students from the instructor. Through this move, students who have completed the class "can still be reflective about their own writing, which is what peer review is supposed to help them do." Although this connection of the student-centered, democratic classroom to the transfer of writing skills into future contexts is clearly discussed as an ideal of collaborative assessment, some anxieties over this approach lingered with instructors, as seen when they mentioned instructor effacement and invisibility.

Theme 4: Transfer of Skills

Collaborative assessment's transferability as a skill that would be useful in other contexts and future writing was mentioned in almost 10% of all utterances, not only as an ideal, but through a variety of examples that might be helpful to other WPAs in training instructors. Helen, one of the ITCs, recounted a successful experience in which a former student from her first-year writing class had asked for feedback on a personal statement for medical school: "And he, at a certain point, without any comment from me, he had sent me his first draft, and he gave me a self-assessment. I was like, 'it works, I did it, oh my gosh!'" Danielle, an instructor, reported that requiring formal self-assessment from her students had transferred into her own writing practice, explaining that she now writes a little self-assessment statement to her advisor every time she submits portions of her dissertation for feedback.

The potential of self-assessment to transfer to contexts outside the classroom was more often mentioned than that of peer review, and two participants specifically mentioned that students were less likely to participate in peer review after the class was over. This view is at odds with the finding in both Brammer and Rees and in our student focus groups that students report that they do participate in voluntary out-of-classroom peer review.

Theme 5: Superficiality of Comments

The concern that students make only superficial comments on peer reviews and self-assessments came up so often we separated it from the broader issue of the difficulty of teaching collaborative assessment, although the two are clearly related. Carla and Danielle particularly worried about the stronger students in their classes, using their own experiences as strong undergraduate writers who were frustrated by superficial peer feedback in explaining that "the better writers don't necessarily get the depth and width they need. They know they'll get it from you, which is why they wait for it" (Danielle). Our participants connected the concern of superficial comments to the larger skill of critical reading, noting that responding to writing requires students to read critically, and might even help them develop that skill.

It seems to us that faculty development workshops with concrete examples of questions that lead students to engage more deeply with the writing they are reviewing—whether their own, a peer's, or a published author's—would be useful in providing instructors tools to combat the challenge of superficial comments. We also wondered if writers were expecting too much direction from their peers. Perhaps instructors were not fully distinguishing the goals of peer review from the goals of instructor feedback and self-assessment. Perhaps the "depth and width" students hoped for from their peers included specific edits that would solve their problems, whereas simply pointing out certain problems might have been a more reasonable expectation.

Theme 6: The Grade

Although we did not ask about grades directly, they were mentioned 32 times by our participants, in a variety of keys. Our participants worried that the importance of the grade had the potential to undermine the value students placed on collaborative assessment, since students would pay more attention to instructor feedback than to their own or their peers' critiques. This problem can be mitigated, some instructors suggested, by grading the collaborative assessments themselves. Although all agreed that such grades should be worth a relatively small percentage of the class grade, discussions about how deeply integrated assessment strategies are with writing development led some instructors who had not previously graded peer reviews and self-assessments—or who had graded them under the rubric of participation—to consider putting a higher numerical value on these activities.

Theme 7: Instructor Effacement

The idea that collaborative assessment allowed an instructor to be "as invisible as possible" (Danielle) in her own classroom came up almost thirty times, and these references were not easily categorized as positive or negative. Members of one focus group expressed agreement at Danielle's approach on peer review days of effacing herself in favor of creating "a day that's just about them and their writing." Much later in the same focus group, Ann imagined peer review and self-assessment working in an idealized way and asked: "So I mean, who needs an instructor at this point?" For these graduate-student instructors, relatively new to teaching, effacing themselves seemed at once philosophically resonant and perhaps all too easy. After all, they were approaching teaching from near the bottom of the academic hierarchy, and they may not have felt they had much power and authority which they could share with students.

THEME 8: INSTRUCTOR DECEPTION

In 2% of utterances, instructors and ITCs admitted that they fear they are deceiving students; this percentage is small, to be sure, but even sixteen mentions of such a delicate matter seem worth exploring. In explaining the principle that all readers are valid in a model of teaching writing that embraces peer review and self-assessment alongside instructor feedback, Gretchen expressed a concern about the potential clash between principles and realities: "I admit that I'm deceiving them. I say, I'm just your reader, but I'm in essence ultimately giving them a grade, so I know that this is difficult to balance." A similar concern came up in one of the focus groups when instructors discussed the ways in which they used student self-assessments as "almost like evaluations all year long." Danielle said "I have to say, it's almost a little selfish as I think about it. But the self-assessments I've had them do so far, I think, are more useful for me necessarily than they are for them...I don't know what they're getting out of it!" It may seem clear to administrators that students actually "get a lot out of it" when instructors closely monitor their progress and respond accordingly. However, to Danielle, this benefit seemed indirect, and thus, requiring self-assessments does not seem truly student-centered; as a result, she admitted, she doesn't always require this practice despite the program mandate to do so. Instructor concerns about "deception" and "selfishness" suggest that their resistance does not merely come from an unwillingness to engage in difficult practices; it grows out of a well-reasoned and considered concern about the trade-offs inherent in creating a collaborative classroom.

THEME 9: INSTRUCTOR EXPERIENCES WITH COLLABORATIVE ASSESSMENT

Our graduate-student instructors knew the collaborative classroom from both sides, and they often referred to their own experiences as students. Participants mentioned positive experiences, especially in considering recent experiences of tough but supportive dissertation groups and the use of self-assessment to communicate more effectively with advisors. In thinking about their undergraduate experiences, though, they focused largely on the negative, and they used quite strong language in doing so. Ann, for example, characterized her undergraduate experiences as "demoralizing" and "traumatic." Carla, in agreement, described undergraduate writing classes in which peer feedback was "either completely useless or incredibly hurtful," saying that she was left feeling that "I'm never going to let anyone see my work ever again as long as I live." Even now, as she neared the end of her doctoral program, Carla said: "I'm just absolutely deathly afraid of anyone reading my work," adding, "except my adviser." For Carla, processing these personal experiences was important as a teacher, since these allowed her to monitor her student reactions. As she said, "I don't want my students to be leaving my class and think they never want anybody seeing their work again. That's absolutely the worst possible scenario."

Our participants also described negative experiences with self-assessment. Ann said she doesn't do self-assessment as a graduate student, "unless you consider harsh, brutal, self-criticism to be self-assessment." Her colleagues did. For Danielle, who was an undergraduate education major, formal self-assessment was a common assignment, and her recollection of the experience was blunt: "I hated writing them as a student, so as a professor, I feel that it's just mean." This observation led to a discussion of resistance summarized by Carla: "Yet even if you try to sell it [self-assessment], it comes through—all the resistance, it comes through."

The resistance to peer review and self-assessment instructors recalled from their undergraduate days was based in different challenges. They tended to see self-assessment as tedious or boring, but characterized peer review as carrying the potential of harm and even "violation" (Ann). Although the two practices have deep philosophical links, such different reactions emphasize the need to also provide instructors with tools to discuss them separately. Our participants' often negative undergraduate reactions to collaborative assessment were mitigated by more positive experiences as graduate students and by seeing both peer review and self-assessment work in the classes they were teaching. It seems likely that discussing such reactions with other instructors—and perhaps even with first-year writing students—would be beneficial in helping instructors move collaborative assessment into their comfort zone.

CONCLUSION

In analyzing our instructor focus groups, we find that instructors, through their own collaborative self-assessment, can productively revise their attitudes towards collaborative self-assessment by recognizing how those attitudes are rooted in their own experiences and prejudgments. We also find that instructors' complex reactions to collaborative assessment—a continuing tension between embracing and resisting the approach—are founded in thoughtful and principled self-assessment and peer review which should be heard out by administrators.

And the communication must be two-way. It is important that WPAs, where possible, share local assessments with their instructors. On a more general level, articles about the theory and practice of collaborative assessment in pedagogy classes might be productively accompanied by studies of student attitudes. For example, Brammer and Rees' study suggests that student attitudes tend toward the mixed rather than the negative. They find, after all, that despite complaints, only 7.3% of their student participants "preferred not to participate in peer review" (77). This correlates with our more anecdotal findings through student focus groups, where they characterized collaborative assessment practices in a number of ways, ranging from "boring" to "very helpful," and where they reported often engaging in informal peer review by asking friends and roommates for feedback on papers.

Rather than pure dislike, we found in instructors true ambivalence: not a lukewarm acceptance or an indifference to these practices, but strong attraction coexisting with strong aversion. On one hand, instructors were drawn to collaborative assessment because it provided a productive context for students to address issues of audience, it promised to shift from them the burden of evaluative power and create a less hierarchical classroom, and they believed it to be a transferable skill that would help students in future writing. On the other hand, they doubted collaborative assessment because it was inherently difficult to teach, it threatened to erode their necessary authority in the classroom, and it concealed their real power rather than honestly distributing some of it throughout the classroom. Instructor attitudes were also heavily inflected by memories of their own often negative experiences with collaborative assessment as undergraduates. Overall, their ambivalence about peer review and self-assessment reflected a sober and realistic view of the risks of collaborative assessment from their perspective at the margins of academia.

For example, despite the program's solid philosophical basis for integrating peer review and self-assessment, perhaps instructors are prudential in separating these practices as they reflect on their teaching experiences; perhaps they have found that the two practices pose different problems, and WPAs should provide instructor training that allows for conceptually distinguishing them instead of (or in addition to) collapsing them. In order to model rhetorical understandings of writing as communication from writer to reader, programs and instructors should provisionally define the roles of writer and reader. Peer reviewers, as readers, can be told that they are not responsible for "fixing" or reconceptualizing the paper, but for telling other writers what they find clear and persuasive and what they do not; the self-assessors, as writers, can be told that they remain "in charge" of the paper and are not responsible for addressing every whim of every reader.

We say "can be told" because models of the reader-writer relationship are many and various; therefore, writing programs should neither rigidly define peer review and self-assessment for everyone, nor allow these terms to remain undefined or hazily defined within each classroom. Writing programs should recognize that instructors—and particularly graduate-student instructors, who may still be negotiating with their committees over ownership of their own writing—may have their own anxieties and misgivings about sharing their own work or explicitly evaluating it for themselves, and may therefore have difficulty asking students to share or self-evaluate without carefully delimiting those activities to create protective boundaries. And other instructors may passionately believe in intense, almost unbounded collaboration between readers and writers. Therefore, we recommend that programs ask instructors to define and delimit the responsibilities of peer reviewers and self-assessors collaboratively within broad parameters informed by the literature (and perhaps using exercises similar to the focus group conversations we used in our study) and that programs also help instructors more specifically define those responsibilities for their own individual pedagogies and courses.

We argue that instructors concerned about possible negative reactions from students should reconsider whether these concerns stem from their own ambivalence about peer review and self-assessment, and that those training new instructors should actively engage with such ambivalence, recognizing its validity without abandoning commitment to the ideals of collaborative assessment. While our graduate-student instructors were ambivalent about teaching collaborative assessment in first-year writing courses, they showed confidence in the value of the conversation they were having, which was essentially a form of collaborative assessment of their own pedagogical practices. For us, the focus groups demonstrated the need for instructors to work together collaboratively and supportively to examine their own experiences and attitudes as writers—particularly in terms of collaborative assessment—and the ways in which these shape their emerging identities as instructors.

NOTES

1. Some utterances were counted under multiple themes, while others mentioned none of these themes. The percentages are calculated by the number of utterances mentioning the theme over the total number of utterances (743).

2. The questions on this and other instruments in the appendices have been edited slightly to remove the name of the university and specific names and numbers of courses.

WORKS CITED

Bedore, Pamela, and Deborah Rossen-Knill. "Informed Self-Placement: Is a Choice Offered a Choice Received?" *WPA: Writing Program Administration* 27.4 (2004): 55-78. Print.

Belcher, Lynn. "Peer Review and Response: A Failure of the Process Paradigm as Viewed from the Trenches." *Reforming College Composition: Writing the Wrongs.* Ed. Ray Wallace, Alan Jackson, and Lewis Wallace. Westport: Greenwood, 2000. 99-111. Print.

Brammer, Charlotte, and Mary Rees. "Peer Review from the Students' Perspective: Invaluable or Invalid?" *Composition Studies* 35.2 (2007): 71-85. Print.

Brooke, Robert, Ruth Mirtz, and Rick Evans. *Small Groups in Writing Workshops: Invitations to a Writer's Life.* Urbana: NCTE, 1994. Print.

Bruffee, Kenneth A. "Collaborative Learning and the 'Conversation of Mankind.'" *College English* 46.7 (1984): 635-52. Print.

Conway, Glenda. "Portfolio Cover Letters, Students' Self-Presentation, and Teachers' Ethics." *New Directions in Portfolio Assessment: Reflective Practice, Critical Theory, and Large-Scale Scoring.* Ed. Laurel Black, Don Daiker, Jeffrey Sommers, and Gail Stygall. Portsmouth, NH: Boynton/Cook, 1994. 83-92. Print.

Elbow, Peter. *Writing Without Teachers.* Oxford: Oxford UP, 1973. Print.

Eubanks, Philip, and Christine Abbott. "Using Focus Groups to Supplement the Assessment of Technical Communication Texts, Programs, and Courses." *Technical Communication Quarterly* 12.1 (2003): 25-45. Print.

Flower, Linda. "Writer-Based Prose: A Cognitive Basis for Problems in Writing." *College English* 41.1 (1979): 19-37. Print.

Hilgers, Thomas L., Edna L. Hussey and Monica Stitt-Bergh. "The Case for Prompted Self-Assessment in the Writing Classroom." Smith and Yancey 1-24.

Huot, Brian. "Toward a New Discourse of Assessment for the College Writing Classroom." *College English* 65.2 (2002): 163-80. Print.

Inoue, Asao B. "Community-Based Assessment Pedagogy." *Assessing Writing* 9.1 (2004): 208-33. Print.

Latta, Susan, and Janice Lauer. "Some Issues and Concerns from Postmodern and Feminist Perspectives." Smith and Yancey 25-34.

Mano, Sandra. "Negotiating TA Culture." Smith and Yancey 157-68.

Moffett, James. *Teaching the Universe of Discourse.* Boston: Houghton Mifflin, 1968. Print.

O'Neill, Peggy. "Reflection and Self-Assessment: Resisting Ritualistic Discourse." *The Writing Instructor* 2.1 (2002): n. pag. Web. 30 June 2010.

Smith, Jane Bowerman, and Kathleen Blake Yancey, Eds. *Self-Assessment and Development in Writing: A Collaborative Inquiry.* Cresskill: Hampton P, 2000. Print.

Spigelman, Candace. "Habits of Mind: Historical Configurations of Textual Ownership in Peer Writing Groups. *CCC* 49.2 (1998): 234-55. Print.

White, Ed. "The opening of the Modern Era of Writing Assessment: A Narrative. *College English* 63.3 (2001): 306-20. Print.

Appendix 1. Relevant Portion of Student Survey[2]

This survey was an extensive assessment tool comparing two versions of a first-year writing seminar. For more detail about its results, please see Bedore and Rossen-Krill. The relevant portions of the survey asked students to compare several skills addressed in the course. N=75

1. How successfully did your writing class focus on satisfying your needs regarding the following skills:

	NOT AT ALL			SUCCESSFULLY	
Reading critically	1	2	3	4	5
Thinking creatively	1	2	3	4	5
Developing a topic	1	2	3	4	5
Formulating a thesis	1	2	3	4	5
Composing an argument	1	2	3	4	5
Engaging counterargument	1	2	3	4	5
Organizing ideas	1	2	3	4	5
Drafting	1	2	3	4	5
Peer reviewing	1	2	3	4	5
Assessing and improving your own work	1	2	3	4	5
Revising	1	2	3	4	5
Editing for correctness and style	1	2	3	4	5
Writing to audience	1	2	3	4	5
Researching	1	2	3	4	5
Using sources effectively	1	2	3	4	5

2. How useful were skills developed in your writing class to writing assignments in future classes? (skills listed as above)

APPENDIX 2. RELEVANT PORTION OF INSTRUCTOR SURVEY

All instructors who had taught the first-year writing course during the semesters assessed by the student survey were given the following survey electronically and on paper. Appropriate spaces were provided for participants to fill in responses. N=19 [several questions collecting demographic data are removed]

1. Thinking back to your most recent first-year writing teaching experience, which skills do students display most strongly when they enter your class?

2. What are the skills they need most work on when they enter your class?

3. Rate your ability to teach the following skills: (skills listed as above)

4. How helpful do you think your class will be to your students in the future?

   NOT AT ALL   1   2   3   4   5   VERY HELPFUL

5. Where do you expect students to use the writing skills developed in the first-year writing class? Please circle as many as applicable.

A. In courses

B. In future research projects (including senior thesis)

C. In applications (ie. for internships, graduate or medical school, scholarships, etc.)

D. In their professions

E. I don't know

6. In your opinion, how useful will skills developed in the first-year writing class be to your students' future writing? (skills listed as above)

7. Do any of the skills listed in question 6 seem unnecessary to a college writing class? Please explain.

8. Are any skills that you focus(ed) on in your class missing from this list?

9. Please describe one cycle of a paper process in your class, indicating the timing of self-assessment, peer review, and instructor feedback.

10. If you use peer review, what is its purpose in your course?

11. If you use self-assessment, what is its purpose in your course?

12. Does self-assessment factor into your grading?   Yes   No
    Please explain.
13. Does peer review factor into your grading?   Yes   No
    Please explain.
14. What kind(s) of strategies, if any, do you use to teach peer review?
15. What kind(s) of strategies, if any, do you use to teach self-assessment?

APPENDIX 3: INSTRUCTOR FOCUS GROUP QUESTIONS

1. How do you define peer review?

[If not answered above, prompt:] Do you think of peer review as a goal? Skill? Assignment? Strategy?

2. How do you define self-assessment?

[If not answered above, prompt:] Do you think of self-assessment as a goal? Skill? Assignment? Strategy?

3. What are your own experiences as a writer with peer review and self-assessment?

[If not answered above, prompt]: Have you been explicitly asked to engage in peer review and self-assessment? In what context(s)?

[also prompt]: To what extent, as a writer, do you seek peer review from other writers?

4. We'd like to get your response to a number of quotations from students about peer review and self-assessment and their relationship to instructor feedback. Please take a look at the handout and share your opinions of these quotations based on your own experiences as instructors.

5. Student Quotations Handout. This included seven quotations about peer review, self-assessment, and the relationship between the two from recent student focus groups. If interested in this handout, please contact the authors, who would be happy to share it.

APPENDIX 4: INSTRUCTOR TRAINING
COORDINATOR INTERVIEW QUESTIONS

1. How do you define peer review?
    1a. [If not answered above, prompt:] Do you think of peer review as a goal? Skill? Assignment? Strategy?
2. How do you define self-assessment?

2a. [If not answered above, prompt:] Do you think of self-assessment as a goal? Skill? Assignment? Strategy?

3. What are some of the different models of peer review used by instructors in the Writing Program? What are the advantages and disadvantages of each?

4. What are some of the different models of self-assessment used by instructors in the Writing Program? What are the advantages and disadvantages of each?

5. What do you see as the relationship between peer review, self-assessment and instructor feedback?

6. In what ways do/did you address peer review and self-assessment in the pedagogy class? In the practicum?

7. How do/did students respond to peer review and self-assessment in the pedagogy class? In the practicum?

Troubling the Boundaries: (De)Constructing WPA Identities at the Intersections of Race and Gender

Collin Lamont Craig and Staci Maree Perryman-Clark

ABSTRACT

This essay forefronts how race and gender play implicative roles in navigating administrative work within the context of writing programs. We situate our understandings of race and gender within the context of our own personal experiences as African American graduate Research Assistants (RAs) while learning to become WPAs at a Land Grant Midwestern university. We call for a racialized and gendered understanding of writing programs. In other words, we look at the ways that both gender and race impact the work that we do as WPAs and provide recommendations for ways that CWPA can acknowledge race more directly in WPA scholarship and the organization.

The role that the writing program administrator (WPA) plays has a tremendous impact on university culture. Much scholarship addresses the challenges for WPAs to transform the institutions that house them (Chiseri–Strater and Qualley; Charlton and Rose; Hesse). Such scholarship generates a forum in the Council of Writing Program Administrators (CWPA) to address issues of institutional change, and we acknowledge this forum for solving institutional matters pertaining to writing program administration. We do applaud venues like CWPA and *WPA: Writing Program Administration* for devoting space for WPAs to work together as we work toward institutional change. As an African American female WPA at a doctoral granting institution, and as an African American male helping to build a new writing program at a small, private liberal arts institution, we value any forum that seeks to improve the institutions where we work, institutions that often bring about conflicts pertaining to our races and genders. However, we also wonder what the relationship is between institutional agency, CWPA, and WPA men and women of color. As first time attendees of one of the CWPA conferences, we noticed the limited representation of people of color, and we were left to wonder why. When and where do we enter this conversation and how might we be more visibly represented in CWPA?

This essay forefronts how looking at WPA work from both a gendered and racial perspective extends the implicative roles of identity politics in navigating administrative work within the context of university writing programs. Furthermore, because graduate students are given limited opportunities to train as WPAs (Enos, "Reflexive"; Dessner and Payne), we situate our understandings of race, gender, and WPA work within the context of our own personal experiences while African American male and female graduate research assistants (RAs) learning to become WPAs at a Land Grant Midwestern university. The purpose of this essay is not to blame CWPA or anyone else for the lack of representation among people of color. Instead, our purpose is to shed light on the obstacles that WPA men and women of color face in the institutions where we serve. Just as we were reminded of the extent that race and embodiment mattered at CWPA, racial corporeality continues to matter in the institutional contexts in which we exist. Our racial and gendered perspectives informed our opportunities as we trained as WPAs.

We foreground our experiences as research assistants by looking at race and gender as they apply first to institutional agency and then race and gender as they apply to CWPA. We argue that both are critical for understanding the contributions of WPA men and women of color who must confront the ways in which they are marginalized and offered few rewards by their departments and institutions, while at the same time, acknowledging the problems they face when entering disciplinary spaces where they are less visibly represented.

In the sections that follow, we first offer a theoretical framework for understanding identity politics as they pertain to race and gender. Based on such scholarship, we argue that experiences embodying both race and gender call attention to the complexities associated with WPA men and women of color. Next, we share personal experiences of the challenges associated with both racism and sexism both at the institutions where we serve and at a CWPA conference that we attended. We conclude this essay by offering recommendations for ways that CWPA as an organization can work to understand and confront the identity politics that often negatively affect minority scholar-administrators in the WPA position.

A THEORETICAL FRAMEWORK FOR UNDERSTANDING
RACE AND IDENTITY POLITICS

We align our experiences within a framework of critical race theory that positions race and gender as "intersecting paradigms" (Collins 42) rather than "mutually exclusive categories" (Crenshaw 139). Kimberle Crenshaw's black feminist theory of intersectionality reveals how both racism and sexism are mutually informing constructs that shape the realities of black female oppression. She argues that we must "account for multiple grounds of identity when considering how the social world is constructed" (1245). While we recognize the necessity of intersectionality to crystallize the black female experiences with patriarchal violence and other forms of oppression—experiences that also reveal the privileges of black men—we also consider black male bodies as constructed within a matrix of interlocking significations that can be oppressive (Matua 22). We also recognize that black men are often the culprits of forms of oppression towards black women that reinforce patriarchal privilege. But this does not negate the reality that black men also experience forms of discrimination such as racial profiling that can be informed by preexisting stereotypes about black male criminality. We follow Athena Matua's nuancing of intersectional theory that constructs the black male at the intersections of corporeality, race and gender in order to reveal how institutional/academic contexts inform how both black female and male bodies are read and treated.

By illuminating how race and gender work together as rhetoric in WPA work, we assert that institutional structures in the academy have particular investitures around identity that align relations of power to representation. Following Patricia Williams in *The Alchemy of Race and Rights: Diary of a Law Professor*, we challenge these institutional "structures of power" that construct "racism [and sexism] as status quo," (49) by factoring our racial and gendered bodies into our ways of knowing and doing WPA work. We do this by "deidentifying" with oppressive discourses that "fix" minority identities as subversive, deviant, or marginal (Munoz 95, 97). In other words, we fully embody the identity of writing program administrators while living in bodies that have historically signified as contested sites of meaning. By situating our narratives in critical race theory, we politicize black bodies and black intersecting identities as sites that challenge the status quo of representation in writing program administration and within the academy at large.

Situating intersectionality in WPA scholarship builds on existing conversations that acknowledge how WPAs learn how to navigate and negotiate their multiple identities for institutional agency and program building

(Adler-Kassner; Rose and Weiser; George). However, intersectionality adds another dimension by revealing how identities "intertwine" in ways that provoke both subtle and blatant forms of discrimination that *other* minorities holding positions as writing program administrators (Knudsen). More broadly within the field of composition and rhetoric, identity politics as a trope has been central when charting the terrain of discourse on power relations between dominant and minority representations. Keith Gilyard's call for a transcultural democracy to challenge asymmetrical power relations suggests that we need a language that effectively allows us to have "cross-cultural conversations" about difference in our field (266-7). Jacqueline Jones Royster states that these dialogues give agency to individual subject positions to interpret "context, ways of knowing, language abilities, and experience" in order to "enrich our interpretive views" and give voice to our own realities (29). Similarly, Nancy Barron reveals "cultural frameworks" in our field and the broader institution that reward folks of color for assimilating "Anglo mainstream" ideologies of how they should see the world (21). Her interrogation of "dual constructions of identity" that Mexican teachers and students experience speaks to a rhetoric of *othering* that maps the margins of Mexican identity in academic discourse. Our narratives extend existing conversations in WPA scholarship and more broadly composition and rhetoric by exploring how gendered and racial identities construct an identity politic within the field and the broader institution.

We also acknowledge that the theme of intersectionality in relationship to WPA narrative-based scholarship is not new. For example, in "Demystifying the Asian-American WPA: Locations in Writing, Teaching, and Program Administration," Joseph Eng addresses the intersections between being Asian American and being in a position of authority. He states that many narratives of Asian scholars in the field "seem to suggest broadly discipline-based and admittedly awkward moments" (154). In relationship to his experiences as a WPA at two different institutions, Eng recounts the following:

> Having been a writing program administrator at two different institutions, I sometimes wonder how issues regarding my communication, authority, and career choice in general might be shaped by my ethnic identity or identities perceived. For instance, some colleagues or graduate students seem to scrutinize every memo I send out—even under informal circumstances—for usage or idiomatic perfection. To many new acquaintances, why and how I have become an English faculty member are their only greeting lines. (155)

Like Eng, we can relate to particular moments of awkwardness. We can also relate to the scrutiny we experienced in the following stories we tell. Eng's narrative further resonates with us because it offers an example of the challenges that WPA men of color face in the administrative roles they assume. From his narrative we learn that CWPA represents all of us, and that we each have significant contributions to make as we work to transform the status of administrators in the profession.

OUR STORIES: INTERSECTING RACE, GENDER, AND IDENTITY POLITICS

Before sharing our stories, we wish to first provide a bit of institutional context relating to our experiences. Our positions as RAs took place at a large Midwestern research extensive university with one of the largest first-year writing programs in the region. In comparison to many first-year writing programs that are traditionally housed in English Departments, our writing program is unique because it is housed separately from the English Department. Its "disciplinary orientation was not rhetoric and composition, or English studies; instead, [it] was historically taught as a history-focused course on Western civilization" (Perryman-Clark 116). We provide an institutional context here because we acknowledge the relationship between independent writing programs and institutional challenges. Like Peggy O'Neil also acknowledges in the book, *A Field of Dreams: Independent Writing Programs and the Future of Composition Studies*, we add to stories of institutional challenges faced by independent writing programs by sharing our own experiences. Prior to our role as RAs, our institution did not have a contractually hired WPA and any research assistant WPA positions, so as the first RAs to the WPA a lot was at stake, and we felt the pressures of having a lot to prove. We build on previous WPA scholarship by addressing how we might view divisions of labor, marginalization, racism and sexism though different lenses. From these stories, hopefully WPAs—as well as those instructors who teach writing—may begin to consider the ways that WPAs become racially and sexually marked in their WPA positions and in the academy at large with greater agency.

A SISTA SPEAKS: CONFRONTING RACISIM AND SEXISM AS A FUTURE WPA

WPA work first began to interest me when I took a course with my institution's director of first-year writing. My professor asked me to assist her in doing a leadership workshop at another Research 1 university for graduate students interested in doing administrative work. I'd previously done administrative work with a local chapter of the National Writing Project (NWP) at the institution where I received my M.A. and wanted to continue doing additional work at my PhD institution. I honestly liked the ways that I had to balance intellectual, delegatory, and even laborious types of work required of the administrative position. And, while I understand the critiques associated with WPA work as menial labor (Micciche; Brown, Enos, and Chaput), I'm less bothered by work that requires a hands-on approach, as long as my intellectual contributions to the position are still valued, an idea that I admit certainly has come into question in the story I wish to tell concerning racism and sexism.

The experience that I wish to tell momentarily similarly reflects my role as anything but intellectual. Instead, it focuses more on sexuality and physical perceptions of attractiveness than the work that women do in the academy, and the fact that race intersects with this role complicates this narrative. This experience occurred quite early on as a RA for my WPA. I was just appointed to the position, and recently finished my first TA orientation as I assisted the WPA in training new first-year writing TAs. During orientation I was assigned various tasks such as checking TA syllabi, and verifying that TAs addressed all of the institutional and department required policies and procedures. I also conducted orientation workshops on addressing issues of race, class, and gender in class discussions, course readings, and course assignments. By the time classes started, I became the peer advisor whom TAs would consult in the event that they encountered any classroom problems. By assuming these responsibilities, TAs and other faculty members in the department attached the role, "the go-to girl" to my WPA identity.

A week after classes started, I was approached by a full professor who helped supervise first-year writing TAs in previous years, yet his expertise fell outside the areas of composition theory and pedagogy.[1] Our conversation went something like this:

"So, what exactly do you do for [the Director of First-Year Writing]?" he asked.

"I'm the RA, and I'm here to assist [the Director] in running pedagogical workshops and conducting weekly TA mentor meetings," I replied.

"Can we step out of the sun and into some shade to talk?'

"Sure."

"Hey, Listen. I've got this African TA whom I've worked with in previous years that I'm really having difficulty with. Perhaps you could talk to him. He might take constructive criticism better from a pretty woman like you than an old white guy like me."

"I'll definitely have to talk this over with my supervisor and see what she says."

The problem with how African American women's bodies are represented extends historically beyond the academy, however. bell hooks writes that this is certainly the challenge facing black women, who must confront the old painful representations of our sexuality as a burden we must suffer, representations still haunting the present. We must make the oppositional spaces where our sexuality can be named and represented, where we are sexual subjects—no longer bound or trapped (132). In "Selling Hot Pussy: Representations of Black Female Sexuality in the Market Place," hooks addresses representations of sexuality in relationship to the media and consumerism. As my own experience demonstrates, though, such allusions to black sexuality are also prevalent in the academy, a space where—at least in my own experiences—any visual reference to sexuality was not welcomed. Limiting a woman's skills and abilities to visual representations when doing intellectual work clarifies how female identity is often fixed by a patriarchal gaze that renders black female bodies primarily as objects for consumption. From my own experience, the professor assumed that the African TA would "need" my race and sexuality to resolve his teaching problems, further undermining men of African descent and their ability to engage their intellect as opposed to sexual desire or attractiveness. The professor assumed that the only way the African TA would be persuaded to adopt different pedagogical practices would be to listen to an attractive woman. As I reflect on this experience, most notable are the power dynamics indicative of the professor's behavior. His physical stature of six plus feet and three hundred plus pounds was nothing to compare to my five foot one frame. In addition, I was a young graduate student RA, and he was a full professor with a reputable career who had been in our program for over a decade. Along with apprehensions about causing a stir with a harassment dispute that bore no witness, I had little faith that the university would handle my concerns adequately.

With this experience, one may further find implications for the division of labor with WPA work. Because I was female, and because I was African American, I was thought better fit by a senior faculty member to confront an African TA. Here we see a diffusion of responsibility and labor that WPAs and faculty of color are often confronted with when it comes to race. The senior faculty member assumed an "it's-not-my-problem" attitude, similarly to the "I-can't-teach-these-people" attitudes adopted by white teachers who are conflicted when dealing with ESL and ESD speakers[2]. His dealings imply that only blacks are equipped to deal with blacks, regardless of nationality, and regardless of the cultural differences between African Americans and Africans. Assuming that all people of African descent share the same ideologies and perspectives (regardless of nationality) undermines the diversity of African and African American cultural experiences, especially when such diversity associated with European Americans' cultural experiences is often acknowledged.

Instead of taking the responsibility and handling the problem himself, the professor attempted to pass the hard work onto someone else, with that someone else being a woman of color. I wonder, though, why the professor felt unequipped to confront the TA previously, especially considering the fact that he had more experience in the classroom than I did. Perhaps the situation may have played out differently had he asked for advice on how to deal with the TA himself, such that the power dynamics would have been different, since doing so would have required more authority and expertise of me. Thus, the division of labor reflects this professor's unwillingness and inability to confront cultural differences himself; it also reflects his unwillingness to consult advice on how to handle cultural confrontations and difference. Furthermore, the professor's comments undermine the intellectual and rhetorical capabilities of both men and women in the academy by suggesting that the only way that men may be persuaded by men is by evoking gender and sexuality. Perhaps the professor relied on me to talk to the TA because women are often expected to nurture men (in a maternal way) while also possessing the ability to lure them into do the right thing (in a seductive way). Whatever the case, comments such as these reduce men to objectifying, and women to seducing, neither of which acknowledges the role that intellect plays in pedagogical guidance or decision making.

I optimistically believed that the professor's intent was not to be blatantly racist or sexist, although his comments reflect racial and gender insensitivity. The question now becomes how we move beyond intentionality (or lack thereof) to accountability. Regardless of whether or not the professor's comments were unintentional or not, he needed to be held accountable for making racist and sexist assumptions and remarks about women of color in the academy. Such accountability, then, requires that he understand why these comments offend in relationship to the historical implications associated with African American women's bodies being put on display for public control and objectification, where those in positions of power take ownership over the validation of black beauty. When faculties understand the historical implications surrounding racist and sexist comments, they can no longer use ignorance as an excuse.

The professor's comments reflect an often excused social incompetence about diversity on a larger institutional scale. His comments also reflect an ongoing trend by white males in positions of power who speak as they wish without any accountability and responsibility. In fact, racist and sexists remarks that demean black women are becoming more a part of our public discourse. From Don Imus's denigration of black female athletes as "nappy headed hoes" to the demonization of Michelle Obama as militant by political right wing politicians, white males in central positions of power are too easily let off the hook for racist and sexist rhetoric that subordinates black female identity. Patriarchal privilege or their dominant racial ethos precludes these men from receiving disciplinary action in the U.S. labor force.

Experiences such as these represent more than faux pas or gaffs. We need to move beyond the notion of unintentional racist or sexist mishaps and hold those who do make racist or sexist comments—whether misinformed or not—accountable for their actions. Suppose the professor was attempting to issue a complement. It is still necessary to have explicit conversations about appropriateness in relationship to race and gender. Such a conversation, then, requires that we ask critical questions of kairos. When we issue remarks that have racial and/or gendered implications, we need to determine the appropriate occasions for our comments and whom and how they might offend. In professional spaces—especially those that involve graduate students—we need to understand why pedagogical training sites are not appropriate occasions for remarking on women's visual appearances. With regard to race, we also need to understand why it's not appropriate to assume that an African American will automatically relate to an African. When we consider appropriateness and occasions for appropriateness, we can begin to rethink accountability as opposed to readily dismissing and attributing offensive speech or actions to ignorance.

In reading this narrative, I urge readers to understand how the race, gender, and power dynamics that played out through my experiences similarly parallel societal roles in relationship to power. I also urge readers to consider how such power dynamics determine who gets to say and do what to whom in our institutional and disciplinary spaces, without being held accountable and responsible for what is said. As we think more about CWPA, we can ask similar questions concerning who gets to do, say, act, speak, and lead the organization. How are women of color represented in CWPA? What tasks does CWPA assign them, and what might these tasks suggest about divisions of labor? When do women of color get to speak, and what do they get to say? How does CWPA hold people accountable and responsible for what is said in relationship to people of color? Posing these questions does not suggest that CWPA marginalizes women of color. Instead, what I am suggesting is that we use women of color's personal experiences in institutional spaces to think more critically and carefully about how representation and power dynamics impact the way that women of color are represented in disciplinary and organizational spaces.

"Black Maybe": Navigating Identity Politics in Wpa Work As an African American

I became interested in WPA work because I believed that a writing program was more than just a place that housed required first-year writing courses. For me the WPA could be a conscious community builder. Yet for many fellow graduate students, the perception of a WPA was as micromanager, a taskmaster of TAs and adjuncts who taught courses that most tenured faculty were not interested in teaching. Although the intellectual work that our WPA produced proved otherwise, perceptions often function as agents of containment in how one can signify in the eyes of others. As a scholar of color in the academy, I learned how perceptions can produce the offspring of covert racism or the intolerance for cultural difference. Being an athletic black male graduate student at a predominately white university came with its own issues, ones that would surface when a black graduate student would be awarded things like highly coveted research assistantships. With that stated, the assistantship I was awarded as research writer for our WPA was met with some disdain. One white male graduate student questioned, "Is Collin even qualified for that position?" and frankly stated that I was "not a hard worker." Other rumors stirred that I had received the position because of how I looked. Such responses speak to the pervasive level of scrutiny students and faculty of color face in justifying their success and presence at predominantly white academies if they are not emptying office trashcans, playing a sport, or mowing university grass.

This assistantship as researcher for my WPA gave me the chance to collaboratively write a teacher training manual and create our first co-edited first-year writing reader. I came with the anticipation that it would allow me the opportunity to participate in building a curriculum that aligned with the shared learning goals developed by our first-year writing taskforce that I was a part of the semester prior. But I would also come to discover a looming reality that subject position mattered in my interactions with other administrators and teaching faculty. I read many of the "Kitchen Cook, Plate Twirler" narrated experiences of overworked and feminized WPAs (Holt; Gillam; Hesse). But here I was, a brotha from an urban black community on the south side of Dallas, TX working the infamous managerial position of composition director, traditionally marked by gender and, as I would learn during my tenure, clearly racialized as well. As a black male who already experienced covertly racist responses to being awarded my assistantship as an RA to the WPA, the politics of representation in academia were nothing new to me. I was also aware of how one's visible identity could predetermine how one might enter into collegial discourses, especially at a university with perennial athletic programs. With athletics being big business at our predominately white public institution, specifically for men's basketball and football—both predominantly represented by black men—black male bodies are made most visible and meaningful in the public domains of athletic performance. Stuart Hall states that the "accumulated meanings" generated from these representations are important for how dominant culture marks the 'Other' as different (232). Within the context of my institution, these meanings enable binary oppositions of signification between black/white and athlete/intellectual. Black athletic masculinity needs to be marked in a certain way to maintain these binaries or else it forces dominant culture to rethink how they define difference. More specifically, it forces dominant culture to reconfigure how athletic black male bodies can signify in a university writing program.

Being a graduate student often found me taken for a university football player much more so than an academic. My athletic build does not always fit my students' image of a writing instructor. And in much of the disciplinary scholarship on gender in the workplace (Baliff, Davis, Mountford, Enos,Gerald), I had not found much that spoke to black male jocks who decided to shelf the football and direct a writing program. Therefore, I was left much to my own devices in managing the discourse that came with my body. As a WPA research assistant, the black body that I inhabit functioned rhetorically as a site of contestation to the traditional WPA identity of white and female I had come to know as a college student. Even in this intellectual space—at this Research 1 University—black corporeality needed to be performed through manual work. I grew to understand how black male corporeality might be read with greater acuity in my day-to-day social interactions while working in our office. In the first few weeks working in my position, our department chair came into our office requesting my assistance with menial labor—"Hey, can I use your big muscles to move a few desks and swivel chairs out of an empty faculty office and transport them to a storage room?" These moments were usually in the form of random interruptions while in the middle of writing the TA training manual that we were preparing for first-year writing instructors, or editing our soon-to-be-published reader. Besides the initial frustration of feeling exploited as a graduate student, the request to use my "strong muscles" to help move office furniture undermined my subject position as a black intellectual. In these moments of interpellation, I was asked to signify as another type of laborer in this working space. I thought about Mark Bousquet's article "Composition as Management Science" and wondered if maneuvering heavy desks down department hallways counted as "organized academic labor" (Bousquet). As far as I knew, it was not part of my original job description as a WPA research assistant. Nevertheless, my department chair saw me through the gaze of servile labor; I was a tool for getting menial things done. "Big muscles" were associated with moving big things—chairs and desks—down an office-building hallway, one that I had walked down many mornings en route to my office to meet students for conferences. But more than that, the big black guy as furniture mover invoked a historical narrative of black labor, one where African Americans are found justifying their value and presence as citizens by the work they do with their hands.

These experiences were framed within a larger context of working with two women in a space traditionally marked as feminine, one where divisions of labor had been gendered. And although their identities as women in the workplace might have brought them different experiences from my own, I understood the rhetorical implications of bodies that are marked in certain ways to maintain systems of power. Thus, I wanted to build a culture of reciprocity with my female colleagues in a way that spoke to the gender and racial dynamics of our workspace and how these dynamics could positively inform the curricular and administrative decisions we made. For example, open and honest dialogue about our differences was an effective practice in thinking through how we would decide how race and gender as influential tropes in literacy learning would be represented in the texts that we chose for our first program-produced reader for first-year writing. Our intellectual efforts often found us in disagreement and having to make hard decisions about which texts to include, and which voices needed to be heard and why. As graduate students our vision for the reader was shaped by our beliefs that how one identifies racially, politically, or by gender gauges literacy practices and how one shapes relationships with others (Mitchell and Weiler x). When choosing selections for our reader, we followed this concept of literacy in choosing writers who demonstrated literacy as a "culturally connected" social practice of entering a range of discourses (Mahiri, Moss, Gee). We believed that this approach would allow first-year writers to see that diverse communities gain access to certain forms of literacy in ways reflective of their racial, gendered or political subject positions. In these moments, listening to my female colleagues became a critical practice for me as a male sharing our workspace. Listening enabled me to take their perspectives seriously as intellectuals who came from different gendered and racial locations. Listening allowed me to effectively see them beyond a patriarchal gaze and to engage them as colleagues and co-laborers whose insights and opinions mattered.

As a black male WPA research assistant, having an understanding of a gendered racial reality of what it means to be a person of color whose identity as male influences the complexity of one's racial subjectivity, allowed me to grasp how one might work towards making the dimensions of race visible in conversations about curriculum building and pedagogy. Furthermore, this allowed me to think through a conceptual framework for WPA work that could be developed through a process of reflexive thinking about how students and TAs might think through their own markers of identification, and how these markers mattered in curriculum development and literacy practices. In helping to shape the curriculum for our writing program, I took an active stance to look at race through a gendered lens while further exploring the dimensions of gender politics by recognizing its racial implications. The diverse feedback we received from TAs of all backgrounds in our program who were using the reader was useful for how we might further think about other intersections, such as class, sexuality, and able-isms. With that stated, some saw the reader as not representative enough of the range of identities they saw as intersecting. Others suggested that online spaces and the proliferation of students creating digital profiles offered another dimension to how identities are either shaped at the intersections of place and space. Overall we felt optimistic about the types of responses the reader generated.

Now our approach in using the intersections of race and gender in thinking about curriculum does not mean that one essentially needs to be a racial minority to fully understand how to address the intersections of race, writing, and difference or to interrogate fixed notions of race that undermine the professional development of writing program administrators and their affiliates. It does, however, suggest that directors of composition must build coalitions with faculty and graduate students across race and gender lines to effectively create a culturally inclusive program and disciplinary perspective that best serves learning objectives.

Bitches and Ball Players, or Just Black Intellectual Folks? Attending CWPA for the First Time

It was our first time attending the annual CWPA conference. We, both African American research assistants to our WPA, decided to participate in the conference that year because we thought we had important stories to share. We wanted to present our experiences associated with confronting racism and sexism as graduate students training to be WPAs. We also wanted to share moments where we found ourselves in peculiar situations: being asked to do manual labor, experiencing excessive monitoring by our department chair, and being asked by tenured white faculty members in our department to handle issues with racial minority students whom they deemed themselves too inadequate to deal with. As African Americans, identity mattered in our administrative roles as assistant WPAs at our institution. And our lived experiences in these roles were connected to how we were visibly marked by our race and gender. So for our conference presentation, we wanted to use our own experiences to shed light on the ways in which future WPAs of color must confront racist and sexist practices at the institutional level. And, we figured that as an organization desiring to include more graduate students, more junior faculty WPAs—more people interested in WPA work in general, our audience would be receptive to what we had to say. And they were, but this did not come without certain tradeoffs.

Prolonged stares made for socially awkward moments with conference participants who did little to alleviate our uneasiness with being some of the few folks of color there. One conference member, whom we had previously met when she attended an annual week-long rhetoric seminar Staci and I both helped to facilitate at our university, assumed an air of familiarity with us that we found both presumptuous and offensive. We only knew her informally as a member of the field who taught college writing and did administrative work at her public university. When introducing us to her network of colleagues she iterated, "These are the WPA's bitches at their institution." We were shocked and did not know what to think. When we both mentioned that we were on the upcoming job market, she then suggested that we consider our advantage as minority scholars and advised us to apply to her institution, which according to her didn't have many African Americans and needed a couple more. Her acerbic comments coupled with the racial homogeny of CWPA attendees that we had already noticed and felt during our short time there exacerbated our anxieties about being new attendees. As newbies, we saw this woman's apparent acquaintance with multiple conference participants as an indicator that she was part of the CWPA community, as anyone would. Whether or not she represented CWPA and its mission is debatable, but how else is CWPA represented if not by and through its members?

Later on in the week, the conference decided to host dinner at a park that was also having a basketball tournament nearby. All of the participants in the tournament looked to be young black males–dressed in their basketball gear–lined up courtside, excited and eagerly waiting for their teams to play. I had noticed them as I was following conference attendees at a distance to the dinner. Upon approaching the dinner pavilion, the door was locked. I saw people I recognized inside eating so I was a bit confused. Then a white woman, who I would later find out was hired by CWPA as security, came to the door and shook her head as if to indicate that I had the wrong place. Without opening the door, she spoke while I read her lips and tried to make sense of her muffled voice against the window glass that separated me and her, "You're not allowed in here; this is for conference attendees only." I stood there, frozen by her words, hoping that someone would recognize me on the inside and intercede. After she finally decided to open then door, I entered, visibly embarrassed and confused, scanning the pavilion in hopes that no one had noticed how I had been constrained by what Henry Louis Gates calls epidermal contingencies (10). To my obvious disposition, this woman retorted unapologetically, "Well you looked like a ball player!" This was in spite of my dress shirt, fresh new tie, and a conference nametag I wore around my neck, just like the other conference attendees. But, the existential truth was that I was still black, still different looking; and learning how to deal with those differences was becoming defined as my rite of passage at this conference.

Later that day, after talking to my academic mentor, she made public on a popular online social network the events that occurred—"I am now officially pissed at CWPA. My stunningly smart, exceptional teacher, African American grad student just got refused entrance to the conference dinner." Our conference drama had officially become public dialogue in a matter of hours. This public scrutiny or rebuke by my advisor, who is an accomplished Native scholar in the field, would soon reach the CWPA president who immediately put the issue on the agenda for the conference Town Hall meeting. The CWPA president also wrote about the issue in her online Presidential Blog entitled "WPA Directions – Issues for Action," reminding members "WPA is all of us." At this point I still had not spoken with the CWPA president about what happened, but I had read her seemingly hasty blog response. The response described the white woman who denied my entrance as one who "was horrified and apologized profusely" to me, when in fact I never received an apology. I read on as the rhetorical impact of racism on my embodied experience was neutralized by a "we are the world" discourse of inclusion. WPA is all of us? I did not feel that way. I became fed up with all that I had experienced at CWPA and what now seemed to be an effort at damage control to quickly clean a spill before it became messy. Hyperconscious and emotionally exhausted, I decided to skip the rest of the conference and resigned to hiding in my hotel room. I became the "obviously upset" black male attendee who was no longer present; one that, in reality, most of the conference members did not really know or had not met. Thus, in my absence I could only be made visible by hearsay and spoken for by the CWPA president. I existed in a place between their imaginations and reality. While the president attempted to give recognition to my issue in blog writing or at the Town Hall meeting, to acknowledge that the proverbial black man had been discriminated against at the conference, my subject position as colleague had already been rendered invisible and incapable by the rhetorical situations that had confined me to exist as Other or more specifically, a "WPA's bitch" or the trespassing "ball player."

As a concession, the CWPA president did take time to shed light on a critical point about the reality of our racial differences: "Because of the bodies we live in, we don't all experience the world in the same way. Last night was a stark reminder to me that as a white person, the ways our colleagues of color encounter small acts of racism in everyday interactions are invisible to me." As people who live in bodies historically marked by difference, we agree. Circumstantial realizations by those who both represent dominant culture and are in positions of power can ignite real progress for change, but they also remind us of the privileges that come with not having to live in a racial consciousness or recognize race *as* a consciousness in one's personal, political, or administrative agendas unless provoked to do so.

In hindsight, the meaning of blackness was fixed in the sure reality of these moments. There were rules as to how we as black graduate students could signify, regardless of our attempts to look, act and fit in as professionals who were part of this academic community. Needless to say, this reaffirmed our subject positions as outsiders at this conference and conjured the all too familiar feelings of isolation we had come to know as African American graduate students on our predominately white campus (Williams; Lewis et al.). Now, we would be remiss to use a lady's racist comments, awkward stares from conference attendees, or being denied entrance into a reception for not "looking" like a conference participant to paint broad brush strokes in describing the overall views and sentiment of CWPA. While we know racism and discrimination can indeed be systemic manifestations, they are also products of individual worldviews and choices. But we also believe that just as CWPA is represented through the astute administrative and intellectual work that continues to advance it as a discipline, it also needs to be held accountable for when its members fall short in making CWPA a habitable space for everyone.

As we seek professional development at conferences and work to build culturally sensitive environments in our writing programs, we speculate on how race and representation factors into the goals and objectives implicated in CWPA's mission and professional practices. More specifically, we bring into question the implications of the scarcity of African Americans participating in CWPA and the sobering reality that WPA men and women of color as practitioners are nearly nonexistent in our field—or at least CWPA as an organization. We offer our narrative experiences in attending the conference of writing program administrators to shed light on how our local issues at our institutions reflect our experiences within the larger discourse of writing program administration. We do this to assert that issues of racial representation should begin to be addressed globally so that we might develop a collective consciousness in building dialogue on how to frame race and difference within WPA discourse.

RECOMMENDATIONS FOR WPAs

We applaud the timely response to these issues that was initiated after our experiences and believe they can serve as catalyst for having a fresh conversation about diversity in CWPA. However, as folks of color who have grown too accustomed to reactive rather that proactive responses to racial insensitivity, we wonder if WPA as a sub-discipline in composition and rhetoric is doing enough in addressing issues that reveal how our disciplinary relations are also mediated by cultural differences. In the service of writing programs to "educate the academic community and the public at large about the needs of successful writing programs," ("WPA Bylaws") race matters in how we embody and perform our roles as program administrators and colleagues. Thus, developing a language that serves the interests of diversity should be factored into the goals of the CWPA's objectives and implemented into the agenda of our national conference and cross-institutional dialogues. While there are no clear-cut answers for the lack of representation of African American WPAs, there are practical steps we can take towards making both the WPA position and discipline habitable spaces for our differences.

Following Joseph Janangelo, we recognize that WPAs are "multiply situated" across ranks, institutions, and identities. Yet we believe that, if equipped with the right rhetorical strategies, we can be conjoined by a common language of activism that demystifies our differences and advocates for better working conditions, visibility, respect and access to resources. We believe that this can first happen by revisiting our institutional documents in our respective institutions. Program policies and learning objectives must reflect an activist agenda to see diversity as more than a "topic," but a part of every scholarly audience, community and university (Powell). Retheorizing and repurposing our institutional documents as artifacts of "rhetorical action" works towards changing the culture of our institutions (Porter, et al.), and we believe and hope such action can also change individual attitudes about difference. We as WPAs must construct our policy statements and program philosophies to reflect a mission to engage, challenge and learn about difference. This is the type of rhetorical action that can work towards a strategic initiative plan for CWPA and our individual institutions to explicitly assert that identity matters in how we as writing program administrators go about shaping the social and cultural infrastructures of our writing programs. Writing program infrastructures are both rhetorical and ideological. Thus, these infrastructures can influence our perceptions on diversity, but they can also be revised through our rhetorical practices. Developing a rhetorical approach to both program and interdepartmental relation building gives us a language to hold each other accountable for how we align our administrative, curricular, and interdepartmental social practices to a commitment to honoring diversity. This makes change possible at our institutions.

We realize that changing individual attitudes or worldviews that are discriminatory can be a daunting or impossible task for any WPA. But this does not mean that institutions cannot be rhetorically structured in ways that impact our actions and attitudes about difference. It does not mean that learning how to honor difference cannot be part of professional development. We designate CWPA's Mentoring Project initiative as the ideal platform where we begin cross-institutional dialogue with WPAs on how to develop a language and collective action plan that serve the interests of cultural differences. Rethinking our administrative responsibilities as a rhetorical process of relation building at every level must be a priority for CWPA if we are to recruit the voices and perspectives of a more diverse body of scholars.

Where Do We Go from Here?: Conclusions and Implications

This essay offers a framework for understanding an identity politic in WPA scholarship that is constructed along an axis of multiple intersecting identities. Exploring how race and gender intersect in our own narrative experiences invokes new conversations that also locate heterosexism, classism, nationalism and other isms as intersecting themes of oppression and discrimination. As demonstrated in our narratives, much of our understanding of these intersections concerns not only the ways that our bodies are visibly marked in institutional spaces, but also the ways in which these bodies become marked in disciplinary spaces, including CWPA. Politicizing these markings reveals how academic communities still need historically marginalized groups to signify in certain ways to maintain a status quo of power relations. We use our narratives to call attention to this status quo and to make visible the interlocking discourses of oppression that we continue to challenge at our institutions. And to the CWPA we ask—Who has the authority to speak for us, and who has the authority to define who we are and what our purposes serve to advance its mission? To echo Toni Morrison, "it is no longer acceptable merely to imagine us and imagine for us…. We are the subject of our own narrative, witnesses to and participants in our own experience…" (31-2). In the wake of the institutional and disciplinary challenges that we face, we take courage in our rhetorical abilities as WPAs of color to use our own voices as agents of change, to define and speak for ourselves, and to make visible our presence as we work alongside our CWPA allies in a spirit of equity and diversity.

Notes

1. The implications of this for WPA scholarship is another essay.

2. See PA Ramsey's "Teaching the Teachers to Teach Black-Dialect Speakers," where Ramsey presents a narrative on being assigned a course on teaching "Black-dialect" speakers because he was African American, even though he had no apparent training or expertise in teaching this course. Also, see Paul Kei Matsuda's "Composition Studies and ESL Writing: A Division of Labor," where Matsuda argues that the history of ESL writing instruction has been traditionally designated the responsibility of TESOL and L2 programs and departments and not writing departments, and that this is problematic, since all writing instruction should be the responsibility of composition.

Works Cited

Adler-Kassner, Linda. *The Activist WPA: Changing Stories and Writing and Writers*. Logan: Utah State UP, 2008. Print

Baliff, Michelle, D. Diane Davis, and Roxanne Mountford, eds. Women's Ways of Making It in Rhetoric and Composition. New York: Routledge, 2008. Print.

Barron, Nancy. "Dear Saints, Dear Stella: Letters Examining the Messy Lines of Expectations Stereotypes, and Identity in Higher Learning." College Composition and Communication 55.1 (2003): 11-37. Print.

Bousquet, Mark. "Composition as Management Science: Toward a University Without a WPA." Journal of Advanced Composition 22.3 (Summer 2002): 493-526. Print.

Brandt, Deborah. Literacy in American Lives. Cambridge: Cambridge UP, 2001. Print.

Carter, Duncan, and Sherrie Gradin, eds. Writing as Reflective Action: A Reader. New York: Longman, 2000. Print.

Charlton, Jonikka, and Shirley K Rose. "Twenty More Years in the WPA's Progress." WPA: Writing Program Administration 33.1-2 (Fall/Winter 2009): 114-45. Print.

Chiseri–Strater, Elizabeth, and Donna Qualley. "Split at the Root: The Vulnerable Writing Program Administrator." WPA: Writing Program Administration 31:1-2 (Fall/Winter 2007): 171-184. Print.

Collins, Patricia Hill. "Gender, Black Feminism, and Black Political Economy." Annals of *the American Academy of Political and Social Science*. 568:1 (March 2000): 41-53. Print.

Council of Writing Program Administrators. "Council of Writing Program Administrators By Laws." Wpacouncil.org. 29 Dec. 1977. 10 Sept. 2010. Web.

Crenshaw, Kimberly W. "Mapping the Margins: Intersectionality, Identity Politics, and Violence against Women of Color." Stanford Law Review 43.6 (1991): 1241-1299. Print.

Dessner, Daphne, and Darin Payne. "Writing Program Administration Internships." The Writing Program Administrator's Resource: A Guide to Reflective Institutional Practice. Ed. Stuart Brown and Theresa Enos. Mahwah: Lawrence Erlbaum, 2002. 89-100. Print.

Edgington, Anthony, and Stacy Hartlage Taylor. "Invisible Administrators: The Possibilities and Perils of Graduate Student Administration." WPA: Writing Program Administration 31:1-2 (Fall/Winter 2007): 150-170. Print.

Eng, Joseph. "Demystifying the Asian-American WPA: Locations in Writing, Teaching, and Program Administration." Untenured Faculty as Writing Program Administrators: Institutional Practices and Politics. Ed. Debra Frank Dew and Alice Horning. West Lafayette: Parlor P, 2007. 153-171. Print.

Enos, Theresa. "Reflexive Professional Development: Getting Disciplined in Writing Program Administration." The Writing Program Administrator's Resource: A Guide to Reflective Institutional Practice. Ed. Stuart Brown, Theresa Enos, and Catherine Chaput. Mahwah, NJ: Lawrence Erlbaum Associates, 2002. 59-70. Print.

Enos, Theresa. *Gender Roles and Faculty Lives in Rhetoric and Composition*. Carbondale: Southern Illinois UP, 1996. Print.

Gates, Henry Louis. *Thirteen Ways of Looking at a Black Man*. New York: Random House, 1997. Print.

Gee, James Paul. "What is Literacy?" *Rewriting Literacy: Culture and the Discourse of the* Other. Ed. Candace Mitchell and Kathleen Weiller. New York: Bergin and Garvey, 1991. 3-12. Print.

George, Diana, ed. *Kitchen Cooks, Plate Twirlers and Troubadours: Writing Program Administrators Tell Their Stories*. Portsmouth: Boynton/Cook, 1999. Print.

Gerald, Amy S. "Rhetorical Listening: Identification, Gender and Whiteness." Composition Studies 35.1 (2007): 142-45. Print.

Gillam, Alice M. "Taking It Personally: Redefining the Role and Work of the WPA". Kitchen Cooks, Plate Twirlers and Troubadours: Writing Program Administrators Tell Their Stories. Ed. Diana George. Portsmouth: Boynton/Cook Publishers, 1999. Print.

Gilyard, Keith. "Literacy, Identity, Imagination, Flight." College Composition and Communication 52.2 (2000): 260-272. Print.

Gunner, Jeanne. "Collaborative Administration." The Writing Program Administrator's Resource: A Guide to Reflective Institutional Practice. Ed. Stuart Brown, Theresa Enos, and Catherine Chaput. Mahwah: Lawrence Erlbaum, 2002. 253-262. Print.

Gunner, Jeanne. «Decentering the WPA.» WPA: Writing Program Administration 18:1–2 (Fall/Winter 1994): 8–15. Print.

Hall, Stuart. "The Spectacle of the 'Other'." Representation: Cultural Representations and Signifying Practices. Ed. Stuart Hall. Thousand Oaks: SAGE Publications, 1997. 223-279. Print.

Hesse, Doug. "The WPA as Father, Husband, Ex." Kitchen Cooks, Plate Twirlers and Troubadours: Writing Program Administrators Tell Their Stories. Ed. Diana George. Portsmouth: Boynton/Cook Publishers, 1999. 44-55. Print.

Holt, Mara. "On Coming to Voice." Kitchen Cooks, Plate Twirlers and Troubadours: Writing Program Administrators Tell Their Stories. Ed. Diana George. Portsmouth: Boynton/Cook Publishers, 1999. 26-43. Print.

hooks, bell. "Selling Hot Pussy: Representations of Black Female Sexuality in the Cultural Marketplace." The Politics of Women's Bodies: Sexuality, Appearance, and Behavior Ed. Rose Weitz. New York and Oxford: Oxford UP, 1998. 122-132. Print.

Janangelo, Joseph. "CCCC Conversations on Diversity." Weblog post. CCCC. 22 July 2010. cccc-blog.blogspot.com. Web.

Karis, Bill. "Conflict in Collaboration: A Burkean Perspective." Rhetoric Review 8.1 (1989):113-126. Print.

Knudsen, Susanne V. "Intersectionality – A Theoretical Inspiration in the Analysis of Minority Cultures and Identities in Textbooks." Caught in the Web or Lost in the Textbook? Ed. Eric Bruillard, Bente Aamotsbakken, Susanne V. Knudsen and Mike Horsley. Paris: Jouve, STEF, IARTEM, IUFM de Basse-Normandie, 2006. 61-76. Print.

Mahiri, Jabari. "Street Scripts: African American Youth Writing About Crime and Violence". What They Don't Learn in High School: Literacy in the Lives of Urban Youth. Ed. Jabari Mahiri. New York: Peter Lang, 2004. 19-42. Print.

Matua, Athena. "Theorizing Progressive Black Masculinities." Progressive Black Masculinities.Athena Matua, ed. New York: Routledge, 2006. 3-42. Print.

McKalister, Ken, and Cynthia Selfe. "Writing Program Administration and Instructional Computing." The Writing Program Administrator's Resource: A Guide to Reflective Institutional Practice. Ed. Stuart Brown, Theresa Enos, and Catherine Chaput. Mahwah: Lawrence Erlbaum, 2002. 341-376. Print.

Matsuda, Paul Kei. "Composition Studies and ESL Writing: A Division of Labor." College Composition and Communication 50.4 (1999): 699-721. Print.

Micciche, Laura. "More Than a Feeling: Disappointment and WPA Work." College English 64.4 (2002): 432-458. Print.

Mitchell, Candace, and Kathleen Weiller, eds. Rewriting Literacy: Culture and the Discourse of the Other. New York: Bergin and Garvey, 1991. Print.

Morrison, Toni. "Unspeakable Things Unspoken: The Afro-American Presence in American Literature." The Michigan Quarterly Review 28.1 (1989): 1-34. Print.

Moss, Gemma. Literacy and Gender: Researching Texts, Contexts, and Readers. New York: Routledge, 2007. Print.

Munoz, Jose Esteban. *Disedentifications: Queers of Color and the Performance of Politics*. Minneapolis: U of Minnesota P, 1999. Print.

Perryman-Clark, Staci. "Writing, Rhetoric, and American Cultures (WRA) 125—Writing: The Ethnic and Racial Experience." Composition Studies 37.2 (2009): 115-125.

Powell, Malea. "CCCC Conversations on Diversity." Weblog post. CCCC. 26 June 2008. cccc-blog.blogspot.com. Web.

Porter, James E., Patricia Sullivan, Stuart Blythe, Jeffrey T. Grabill, and Libby Miles. "Institutional Critique: A Rhetorical Methodology for Change." *College Composition and Communication* 51.4 (2000): 610-642. Print.

Ramsey, PA. "Teaching the Teachers to Teach Black-Dialect Speakers." *College English* 41.2 (1979): 197-201. Print.

Rose, Shirley, and Irwin Weiser, eds. *The Writing Program Administrator as Researcher*. Portsmouth: Boynton/Cook Publishers, 1999. Print.

Royster, Jacqueline Jones. "When the First Voice You Hear is Not Your Own." College Composition and Communication 47.1 (1996): 29-40. Print.

Soper, Kerry. "RateMyProfessor's Appearance.com" The Chronicle Review 12 Sept. 2010. 15 Sept. 2010. Web.

Villanueva, Victor. "On the Rhetoric and Precedents of Racism." College Composition and Communication 50.4 (1999): 645-661. Print.

William, Patricia J. *The Alchemy of Race and Rights: Diary of a Law Professor*. Cambridge: Harvard UP, 1991. Print.

Lessons about Writing to Learn from a University-High School Partnership

Bradley Peters

ABSTRACT

This essay focuses on a university-high school partnership that emphasized the design and implementation of writing-to-learn tasks in the curriculum of a low-income school on "Academic Watch." A university coordinator of writing across the curriculum (WAC) teamed up with a special education high school instructor to teach a professional development course, which was sponsored by a federal Teacher Quality Enhancement grant. Replicating National Writing Project research methods, a follow-up exploratory study yielded statistically significant quantitative data and supportive qualitative data that together demonstrated how writing to learn exerts positive effects on student learning outcomes ("NWP Research Brief"). In its emphasis on quantitative data, the study sought to avoid what meta-analysts have identified as problems of reliability, validity, and control in research on writing. The study's findings contribute to what such analysts call a more "pedagogically useful theory" for implementing writing to learn in secondary and post-secondary settings.

I. PROBLEMS WITH STUDIES OF WRITING TO LEARN

The history of scholarship in WAC espouses informal, write-to-learn tasks as the supplementary or default method for integrating writing in cross-disciplinary courses—especially when faculty in universities and high schools shy away from assigning written projects that require research, multiple drafting, and feedback (e.g., Fulwiler 24-25; Zinsser 154-56; McLeod 4; Walvoord, et al. 91-92, 100-102; Bean 97-98; Duffy 118-121). Recent work by the Consortium for the Study of Writing in College (CSWC)—a joint project between the Council of Writing Program Administrators (CWPA) and the National Survey of Student Engagement (NSSE)—reiterates the importance of writing to learn in a new light. In 2008, researchers administered 27 supplemental questions about writing practices in the NSSE. They drew response from approximately 23,000 students in 82 four-year, postsecondary institutions selected at random. As the researchers assert:

> Results suggest that faculty can increase student engagement in deep learning activities and also increase student learning by including interactive activities, assigning meaning-constructing writing projects, and clearly explaining their expectations. The results also suggest that these factors contribute more to the achievement of desirable learning outcomes than does the amount of writing faculty assign (Anderson, Anson, Gonyea, and Paine).

Based on the CSWC's indirect measures, the implications for writing to learn could persuade many more cross-disciplinary faculties to incorporate writing into their pedagogies for the benefit of their students.

However, two contemporary meta-analyses of research on writing to learn warn against oversimplifying such claims. The authors of these meta-analyses, hailing from educational theory, practice, and curriculum development, find that the act of writing itself "does not automatically yield large dividends in learning"(Klein 206; Bangert-Drowns, et al. 29). Both meta-analyses suggest that to get the promising results that the CSCW recounts, proponents must heed four theoretical claims which have shaped our current understanding of writing to learn (Klein 211; Bangert-Drowns, et al. 30, 32-33).

First, to deal with unfamiliar materials, students need to use writing to generate response, personally translate, and collectively share their thoughts. Such writing, "being the form of writing nearest speech, is crucial for trying out and coming to terms with new ideas" (Martin, et al. 43; also see Britton; Vygotsky). Second, to acquire and practice the critical thinking that structures relationships among ideas, students should develop a repertoire of learning strategies such as defining, classifying, explaining cause-effect, and substantiating claims (e.g., Emig; Bereiter and Scardamalia; Langer and Applebee; Newell; Newkirk). Third, to transform unfamiliar material into knowledge, students must review their initial writing, so as to elaborate upon, evaluate, organize, and revise what they've produced (e.g., Bruner, Bereiter and Scardamalia; Flower and Hayes, 1980, 1981). Fourth, to develop the metacognitive skills characteristic of self-directed learners, they must write to reflect upon "their current understandings, confusions, and feelings in relation to the subject matter" (e.g., Bangert-Drowns, et al. 47; McCrindle and Christensen; Yancey). Both meta-analyses agree that to formulate "a more pedagogically useful theory of writing to learn," classroom practices must draw upon each of these four theoretical claims in complementary fashion (Klein 255; Bangert-Drowns, et al. 50).

At the same time, both meta-analysts note that most empirical studies of writing to learn do not elaborate sufficiently on how instructors are trained to apply these four claims, how students are taught to compose with them, or how the students' social context affects their composing (Klein 207; Bagert-Drowns, et al. 36). Furthermore, they note that even the best studies of writing to learn lack control groups, pre/post measures of learning, consistent methods, or the detail that compelling ethnographic research requires (Klein 205; Bangert-Drowns, et al. 39, 40-41). According to this criticism, a dearth of quantitative evidence confirming benefits of writing to learn keeps WAC proponents from validating a rigorous theory that manages to "generalize across task content," posit strategies that "fall within the zone of proximal development of many students," and "include readily teachable strategies" (Klein 255).

Within composition studies, disciplinary critics agree. Portfolio experts Liz Hamp-Lyons and Bill Condon observe that even the assessment of a more robust model of writing—including multiple drafts, peer review, instructor feedback, revision, and editing—relies upon "the traditional crude measures of interrater reliability and criterion validity" (136-137). Tougher questions about reliability remain unanswered. Richard Haswell, co-author of *CompPile*, the discipline's most comprehensive publication data base, reports a paucity of "replicable, aggregative, and data-supported" studies on theories of writing pedagogy (2005, 210). He notes that neither the National Council of Teachers of English nor the Conference on College Composition and Communication encourages such studies. Doug Hesse, former program chair of CCCC, and Chris Anson, past president of the CWPA, both warn that "the lack of compelling findings on pedagogies" undermines the power of writing instructors and administrators "to respond critically to reports of research that will be used to decide how they will teach, what they will teach, and to what ends" (Hesse W421; Anson 28).

The following pages detail an exploratory project that begins to address these problems. I start with brief descriptions of how the project was supported, where the project took place, who the participants were, and how the professional-development course was designed. An account of the follow-up assessment ensues, in terms of who took part in it, how subjects were selected, what procedures were established, and how the teachers were prepared for the final rating of student learning outcomes. An explanation of what quantitative data were collected and how those data were analyzed comes next—substantiating why such data might matter to high school teachers, composition instructors, cross-disciplinary faculty, writing program administrators, and other stakeholders. This essay ends with a discussion of how certain qualitative data help illuminate the quantitative data further, indicating where the follow-up study's more promising results—as well as its limitations—open the way for improved research design, methods, and future meaningful investigation.

II. A WAC Course in a Rough Environment

This project began when my university's College of Education responded to the federal call of No Child Left Behind to intensify coordination between higher education and school districts. The Dean successfully applied for a five-million dollar Teacher Quality Enhancement (TQE) grant sponsored by the US Department of Education. She invited the College of Liberal Arts and Sciences—where secondary teacher certification programs are housed—to participate. The TQE grant would fund a partnership with an urban district, where several of the professional-development schools at the elementary and secondary levels were on Academic Watch. As WAC coordinator and instructor of a teacher certification course in writing methods for middle and high school, I saw a promising opportunity to implement National Writing Project methods and materials without also getting caught up in the extensive fundraising, cost-sharing, and accounting practices that federal law requires (NCLB, Title II, Part C, Ch. C, Subpart 2, Sect. 2332).

Setting

The professional-development high school that the TQE grant identified had a poverty-income index of 58%, with an ethnic mix of 28% black, 20% Hispanic, 47% white, and 5% "other" ("Great Schools"). The potential for ethnic tensions—in combination with egregious inequities in state school funding[1]—contributed "to the social turbulence of adolescents in so many schools like this" (Kozol 28). About 25-30% of the teachers transferred out annually (*JHS Improvement Plan* 3). One semester during the school's involvement with the TQE grant, nearly three-quarters of the math department resigned. Another semester, a reading teacher was thrown against a wall when she attempted to stop a fist-fight. After she got out of hospital, she never returned.

Administrators used the same revolving door. Four different principals served throughout the grant's five years. The district transferred one principal to another school. In a highly racialized controversy, another was fired because he changed 842 failing grades to passing, to improve the school's annual state report card ("Preliminary Report" 9). Two bomb threats, student protests, and school closings occurred while a substitute principal tried to restore order. Peace only came when the fourth took over.

Participants

Experienced participants in university-high school collaborations elsewhere assert that teachers need the opportunity "to experience education as a working continuum, not as a fragmented system in which their individual voices cannot be heard" (Morris, et al. 169). Participants in this project were all too familiar with such fragmentation. Because this professional-development school was on Academic Watch, district administrators required teachers to take several weeks away from content instruction every semester, to have students practice as well as take the requisite battery of standardized tests. The tests often did not coincide with what teachers taught, e.g., students had test questions on earth science, but no high school courses in earth science (*Prairie State Achievement Examination* 55-59; "Science Curriculum"). To teachers' further frustration, district administrators micromanaged curriculum, imposing new test-score improvement programs upon all content areas, sometimes on a per-semester basis.

Surprisingly, when several teachers in the high school met to discuss implementing WAC as part of the TQE grant's objectives, they showed keen interest. In particular, they speculated that integrating writing-to-learn activities might provide a consistent method to shore up the teaching of content in their subject areas, offsetting—as one teacher put it—the school district's predilection for "prescribing fad-of-the-month gimmicks to bolster test scores." We agreed upon three main goals:

- Offer an on-site course to teach writing in various subject areas
- Work with faculty to enhance writing/ reading in their individual classes
- Coordinate with faculty to design authentic assessment of writing

A special education reading teacher with strong experience, energy, and commitment to writing joined me as course co-facilitator. During the next three years—despite the dramatic distractions—31 teachers from 11 different disciplinary areas enrolled (zoology, business, economics, English, French, history, physical education, math, music, Spanish, reading, and special education). Three administrators participated as well: a counselor, a truant officer, and one of the principals. This enrollment represented 20% participation from a high school with 100 full-time teachers and 21 paraprofessionals. The course turned out to be the single-most sustained part of the TQE grant's high school involvement, while unrepeated classes or single workshops predominated (*JHS Improvement Plan* 18-21).

Course Design

We based the WAC course on four best practices identified by the 1998 National Assessment of Educational Progress. The practices corresponded closely to the four theories that this essay mentioned previously:

- Get students to plan informal writing at least twice a month
- Discuss students' writing strategies with them, in the context of course content
- Have students do some form of redrafting
- Ask students to collect their writing, so they can examine and reflect upon what they've learned (Nagin 44)

The teachers themselves engaged in these four practices. They welcomed the notion that assigning long, formal papers was unnecessary (see Bean 117). Course activities involved developing a series of four sets of closely linked, informal prompts for a semester. Each set asked students to write three or four brief, impromptu responses about a central concept that students needed to learn. Each impromptu response comprised a separate day's 5-10 minute writing activity. An interactive discussion or reading assignment about the concept preceded or followed. Each prompt encouraged students to engage in what teachers defined as one or two specific learning strategies, leading up to a slightly longer 10-15 minute activity that required students to redraft and synthesize what they'd written before. A short, reflective prompt wrapped up each set. Just so, this sequenced approach applied the four theoretical claims of writing to learn.

To illustrate, a zoology teacher developed this set of prompts on flat-worms:

- Write a paragraph about general traits of the phylum Platyhelminthes, and describe traits that differentiate the four classes.
- Choose two parasitic flatworms that we've read about or studied online, comparing their life cycles. Identify intermediate and determinate hosts, and the stage of development that the flatworms are found in each host. Then draw two comparative charts, using scientific and common names.

- Choose a third parasitic flatworm that we've researched. Write about the disease that it causes, where and how people 'catch' the disease, what symptoms occur, how the disease is cured, and how you'd avoid it.
- With two other students, write a public health pamphlet informing a community about the health problems that one specific species of flatworm cause. Provide information about its life cycle, prevention, symptoms, and public health sources. Include photos and drawings.
- What were the three most important things you learned from writing about flatworms? Identify what was most difficult, and explain why. What did we do that was most helpful to you? Again, explain why.

Although we didn't suggest that teachers grade student responses to these prompts, we developed a rubric that incorporated state standards, to evaluate if students met expectations, missed, or excelled (see Elbow 86-87). The rubric's third criterion also included learning strategies that Klein and Bangert-Drowns, et al. had identified.

Table 1: Rubric (Score = sum of ratings for each criterion divided by 4 and rounded to nearest tenth)

CRITERIA	3-exceeds expectations	2-meets expectations	1-misses expectations
Comprehension of Task—ability to respond informally to what a writing prompt asks	Student always understands and follows instructions exactly.	Student usually understands and follows instructions.	Student often misunderstands or disregards instructions.
Content—ability to convey knowledge of course content obtained from reading or listening	Student provides information that is accurate and detail that supports it very well.	Student provides information that is mostly accurate and detail that is adequate.	Student provides information that is not accurate and/or detail that is insufficient.
Strategies—ability to apply, analyze, back up, compare, classify, critique, define, describe, evaluate, explain, exemplify, illustrate, interpret, question, reflect, review, show cause-effect, solve, synthesize, translate, etc.	Student shows clear control over the strategy or strategies that the prompt requires.	Student shows satisfactory evidence of understanding and practicing the strategy or strategies required.	Student shows little or no evidence of understanding the strategy or strategies required.

CRITERIA	3-exceeds expectations	2-meets expectations	1-misses expectations
Language usage—ability to develop a readable response and to use conventions of grammar and punctuation	Student's response is very articulate, and errors are too minimal to worry about.	Student's response is fairly easy to read, and errors do not keep me from understanding.	Student's response is illegible and/or difficult to understand, and errors confuse me.

At the end of the course, the teachers reviewed their folders and reflected on what was especially valuable about designing and incorporating these informal, write-to-learn tasks into their curricula. The zoology teacher said: "The most valuable part of this second-semester project was putting together more than one linked set of writing assignments... I have learned a very different approach to getting students to write." A math teacher noted that he now wanted to use writing to help students realize how course content was applicable to their lives—and "not just another hoop to jump through for that doggy treat of a diploma.... To make this work, I have to rethink how and what I am teaching." An English teacher offered the following comments:

> Writing good prompts depends on many different factors—breaking a task down, audience, timing, talking about yourself as a writer, helping students develop a knowledge base, explaining terms, and a classroom's behavioral context. I know a lot of these ideas already, but making me think about them, sort them out, and use them has been really beneficial.

III. The Follow-up Assessment

Although the WAC course had encouraged teachers to rethink their teaching practices, my co-facilitator and I wondered who would go on applying the principles they'd learned, and what outcomes might emerge. Four of our alumni from zoology, economics, English, and history volunteered to give at least a year to do an assessment project. The co-facilitator added reading to the mix. Later, the history teacher had to withdraw for personal reasons.

Selection of Subjects and Procedures

The follow-up project drew students from various disciplines and grade levels (9 through 12) who engaged in sustained, impromptu writing and assembled it in folders that we assessed. Students did a final reflection letter that:

- Explained which they thought was their strongest example and why
- Critiqued which was weakest and why
- Defined which three concepts they felt they had learned best
- Reflected on how writing had helped them learn those concepts

Participating teachers identified one class where students would do sustained, informal writing and another, like class where students would not. Students in both the "writing-folder" and "non-folder" classes completed all other coursework (e.g., worksheets, lab reports, term papers, collaborative projects, exams). They all wrote a brief piece before and after their coursework, so we could gauge if the writing-to-learn groups had made any gains. For instance, "pre-course" economics students in both the writing-to-learn and control classes wrote about a personal problem (financial or otherwise) they had worked through. For the "post-course" activity, the same students identified what they thought was America's most compelling economic problem, how it affected them or their families, and how the country might work through it to achieve a stronger recovery from the recession. Such pre-/post- writing samples are valid and may show statistically significant gain "if exact measures match what teachers are actually teaching and students actually practicing in their writing" (Haswell, "Assessment").

The teachers from senior economics and junior zoology participated for one year, while the teachers from sophomore AP English and freshmen special education reading volunteered for two. During the first year, I observed classes in zoology, English, and reading, to get a clear idea of classroom dynamics. I also visited an economics class once. Both years, we all met every two weeks to compare several factors, including:

- Design of the sequenced writing prompts
- Feedback students received (commentary and primary-trait scoring[2])
- Gains that students ostensibly made from writing to learn
- Progress in the "folder" and "non-folder" classes

All teachers wrote quarterly reflections to detail what insights they were gaining about their students' learning outcomes and their own teaching. For one semester, a student teacher in economics joined our bi-weekly discussions, so he could understand the project and consistently administer the prompts that the economics teacher designed.

Preparation and Final Assessment

Every quarter during the two years, we rated sample folders from a stronger and weaker student in each course. The teachers and I used the rubric shown in Table 1, based on the three-point scale. Then we discussed how and why we rated the four criteria.

At the end of each year, two teachers other than the teacher of record rated the teacher of record's folders (e.g., the special education and English teachers rated zoology folders). For the first year, two teacher-certification specialists from my university—one in history and one in English—also rated each class set. I served as a rater for both years. Being the only reader who had rated all student work, I also used the rubric to rate the pre/post writing samples from all folder and non-folder classes. After rating the pre/post writing, I checked my scores against the pre/post scores that each teacher of record had assigned. Finally, each teacher wrote a reflection about what they had learned that year.

Under these protocols, we hoped to control not only for validity, as researchers advise, but also for reliability, given the primary variables of grade level, subject area, length of participation, and ability grouping (see Hamp-Lyons and Condon 137-138).

IV. Findings

The quantitative data in this section provide insights about student learning outcomes in ways that indirect methods or qualitative data cannot. Brief rationales accompany each statistical measure, to validate assessment methods and to explain the extent to which writing to learn may have exerted a positive effect.[3]

Basic Data and Statistical Measures

Raters assessed a total of 88 folders: 49 at the end of the project's first year and 39 at the end of the second. In 2008, the three high school teachers, two university teacher certification specialists, and I rated each of 49 folders for a total of 245 scores. In 2009, the three high school teachers and I rated each of 39 folders for a total of 117 scores. In addition, I rated 61 pre-/post-course writing samples from the folder group and 55 pre/post samples from the non-folder group.

Pearson *r* was calculated to correlate interrater reliability between different pairs of raters. Means and standard deviations were calculated for scores on each of the four rubric criteria—comprehension of task, content, strategies, and language usage—to find the students' collective central tendencies as well as their central tendencies in each subject area. Percentages were calculated for scores on each of the rubric's criteria to compare the students' overall dispersion of written performances and the dispersion of their written performances in each different subject area, grade level, and ability group. A t test for unequal samples was calculated between the scores for the pre-/post-course writing samples, both for the folder groups and the non-folder groups, to see: (A) what differences existed between the groups, and (B) if those differences might be statistically significant (see Steinberg 235). Effect size was calculated to judge if any statistical significance between scores for pre-/ post-course writing samples might be large enough to claim that writing to learn indeed did make an impact on the folder groups' learning outcomes. Finally, means, standard deviations, and percentages were calculated for each rubric criterion in the pre-/post-course writing samples, to compare in more detail where the folder and non-folder groups' strengths and weaknesses lay.

Interrater reliability

Pearson r is a common calculation to determine correlations between pairs of scores.[4] Tables 2 and 3, below, identify the Pearson r correlations for each pair of raters. To illustrate, the Table 2 correlation of scores between raters NC and LG in special education reading 2008, which had 9 students, is $r(7) = .88$, $p < .01$. This result shows that Pearson r at 7 degrees of freedom is +.88, with less than a 1% probability, p, that the correlation of scores is due to chance (see Steinberg 409). To state that the raters agreed upon the benefits that students in special education reading gained from writing to learn is overly optimistic, however, because 9 constitute such a small sample size.[5] A more convincing correlation exists between DS and BP (me) in zoology 2008, where $r(18) = .91$, $p < .01$. The result comes from a larger group of 20 students (18 df), showing that there is less than a 1% probability, p, that the correlation occurred by chance.

Interrater reliability was strongest and most consistent for the zoology 2008 and economics 2009 folders. It was the weakest and least consistent for English 2008 and special education reading 2009. The seemingly high 2009 special education correlation coefficients yield lower or no statistical significance because there were only 6 students who completed folders by the end of that year. As seen, a fairly diverse range of correlations showed up among pairs of raters. Yet many more correlations were statistically significant than not, with p ranging from <.01 to <.05. I tended to give the lowest ratings, accounting for three of the Pearson r coefficients that failed to demonstrate statistical significance. The university teacher certification

Table 2. Pearson r Calculated for Pairs of Readers, Year One

SP ED READING 2008		ZOOLOGY 2008		ENGLISH 2008	
Raters	Correlation of Scores	Raters	Correlation of Scores	Raters	Correlation of Scores
NC/LG	$r(7) = .88, p < .01$	DS/BP	$r(18) = .91, p < .01$	JP/JH	$r(18) = .82, p < .01$
LG/JH	$r(7) = .86, p < .01$	DS/LG	$r(18) = .87, p < .01$	DS/JP	$r(18) = .67, p < .01$
JP/JH	$r(7) = .74, p < .05$	DS/JH	$r(18) = .78, p < .01$	DS/JH	$r(18) = .66, p < .01$
BP/JH	$r(7) = .72, p < .05$	DS/JP	$r(18) = .77, p < .01$	DS/BP	$r(18) = .51, p < .05$
LG/BP	$r(7) = .70, p < .05$	LG/BP	$r(18) = .77, p < .01$	BP/JP	$r(18) = .49, p < .05$
LG/JP	$r(7) = .69, p < .05$	LG/JH	$r(18) = .74, p < .01$	NC/DS	$r(18) = .42,$ not significant
NC/BP	$r(7) = .68, p < .05$	JP/JH	$r(18) = .72, p < .01$	NC/JH	$r(18) = .41,$ not significant
BP/JP	$r(7) = .67, p < .05$	BP/JH	$r(18) = .69, p < .01$	NC/JP	$r(18) = .39,$ not significant
NC/JH	$r(7) = .67, p < .05$	LG/JP	$r(18) = .69, p < .01$	BP/JH	$r(18) = .37,$ not significant
NC/JP	$r(7) = .48,$ not significant	BP/JH	$r(18) = .66, p < .01$	NC/BP	$r(18) = .32,$ not significant

Table 3. Pearson r Calculated for Pairs of Readers, Year Two

SP ED READING 2009		ECONOMICS 2009		ENGLISH 2009	
Raters	Correlation of Scores	Raters	Correlation of Scores	Raters	Correlation of Scores
DC/LG	$r(4) = .91, p < .02$	DS/LG	$r(15) = .88, p < .01$	DC/DS	$R(14) = .85, p < .01$
DC/BP	$r(4) = .87, p < .05$	DS/BP	$r(15) = .64, p < .01$	DC/BP	$R(14) = .61, p < .01$
LG/BP	$r(4) = .72$, not significant	LG/BP	$r(15) = .58, p < .01$	DS/BP	$R(14) = .59, p < .02$

specialists did not join the second year of assessments because funds were cut back. Further comments on these and other results appear in the discussion section that follows.

Central Tendencies and Dispersion of Scores

Calculating central tendencies and the dispersion of scores makes it easier to aggregate and compare groups of different sizes, by "mapping" results back to criteria such as those in the rubric used for this project (Suskie 258-260).

Table 4, below, provides means, standard deviations, and a percentage dispersion of scores. An immediate good sign that writing to learn might have had a positive impact is that the means for the rubric's individual criteria, as well as overall scores, tended to range no more than .5 beyond 2, the point for meeting expectations. The means tended to be lowest and standard deviations highest with the most challenging criteria—content accuracy and learning strategies. Comprehension of written tasks generally appeared to present less of a challenge, as did language usage. In general, the means for AP English tended to skew higher as might be anticipated.

An aside: it is preferable to calculate standard deviation with no less than 30 subjects. But in these data sets, calculating standard deviation for the means of smaller groups seemed appropriate and instructive because the numbers satisfied another important condition: overall dispersion of percentages in each subject area, as well as in all subject areas combined, approximated a typical bell curve (see Steinberg 453). Standard deviation was also necessary for calculating the overall percentage dispersions.

Table 4. Scores analyzed by Means, Standard Deviations, and Percentages

Student Learning Outcomes	Mean	S.D.	Exceeds	Meets	Misses
All subjects (Grades 9-12, two years, n=88, 362 readings)					
Comprehension of task	2.17	.58	27%	63%	10%
Content	1.98	.69	23%	52%	25%
Strategies	2.09	.69	29%	51%	20%
Language usage	2.25	.66	38%	50%	12%
OVERALL	2.15	.54	23%	58%	19%
AP English (Grade 10, two years, n=36, 148 readings)					
Comprehension of task	2.43	.51	43%	56%	1%
Content	2.36	.56	40%	56%	4%
Strategies	2.5	.55	52%	45%	3%

Student Learning Outcomes	Mean	S.D.	Exceeds	Meets	Misses
Language usage	2.55	.49	55%	45%	0%
OVERALL	2.48	.40	20%	73%	7%
Zoology (Grade 11, one year, n=20, 100 readings)					
Comprehension of task	1.95	.56	13%	69%	18%
Content	1.64	.67	11%	42%	47%
Strategies	1.77	.69	15%	47%	38%
Language usage	1.99	.64	19%	60%	21%
OVERALL	1.86	.52	17%	63%	20%
Economics (Grade 12, one year, n=17, 51 readings)					
Comprehension of task	2.18	.51	23%	71%	6%
Content	1.98	.61	18%	63%	19%
Strategies	1.94	.65	17%	59%	24%
Language usage	2.62	.49	63%	37%	0%
OVERALL	2.21	.45	19%	59%	22%
Sp. Ed. Reading (Grade 9, two years, n=15, 63 readings)					
Comprehension of task	1.94	.59	14%	65%	21%
Content	1.66	.62	8%	51%	41%
Strategies	1.75	.54	5%	65%	30%
Language usage	1.65	.51	1%	62%	37%
OVERALL	1.77	.43	14%	67%	19%

Setting up a percentage dispersion of scores for each criterion provides a more detailed comparison of how the students performed in their different subject areas, grade levels, and ability groups (Suskie 258-259). For instance, even though the language usage of grade 12 economics students was hands down the strongest, that skill did not help them outdo the grade 10 AP English students in content mastery and learning strategies. Indeed, economics students' overall dispersion compared more readily to zoology and special education reading.

AP English dispersions seem less of an anomaly when separated out over the two years, in Table 5. Very similar central tendencies and percentages of dispersion emerged:

Table 5. Comparison of Scores/Percentages for 1st and 2nd-Year AP English Folders

Student Learning Outcomes	Mean	S.D.	Exceeds	Meets	Misses
1st YEAR: AP English (Grade 10, n=20, 100 readings)					
Comprehension of task	2.42	.50	42%	58%	0%
Content	2.34	.57	39%	56%	5%
Strategies	2.52	.52	53%	46%	1%
Language usage	2.55	.50	55%	45%	0%
OVERALL	2.48	.39	20%	53%	27%
2nd YEAR: AP English (Grade 10, n=16, 48 readings)					
Comprehension of task	2.44	.54	46%	52%	2%
Content	2.40	.54	42%	57%	1%
Strategies	2.46	.62	52%	42%	6%
Language usage	2.56	.50	56%	44%	0%
OVERALL	2.48	.43	21%	52%	27%

What stands out at once is the near-exact overall dispersion of percentages for both years, along with the large percentage of folders that seemed to miss expectations. Means in AP English were so high that when analyzed apart from other subject areas, folders receiving overall scores of 2, "meets expectations," fell into the category of "misses" instead.

Unlike AP English students, Table 6, below, shows that special education readers in the first year seemed to have stronger means than those in the second year—even though the second-year students seemed to have put in a stronger performance overall:

Table 6. Comparison of Scores/Percentages for 1st and 2nd-Year Special Ed Reading Folders

Student Learning Outcomes	Mean	S.D.	Exceeds	Meets	Misses
1st YEAR: Sp. Ed. Reading (Grade 9, n=9, 45 readings)					
Comprehension of task	1.93	.61	16%	62%	22%
Content	1.69	.67	11%	47%	42%
Strategies	1.78	.56	7%	64%	29%
Language usage	1.69	.51	2%	65%	33%
Overall	1.79	.47	18%	60%	22%

Student Learning Outcomes	Mean	S.D.	Exceeds	Meets	Misses
2nd YEAR: Sp. Ed. Reading (Grade 9, n=6, 18 readings)					
Comprehension of task	1.94	.54	11%	72%	17%
Content	1.56	.51	0%	56%	44%
Strategies	1.61	.5	0%	61%	39%
Language usage	1.5	.51	0%	50%	50%
Overall	1.67	.31	22%	67%	11%

Closer examination of the two sets of scores suggest that even with weaker language usage, the year-two special education students comprehended the writing tasks better. However, they appeared to be less proficient at relaying content, and they perhaps found exercising the learning strategies more of a challenge than the year-one students.

Statistical Significance and Meaningful Difference

The pre-/post-writing samples from folder and non-folder groups in this project came from students in separate sections of the same class in each subject area. The folder and non -folder groups were of unequal sizes. For such independent groups, a t-test with unequal sample sizes was the appropriate calculation to determine how probable it was that a specific treatment, such as engaging students in writing-to-learn tasks, might result in a difference in the folder groups' outcomes (Steinberg 235; 454).[6]

As with Pearson r, the final calculation, t, for this two-sample test yields a figure that translates into probability, p. For example, in Table 7, t for the combined folder and non-folder groups (114) equals 7.581. Probability, p, is less than one chance in a thousand that the difference in post-course means between folder and non-folder groups is due to mere chance (see Steinberg 239).

Table 7. Statistical Significance of Score Differences between PRE/POST Writing Exercises*

Subject Areas	Pre-Course Means	S.D.	Post-Course Means	S.D.
COMBINED				
Folder group (n=61)	1.98	.39	2.33	.46
Non-Folder group (n=55)	1.97	.44	1.72	.40

Subject Areas	Pre-Course Means	S.D.	Post-Course Means	S.D.
SIGNIFICANT?	No		Yes	
			$t(114) = 7.581, p < .001$	
AP ENGLISH				
Folder group (n=32)	2.11	.38	2.36	.35
Non-Folder group (n=35)	2.17	.35	1.88	.37
SIGNIFICANT?	No		Yes	
			$t(65) = 5.516, p < .001$	
ECONOMICS				
Folder group (n=19)	1.93	.33	2.35	.66
Non-Folder group (n=11)	1.77	.33	1.42	.28
SIGNIFICANT?	No		Yes	
			$t(28) = 4.494, p < .001$	
SP. ED. READING				
Folder group (n=10)	1.59	.30	2.19	.32
Non-Folder group (n=9)	1.41	.33	1.48	.34
SIGNIFICANT?	No		Yes	
			$t(17) = 4.7059, p < .001$	
*Pre/Post data from zoology incomplete.				

Although the folder and non-folder groups scored very similar means on the pre-coursework writing samples, the statistical differences between the folder/non-folder groups on the post-coursework writing samples were consistently significant, suggesting higher learning outcomes in writing for the folder groups. Moreover, calculations for the non-folder groups in AP English and economics show that the means of their post-coursework writing scores even dropped a bit, as did combined groups.

Numbers of pre/post writing samples (61) for the folder groups in Table 7 do not match numbers of folders (88) in Table 5 for several reasons. A few students in the folder groups for AP English and special education reading did not do both a pre- and post-coursework writing sample. Two economics students' folders did not get read during the scoring sessions, but this oversight did not present a reason to exclude scoring their pre/post samples. More unfortunately, data for post-coursework writing from the non-folder zoology group was not collected, and the pre/post data set for the folder group in zoology was too small to be representative of the class (only six students did pre- and post-coursework writing). Despite the missing data, the theory that writing to learn makes an impact on student learning outcomes strengthens with these statistics.

Yet again, calculating statistical significance for a *t*-test with unequal sample sizes does not suffice because it does not determine the practical importance of an outcome. That is, a calculation to measure effect size had to be performed to determine if the difference between the folder/non-folder groups was in fact not only statistically significant but also large enough to suggest a meaningful impact on common practice (Steinberg 364). The formula for calculating effect size for a two-sample t test is called effect size *r*. The acceptable range for a small effect is less than .25; a medium effect, .25 to .40; a large effect, .40 or more (366). Table 8 shows that not only was it highly probable that the writing-to-learn tasks had a statistically significant impact on student learning outcomes, but that the correlation between writing to learn (WTL) and student learning outcomes—in the context of this research—was also consistently large:

Table 8. Effect size *r* of Writing-to-Learn Tasks

Subject Area	Effect size	Correlation of WTL to Outcomes
Combined	.579	Large
AP English	.565	Large
Economics	.647	Large
Sp. Ed. Reading	.752	Large

Table 9 returns to the method of breaking down percentages on how folder and non-folder groups performed on different criteria in the post-coursework writing samples. Although it might have been instructive to separate out all subject areas as well as examine the combined subject areas (as in Table 4), such an extensive analysis did not seem appropriate because of the more informative measures of statistical significance and effect size. A look at the "larger picture," on the other hand, did seem useful:

Table 9. Scores/Percentages for POST Writing Exercise, Folder/Non-Folder Groups

Student Learning Outcomes	Mean	S.D.	Exceeds	Meets	Misses
FOLDER groups in Econ, AP Eng & Sp. Ed. Reading (n=61)					
Comprehension of task	2.13	.53	21%	71%	8%
Content	2.38	.64	46%	46%	8%
Strategies	2.51	.57	54%	43%	3%
Language usage	2.28	.55	33%	62%	5%
Overall	2.33	.46	28%	59%	13%
NON-FOLDER groups in Econ, AP Eng & Sp. Ed. Reading (n=55)					
Comprehension of task	1.72	.53	4%	65%	31%
Content	1.54	.63	7%	40%	53%
Strategies	1.51	.61	5%	40%	55%
Language usage	1.98	.30	4%	91%	5%
Overall	1.72	.40	11%	65%	24%

While folder groups appear to have benefitted more from writing to learn overall, neither the folder nor the non-folder groups fell more than 5% below expectations in language usage. These descriptive measures suggest the students in the folder group were not necessarily better writers. Yet the difference between dispersion of other scores for folder and non-folder groups was as dramatic as the differences among means. Therefore, although we must exercise caution in making too much of data collected from only one post-coursework writing exercise, it appears that systematically designed write-to-learn tasks did have a positive impact. The folder group showed greater ability to retain course content. The folder group also had a greater command of strategies for thinking critically about that content, whether the students were low-achievers or high, across grade levels 9, 10, and 12.

V. Discussion

In this project, we wondered if quantitative data would support the CSWC's claim that short writing-to-learn tasks not only engage students in deep learning, but also increase it. Our results promise to contribute to a validation of writing to learn as sound pedagogical practice. However, we discovered an underlying statistical problem: the relation of the number of variables to the number of tests of significance greatly increased the chance that significant effects would be found. Future studies should avoid such a design flaw. Moreover, two aspects of the study's design created limitations that must be addressed: (1) how interrater reliability was established; and (2) how the classes were chosen. Examining these two aspects again leads to insights about method and biases. These limitations can, in turn, become research questions about best practices that may guide future research toward more rigorous controls and, ultimately, toward a more robustly developed, pedagogically useful theory of writing to learn.

This discussion must also focus on a third concern: what happens to research when one of its participants becomes a target of administrative disapproval because of her commitment to a project? Such a concern speaks to the political reasons why quantitative data must become an essential part of our understanding of a pedagogical theory whose roots drink so deeply from humanism and its ethical traditions.

How do we best establish reliability?

The argument that raters need only to decide, essentially, whether a students' collection of written work meets, doesn't meet, or exceeds expectations has existed in our discipline's assessment literature for several years, and it is persuasive (Elbow 1996). Yet if this approach to writing assessment is as reliable as it is persuasive, it should stand up to a measure of co-efficiency such as Pearson r, which checks to see if "the values of accuracy, dependability, stability, consistency, or precision" are "operationalized" between pairs of raters (Parkes 2). The findings indeed suggested as much, but even under carefully established controls and a reasonably well-developed rubric, reliability can be compromised if raters are unsure about assessing student learning outcomes in a subject area different from their own.

Yet again, this project also heeded the caveat that good writing assessment must be balanced with ongoing, thoughtful discussion among the teachers who assess. Only so can a "reading community" evolve "in which reliability grows out of the readers' ability to communicate with each other, to grow closer in terms of the ways they approach the samples" (Hamp-Lyons and Condon 133).

Our qualitative evidence supports this assertion. During the first-year's third-quarter session, teachers rated sample folders which, by then, contained a substantial amount of writing. The zoology teacher remarked:

"Getting to this point takes a long time, but putting everything together and looking at it as a whole was very exciting." She saw that students "showed consistent writing" and also "showed work that scored consistently" on the rubric. At the end of the year, when it was time to score the entire class set of folders, her colleagues confirmed her remarks. In looking over what students had written, the special education teacher said, "You could actually see the progression of growth through the different animals." Both the zoology teacher and the special education teacher were struck as well by the similarities between their students. The zoology students were struggling with Latinate terminology that presented as much of a reading challenge to them as the "remedial" material posed to the special education students.

A similar response governed the scoring during the second year. The AP English teacher noted in particular why she scored the special education students' folders as she did:

> The success that stood out most was with [the special education] group. As I read those folders, I struggled. It was a really good struggle, though. The pile of entries that was the smallest would be the one you would think would take the least amount of time. It actually took me the longest. You could see such thought going on in the minds of the students.

The economics teacher agreed, adding, "Often the concerns and successes I had in my room were the same as my colleagues despite the variety of subjects and classroom settings in which we teach."

The teachers found that meeting regularly throughout the year and talking about the learning objectives they were trying to accomplish with their students in different subject areas ultimately helped them assess the learning outcomes in those subject areas with more confidence. The economics teacher verified as much: "The process allowed us to identify common challenges, successes, strategies, and brainstorm solutions to problems."

Occasions for such closely controlled inter-disciplinary collaboration are rare, however. Future research—especially in a high school setting— might best be conducted among teachers in the same subject area, where they more uniformly understand the specific content and disciplinary conventions of writing and believe they have the knowledge to assess their students' mastery of each.

How do we best choose our research samples?

In this project, each teacher chose which class did the writing-to-learn tasks, and which did not. At the very least, this liberty could lead to sample bias because of the likelihood that teachers chose an available folder-group whom they hoped would perform well, or conversely, chose an available non-folder group whom they suspected would perform not so well (see Gay 100). As the project progressed, teachers invested time and effort in developing or revising writing-to-learn tasks, adding to the possibility that experimenter bias could also have increased in concert with their expectations of improved student learning outcomes (219). Moreover, students themselves knew that they were involved in a university project that accounted for the extra writing they were doing, which could have invoked a sense that the folder groups were somehow special—and which could even have caused them to become more interested in (or aloof to) the writing-to-learn tasks.[7]

At the same time, the teachers chose their folder and non-folder classes at the year's beginning when they didn't know the students in either group very well. As the study progressed, developments occurred in the folder groups, causing the teachers to make adjustments that seemed to have an equalizing impact on how they treated both the folder and non-folder classes. For instance, the AP English teacher felt that the students in her year-one folder group sometimes tended to write responses that didn't answer her questions, or more often, didn't demonstrate sufficient use of the learning strategies she wanted them to master. She asked herself: "Why am I doing what I am doing—how am I teaching the material to best fit the needs of my students? Am I accurately measuring their growth and learning?" Consequently, she not only expected students to revise, but she revised her prompts as well. Comparing two of her tasks on *Twelve Angry Men* demonstrates:

   Year one:

   • Discuss any experiences you have witnessed with our jury system (for example, on television).
   • Do you think juries are always fair to the person being tried?

   Year two:

   • Discuss a time when you worked with a group, explaining trouble, conflicts, satisfaction. Compare it to a situation in the play, where the jury does or doesn't work together. How do such examples affect your opinion of how people work together?

• After reading the play, discuss why you do or don't think people are truly granted a fair trial. Why do or don't you believe our system works?

Such revisions also affected how she taught her non-folder classes. "I think both classes compare," she observed. "I ended up having the same discussions in both classes. It was as though my prompts guided our class discussions and questions without me even knowing it."

The zoology and economics teachers observed as well that their folder classes informed them how to teach their non-folder classes more effectively. During the first quarter, for instance, the zoology teacher became concerned about her weaker students in the folder class "just copying down information without truly understanding." One student confirmed her suspicions by asking why the class was studying protozoans, why they were looking at these creatures under a microscope, and what protozoans had to do with him. Why indeed? She started to incorporate the kinds of questions he asked, not only into her consequent writing-to-learn tasks, but into her discussions with folder and non-folder classes alike. At the quarter's end, she reported that "most of my students now have an appreciation for the environmental and human connections of the phyla we have studied, including water quality, parasitism, and other dangers to humans." The insight she gained carried through to other units in both the folder and non-folder classes.

In a similar vein, the economics teacher observed: "The students in both classes completed numerous short-answer quizzes as the units progressed and scored very similarly." Moreover, he—along with the student teacher he had the first semester—both noticed that the responses his folder class wrote to the writing-to-learn tasks helped them as teachers develop better test questions and conduct more focused, thorough discussions for the folder and non-folder classes alike.

The economics teacher wanted his students not merely to understand economic principles, but to realize how those principles affected their lives. The writing-to-learn tasks helped him see how he might develop the kind of teacher-student dialogue that could sustain such an objective. He reflected:

> On both the final writing prompts and the multiple-choice tests, there was a clear difference in the basic understanding of the units as well as the personal connection that the students [in the folder class] made with the material. I think this outcome is largely due to the

feedback I provided on the prompts, the discussions we had based on the prompts, and the personal insight I gained as a result of reading their written responses to the prompts.

Given the foregoing qualitative data, it seems reasonable to speculate that the participating teachers' concern about their students learning outcomes in both the folder and non-folder classes helped offset some of the biases that this project failed to avoid. And even if the biases still had an effect on the quantitative results, the efforts that the teachers made to create a balance between folder and non-folder classes seem to have helped the results remain meaningful as well. Moreover, the teachers came to appreciate the student outcomes that writing to learn enabled in a variety of academic subject areas, grade levels, and above all, ability levels.

Why do we do research?

Even the best findings in a research project are diminished if they do not have an impact on the context in which the research takes place. This assertion is especially true in a school beset by the everyday problems that accompany high levels of poverty among the students.

During the first year of the project, the special education teacher did not expect that the class she chose to study would present such a major challenge. Black males predominated. As the project moved forward, she suspected that many of the young men had been placed in the class for behavioral issues rather than learning disorders. Accordingly, many of them tended to resist everything she asked them to do—and she had to find ways to work with their resistance. Bit by bit, she began to focus less on the reading program that the district expected her to teach. They hated it. She searched for supplemental materials that she felt were more relevant to her students and deployed the writing-to-learn methods that the program didn't recommend. She knew her students needed more and that state law would back up her efforts (see Quenemoen, et al.).

To illustrate, when the special education students began Mildred Taylor's *The Well: David's Story*, she set the following prompt: "Although it is never said, prejudice plays an important part in *The Well*. Why did Charlie hate the Logans so much?" The students read and reread the relevant passage. Then they discussed the answer. Finally, they wrote. One of her more recalcitrant students turned in a response that said: "Hammer David beat. Knock his ass, No." The special education teacher asked him to read it aloud. He laughed and exclaimed, "What the hell does that say!" She smiled in reply: "You wrote it. You tell me." He revised his answer as follows: "Hammer and David got beat because Hammer hit Charlie. It wasn't fair, cuz Charlie hit David first. Charlie should have been punished too but he white so he don't get punished"—a concise summary and an accurate interpretation, but one which required extra patience and persistence to elicit.

The high school principal at that time did not support the special education teacher's efforts. Instead, he seemed to hold her responsible when six of the students in her folder group either stopped coming or got expelled, so she had to assign them failing grades. He denied her requests to get involved in school leadership opportunities. He dismissed her expertise in faculty meetings. He cast so many doubts on her teaching abilities and her "reluctance to teach by the book" that at one point, she seriously considered resigning.

Notwithstanding, when the time arrived for the school to do the year's battery of standardized tests, the special education teacher decided that she would do writing-to-learn exercises with her students to help prepare them. She suggested to the principal that the school sponsor a workshop to show other teachers how to do the same. He ignored her. "If he fires me," she said, "maybe I'll go back to school to get my PhD." She redoubled her efforts with her students and did only the most minimal work with the district's required reading program. The result? All of her students who continued to attend class and put forth an effort to do their work managed to pass the tests. At the end of the year, she wrote a kind of contract with herself, drawing up four resolutions:

- Do more writing, even if it's shorter than a paragraph
- Do more scaffolding to get more extended responses
- Create opportunities for more personal connections to the reading
- Don't get sidetracked or discouraged by behavior

In the second year of the project—after the district dismissed the principal—two of her folder-group students who had failed other courses were assigned again to a class of hers for further "remediation." She chose that class as her folder group. She knew they would benefit from another year of writing to learn.

Results from this project may not substantiate the broad claim that special education readers in ninth grade may demonstrate better student learning outcomes if they practice writing to learn. But the results can quantitatively and qualitatively challenge the lacuna in our research that leads critics to say: "For poor writers, or students with little confidence or interest in writing, writing tasks can be detrimental to motivation.... The content learning of poor writers may not benefit from writing to learn" (Bangert-Drowns, et al. 6; 53). However, to lead teachers away from more narrowly defined classroom assessments that have no connection to valid learning strategies, our research must examine many more "combinations of writing ability and subject area competence," to produce the "complex interactions" of data that will not only convince teachers, but their administrators as well (6; 53).

VI. CONCLUSION

Collaboration between university writing program administrators and high school teachers most commonly takes place at National Writing Project sites. Nevertheless, educational grants also present an opportunity to pilot productive professional development partnerships. This exploratory project suggests that such partnerships can provide the training and follow-up necessary for cross-curricular faculty to produce statistically significant student learning outcomes through the implementation of writing to learn. This project also suggests the efficacy of specific practices in writing to learn, even in difficult learning environments. By replicating appropriate controls and practices in other secondary and post-secondary settings, future research promises to substantiate a robust pedagogical theory of writing to learn that is solidly based upon quantitative rather than anecdotal evidence. Such quantitative evidence, in turn, can help cross-curricular teachers and writing specialists resist overreliance on standardized tests as the preferred—or oftentimes the only—measure of student learning.

NOTES

1. In Illinois, where the study occurred, public schools rely primarily on local tax bases. Low-income neighborhoods always suffer (Street 54-55).

2. Commentary was very brief, e.g., "Why do you make this claim?"; "What did you leave out of your explanation?" While the reading and English teachers used the general rubric, the zoology and economics teachers substituted descriptions of primary traits for "Content" that more specifically reflected their subject areas—i.e., "understands key concepts in zoology"; "reports accurate economic facts."

3. Professor Balikrishna Hosmane and graduate assistant Ujjwal Das, checked and provided feedback on this study's calculations. Professor David Walker, editor of *Multiple Linear Regression Viewpoints*, gave advice on interpreting and presenting results. An anonymous reviewer also offered valuable critique of the "Findings" section.

4. Cohen's Kappa, another measure of interrater reliability, was not used because the rubric did not deploy absolute scoring, e.g., past/fail (see Wood).

5. Our statistical consultants did not suggest calculating effect size here—a measure described below for a t-test—because this use of Pearson r focused on the similarities or differences between readers, not between scores.

6. Pearson r was not calculated for the ratings of the pre/post writing samples between folder and non-folder groups because rating conditions were different. I compared but did not average my own ratings with each teacher of record's. I disagreed with teachers' ratings in 5 instances (3 economics non-folder students; 1 English non-folder student; 1 English folder student). I consistently rated lower overall, and on all disagreements rated lower (e.g. 1.5 to 2.5).

7. This first type of bias among research subjects is known as the "Hawthorne effect," while the second is called a "novelty effect" (Gay 431, 433).

Works Cited

Anderson, Paul, Chris Anson, Bob Gonyea, and Chuck Paine. "A National Study of Writing's Contributions to Learning in College: Major Findings and Practical Implications for All Writing Programs." July 17, 2009. Council of Writing Program Administrators Summer Conference, Minneapolis, MN. Print.

Anson, Chris. "The Intelligent Design of Writing Programs: Reliance on a Belief or a Future of Evidence." *WPA: Writing Program Administration* 32.1 (Fall 2008): 11- 36. Print.

Bangert-Drowns, Robert, Marlene Hurley, and Barbara Wilkinson. "The Effects of School-Based Writing-to-Learn Interventions on Academic Achievement: A Meta-Analysis." *Review of Educational Research* 74.1 (Spring 2004): 29-58. Print.

Bean, John. *Engaging Ideas: The Professor's Guide to Integrating Writing, Critical Thinking, and Active Learning in the Classroom.* San Francisco: Jossey-Bass, 2001. Print.

Bereiter, Carl and Scardamalia, Marlene. *The Psychology of Written Composition.* Hillsdale: Lawrence Erlbaum, 1987. Print.

Britton, James. *Prospect and Retrospect: Selected Essays.* Ed. Gordon Pradl. Upper Montclair: Boynton/Cook , 1982. Print.

Bruner, Jerome. *Toward a Theory of Instruction.* Cambridge: Harvard UP, 1966. Print.

Duffy, Sean. "Writing in Political Science." *Direct from the Disciplines: Writing Across the Curriculum.* Ed. Mary Segall and Robert Smart. Portsmouth: Boynton/Cook, 2005. 115-24. Print.

Elbow, Peter. "Writing Assessment in the 21st Century: A Utopian View." *Composition in the Twenty-First Century: Crisis and Change.* Ed. Lynn Bloom, Donald Daiker, and Edward White. Carbondale: Southern Illinois UP, 1996. Print.

Emig, Janet. "Writing as a Mode of Learning." *College Composition and Communication* 20 (1977): 122-28. Print.

Flower, Linda, and John Hayes. "The Cognition of Discovery: Defining a Rhetorical Problem." *College Composition and Communication* 31 (1980): 21-32. Print.

---. "A Cognitive Process Theory of Writing. *College Composition and Communication* 32 (1981): 365-87. Print.

Fulwiler, Toby. "The Argument for Writing Across the Curriculum." *Writing Across the Disciplines: Research into Practice.* Upper Montclair: Boynton/Cook, 1986. 21-32. Print.

Gay, L. R. *Educational Research: Competencies for Analysis and Application, 2nd Edition.* Columbus: Charles E. Merrill, 1981. Print.

GreatSchools.net. "Rockford School District 205." http://www.greatschools.net/city/ Rockford/IL. (28 March 2009). Web.

Hamp-Lyons, Liz, and William Condon. *Assessing the Portfolio: Principles for Practice, Theory, and Research.* Cresskill: Hampton P, 2000. Print.

Haswell, Richard. "NCTE/CCCC's Recent War on Scholarship." *Written Communication* 22 (2005): 198-223. Print.

---. (2009, September 8). Re: Assessment. *Writing program administration mailing list.* WPA-L@asu.edu. Archives of WPA-L@asu.edu. http://lists.asu.edu/archives/wpa-l.htm (12 Sept. 2009). Web.

Hesse, Doug. "The Nation Dreams of Teacher Proofing: Neglected Expertise and Needed Writing Research." *College Composition and Communication* 60.1 (2009): W416-W423. http://www.ncte.org/library/NCTEFiles/Resources/Journals/CCC/0611sep09/CCC0611/Exploring.pdf. (10 Oct. 2009). Web.

Jefferson High School Improvement Plan. Rockford: Jefferson High School, 2005. Print.

Kozol, Jonathan. *The Shame of the Nation: The Restoration of Apartheid Schooling in America.* New York: Three Rivers P, 2005. Print.

Klein, Perry. "Reopening Inquiry into Cognitive Processes in Writing-to-Learn." *Educational Psychology Review* 11.3 (1999): 203-70. Print.

Langer, Judith, and Arthur Applebee. *How Writing Shapes Thinking: A Study of Teaching and Learning.* Urbana: National Council on Teachers of English, 1987. Print.

McCrindle, Andrea R.. and Carol A. Christensen. "The Impact of Learning Journals on Metacognition and Cognitive Processes and Learning Performance." *Learning and Instruction* 5 (1995): 167-85. Print.

McLeod, Susan. "Introduction." *Writing Across the Curriculum: A Guide to Developing Programs.* Ed. Susan McLeod and Margot Soven. Newbury Park: Sage Publications, 1992. 1-11. Print.

Martin, Nancy, Pat D'Arcy, Brian Newton, and Robert Parker. "The Development of Writing Abilities." *Landmark Essays on Writing Across the Curriculum.* Davis: Hermagoras P, 1994. 33-49. Print.

Morris, Barbara, George Cooper, Constance Childress, Mary Cox, and Patricia Williams. "Collaboration as Sharing Experience: A Detroit Public Schools/ University of Michigan Course." *Programs and Practices: Writing Across the Secondary School Curriculum.* Ed. Pamela Farrell-Childers, Anne Ruggles Gere, and Art Young. Portsmouth: Boynton/Cook/Heinemann, 1994. 154-70. Print.

Nagin, Carl, and National Writing Project. *Because Writing Matters: Improving Student Writing in Our Schools.* San Francisco, CA: Jossey-Bass, 2003. Print.

National Writing Project. "Research Brief: Writing Project Professional Development for Teachers Yields Gains in Student Writing Achievement." Berkeley: NWP, 2008. www.nwp.org (3 Sept. 2009). Web.

Newell, G.E. "Learning from Writing in Two Content Areas: A Case Study/Protocol Analysis. *Research in the Teaching of English* 18 (1984): 265-287. Print.

Newkirk, Thomas. "The Non-narrative Writing of Young Children. *Research in the Teaching of English* 21 (1987):121-44. Print.

"No Child Left Behind Act of 2001." http://www2.ed.gov/policy/elsec/leg/esea02/107- 110.pdf. (20 June 2010). Web.

Parkes, Jay. "Reliability as Argument." *Educational Measurement: Issues and Practice* 26.4 (2007): 2–10. Print.

Prairie State Achievement Examination: Teacher's Handbook 2004-205. Springfield, IL: Illinois State Board of Education, 2004. Print.

"Preliminary Report to be Released to Senior Management and Board Members of the Rockford Public Schools, District 205." Rockford, IL: Hinshaw and Culbertson, LLP, 2007. http://data.e-rockford.com/upload/files/1/school.pdf. (3 May 2007). Web.

Quenemoen, R. F., Lehr, C. A., Thurlow, M. L., Thompson, S. J., & Bolt, S. *Social Promotion and Students with Disabilities: Issues and Challenges in Developing State Policies* (Synthesis Report No. 34). Minneapolis, MN: University of Minnesota, National Center on Educational Outcomes. http://education.umn.edu/NCEO/OnlinePubs/Synthesis34.html. (7 Aug. 2010). Web.

"Rockford District 205 Science Curriculum." http://webs.rps205.com/curriculum/ science/. (12 June 2010). Web.

Rose, Reginald. *Twelve Angry Men.* New York: Penguin Classics, 2006. Print.

Steinberg, Wendy. *Statistics Alive!* Los Angeles: Sage, 2008. Print.

Street, Paul. *Segregated Schools: Educational Apartheid in Post-Civil Rights America.* New York: Routledge, 2005. Print.

Suskie, Linda. *Assessing Student Learning: A Common Sense Guide, Second Edition.* San Francisco: Jossey-Bass, 2009. Print.

Taylor, Mildred. *The Well: David's Story.* New York: Puffin, 1998. Print

Vygotsky, Lev. *Thought and Language.* Trans. Eugenia Hanfmann and Gertrude Vakar. Cambridge: MIT P, 1962. Print.

Walvoord, Barbara, Linda Hunt, H. Fil Dowling, and Joan McMahon. *In the Long Run: A Study of Faculty in Three Writing-Across-the-Curriculum Programs.* Urbana: National Council of Teachers of English, 1997. Print.

Wood, James. "Understanding and Computing Cohen's Kappa: A Tutorial. *WebPsychEmiricist.* Retrieved May 28, 2010 from http:///wpe.info/papers_table.html. Web.

Yancey, Kathleen Blake. *Reflection in the Writing Classroom.* Logan: Utah State UP, 1998. Print.

Zinsser, William. *Writing to Learn: How to Write—and Think—Clearly about Any Subject at All.* New York: Harper & Row, 1989. Print.

Cohorts, Grading, and Ethos: Listening to TAs Enhances Teacher Preparation[1]

Amy Rupiper Taggart and Margaret Lowry

ABSTRACT

After the "practicum" is over, graduate student teaching assistants (TAs)[2] know a lot about how the teacher preparation course helped and sometimes hindered their teaching, and they understand many of the pedagogical underpinnings of the course, but they rarely get to offer frank feedback to their instructors. Recognizing the valuable resource in TAs who have completed their programs' teacher preparation courses, the authors developed a survey, conducted at two institutions, of TAs instructed by prior WPAs. Our research adds to the existing discussion of how best to support new teachers of undergraduate writing. Our findings have led us to develop pedagogical responses that help mitigate TAs' primary concerns in three areas: building cohorts, grading and responding, and developing teacher ethos (classroom management).

It is clear that graduate students have become the "experiential experts" in the field of composition. We decided that it was time for the graduate-student voice to be recognized as authoritative and useful in the field of composition studies.

—Tina LaVonne Good and Leanne B. Warshauer

A good program is one that, first, serves the needs of the students; second, prepares graduate students to teach both curriculum and individual students; and third, encourages the developing faculty member to reflect upon and learn from practice. It thus is a model that is itself theorized and that fosters the identity of the developing teacher. As important, it's a model of TA development that welcomes and socializes the TA without scripting him or her.

—Kathleen Blake Yancey

When students are deeply committed to teaching and learning and are teachers themselves, shouldn't we take the opportunity to draw on their insights into our teaching?[3] In terms of new teacher preparation, present and former TAs have important perspectives to offer. While not experts in the field yet, they are experts of their learning experiences who can help us to see our preparation course sequences and materials from their viewpoint. Learner-centered education specialists (Angelo and Cross; Blumberg; Brookfield; Huba and Freed, among others) and many in writing studies believe we can learn much about our teaching and our students' learning from the learners themselves. As a discipline, we value using the wide array of classroom assessment techniques (CATs, e.g., minute papers, muddiest point, critical incident questionnaires) at our disposal to find out how our students are experiencing our courses. Therefore, it seems right to seek similar information from the students we teach at the graduate level, particularly those who will teach others, since the teacher preparation course models many of the teaching techniques we use to teach undergraduates.

Indeed, in texts such as *In Our Own Voice: Graduate Students Teach Writing*, TAs themselves argue that they are developing experts who are able to contribute a great deal to the writing programs in which they teach. Compellingly, they note that they are the group teaching far more sections of first-year writing than the senior faculty in our field (Good and Warshauer x). They also suggest that those of us with more experience may sometimes be unable to bridge the experience-inexperience divide and might even cause graduate students dismay when they are unable to produce the same results we do in the classroom (Bettencourt 10-11). As a result, they often need to learn from one another, and we need to listen to them to understand where they stand intellectually, emotionally, and experientially in relation to teaching if we are to have any chance of effectively crossing that divide.

Our study arose during transition periods from one WPA to another at our respective institutions, which prompted us to think about where there might be knowledge about teacher professionalization that we could tap to best construct and develop teacher preparation under our supervision. Both WPAs inherited solid programs from supportive predecessors; therefore, we both wanted to maintain continuity while adding any needed improvements. We wanted to think about the form, function, and effectiveness of the course from more than one perspective. We both planned to consult with our predecessors, as many new WPAs do. But we saw an "opportunity space" to learn from other stakeholders (Guerra and Bawarshi 54), specifically the present and former TAs still in our programs or within email contact. We planned to correlate our knowledge of discipline, program, previous directors' visions of the course, and graduate students' perceptions and values regarding the course. And we both believed we would benefit from conducting this kind of study consistently at both institutions, so we could see what kinds of issues might be contextual and which more broadly applicable, in the field, or even in teacher preparation in higher education.

One of our claims in this article, then, is that surveying experienced TAs trained in a writing program is valuable to shaping ongoing teacher preparation programs. It can be particularly productive when the program is in transition either from one director to another or from one paradigm to another (such as a shift from modes to genres as a programmatic focus). We also offer here a method for getting information quickly, efficiently, and anonymously from program stakeholders at these key moments of transition.

Further, this study addresses Kathleen Blake Yancey's suggestion that in composition studies we don't think enough about how to instruct TAs well, attending as we do so much to teaching undergraduates how to write (63). Proportionally in our field, much more time and intellectual energy is spent on discovering how undergraduates write and learn to write than on how graduate students teach and learn to teach. That is understandable, given how few in the field actually train those teachers; however, we'd like to suggest that that very scarcity places the burden on us to conduct these studies when we train TAs. Our impact is exponential, affecting the teachers and all of their students. In that spirit, then, our survey research adds to the existing discussion of how best to prepare new teachers of undergraduate writing. Our findings have led us to develop pedagogical responses that seem to help mitigate TAs' primary concerns in three areas: grading and responding, building cohorts, and developing teacher *ethos* (classroom management).

What Does the Existing Research Suggest About Ta Preparation?

While interested in a wide range of issues regarding teacher preparation, we focused on TAs' responses to workshop and course content and day-to-day facilitation. The existing research informs our understanding of the nature of graduate-level teacher education and provides a range of models and practices against which to place the methods and models we studied.

One of the strands in the literature regards what we might term the course's identity crisis, centered mostly on a theory-practice debate but also on what type of orientation to offer: pre-semester workshops, a full-semester course prior to teaching, a course during the first semester of teaching, for-credit courses versus mentor teams, a workshop plus a course, a full year of courses, a course plus a mentorship, etc. The teacher preparation course is often not treated as a serious class, and aspersions are cast on the notion that there might be a practical graduate-level course. Scholars warn that teacher preparation must involve theory and practice, lest we teach tips and tricks without pedagogical rationales (Dobrin; Payne and Enos; Stancliff and Goggin). Although we agree that theory and practice should come together, we did not put the theory-practice balance at the center of our study. We began with the assumption that some pedagogical and writing theory should inform practical instruction. At The University of Texas at Arlington (UTA), readings on the history of the field and debates within the field have been a core component of the summer TA preparation course. At North Dakota State University (NDSU), the course introduces genre theory since the program takes a genres approach, and adds pedagogical theory to underscore how teachers can think about structuring courses and addressing a range of learners. We also did not directly raise questions about the present overall structures of our training, though working together has led us to begin to think about the range of models for teacher preparation course sequences.

Other studies of TA preparation look at particular practices, such as journals (McKinney and Chiseri-Strater), mentoring (Ebest), and portfolios (Winslow) to consider the roles, best practices, and pitfalls of each of these course and program components. While we didn't enter this study looking to understand any single pedagogical practice, by listing existing and possible new practices for TAs to evaluate in our survey, we offer others insights into how generative each practice is in the eyes of the newly professionalized teacher (see Appendix).

A third strand of research explores concerns about teacher preparation courses as sites of "indoctrination" (Dobrin), focusing both on the implications of considering such courses as "undemocratic" (Latterell) and on ways to provide TAs with agency within the courses. This aspect of the scholarship has been particularly important to us as we try to balance the challenges inherent in helping TAs to master—and then move beyond— the pedagogical frameworks provided by our programs. Scholars who argue that teacher preparation courses create an "undemocratic" division of authority note that WPAs impart knowledge to TAs and TAs impart knowledge to students (Latterell 19). Dobrin maintains that recognizing teacher preparation courses as sites of indoctrination means also acknowledging the importance of such courses to the program and the field—as the places where knowledge about the field is disseminated to its practitioners, particularly those who may never take other courses in composition theory or pedagogy. Bellanger and Gruber work to unravel these "generative tensions" in the teacher preparation course by asking TAs to critique the course. Other WPAs also solicit TAs' input, feedback, or experiences during the course, for instance by enlisting experienced TAs to participate (Martin and Payne), asking new TAs to analyze the program's writing policies as they develop their own course policies (Stancliff and Goggin), and "authorizing" TAs' stories as important sources of knowledge within a TA preparation program (Boardman).

One of the articles most like our own is Irwin Weiser's 1990 "Surveying New Teaching Assistants: Who They Are, What They Know, and What They Want to Know." Like us, Weiser wanted to learn from the TAs as a population. Differently, however, he surveyed the TAs entering his course to find out more about the people he would orient. He was less focused on post-course feedback. Brian Bly's survey of other TAs in programs around the nation has the same set of questions as our study at its core: what do TAs value and not value in their preparation, and what can programs do better to support them as they transition into the classroom, often rather quickly? Indeed, as Bly's survey—and our own—indicate, many TAs feel that their experiences should be included in discussions of teacher preparation because they are in the trenches teaching the courses.

In balance, then, the field is concerned with practices, but often as they intersect theory. Teacher-scholars are also concerned with how this course and its related components represent and contribute to forming the field of composition studies, as it is often an entry point for newcomers to the field. Our study concerns itself with how TAs' experiences in our teacher preparation programs have shaped our revisions of those programs. As a result, the study errs on the side of practice and adds to the discussion of which pedagogical practices and materials are most valued by TAs, as well as the major issues that emerge from their sense of what helped them most and for what they were least prepared.

METHODS

Our data collection was a two-part process: trying to understand the teacher's approach from his or her perspective and then determining the TAs' reception of that instruction and their perspectives on it. We began by gathering the former directors' materials and discussing extensively how these instructors structured their courses, which methods they used, and which resources were key to retain. Rupiper Taggart worked from Kevin Brooks's archived teaching folders, including electronic copies of the syllabus, schedule, assignments, readings, and even class preps. She also received a binder of printed teaching materials, including extra articles, plans, notes, and other related documents but relied most heavily on the electronic files and conversations with Brooks for understanding the course. Lowry similarly worked from Audrey Wick's materials, which included readings, handouts, discussion questions, and assignments. More importantly, Lowry had seen the course in action and assisted with it, although she had not been its designer.[4] We both had the benefit of having seen parts of the teacher preparation process in action and heard conversations about it. Those who want to discover the practices of a former director no longer at their institution could simulate most of this process by accessing any materials posted to a program repository, requesting electronic materials via email, or, in the case of no access to previously used materials, by developing more generalized questions (see our "Implications for Transitioning"). This pre-process gathering of resources was key to developing a survey that asked about materials and activities rooted in the context.

The resulting survey was ten questions long (see Appendix), though a few of the questions involved responding to multiple items. Most of the questions were standard, used for both institutions, but given the contextual practices we were studying, we each adjusted a few of the most complex questions (8, 9, and 10) to get information specific to our programs.[5] Using SurveyMonkey—which allowed respondents to be anywhere, any time, and anonymous—we sent the link to teachers who had been instructed by the previous WPA. Many were still teaching at our respective institutions and were therefore accessible through departmental listservs, and some we contacted via email in their new locations. We asked questions about perceptions of practices and materials used in the previous preparation sequence, as well as their opinions about adding practices and materials as possibilities for a revised course. We both wanted to know how satisfied respondents were overall with the preparation they had received and which materials and methods best prepared them from their experiential perspective.

According to Fred Van Bennekom, there are four factors to consider when determining whether you have a large enough pool: "size of the population," whether you want to look at just a segment of that population, the "degree of variance in responses," and the researcher's "tolerance for error." Lowry received a strong response to the UTA survey. Of the 41 current and former TAs she queried, 24 (58.5%) completed the survey. Of those 24 respondents, 9 (37.5%) took the TA course from Audrey Wick and Nancy Wood, the previous team teachers, and 15 (62.5%) took the course when it was team-taught by Lowry and other instructors. The NDSU responses were in the low acceptable range, 9 out of 26 (34.6%). However, there was little variance in responses, which suggests that the data were relatively reliable. All respondents were trained by Kevin Brooks.

RESULTS OF THE NDSU STUDY

The NDSU training sequence begins with a one-week, pre-semester intensive workshop. The content of this workshop has focused on general pedagogical principles (Merrill) combined with an introduction to the program focus on genres (Dean), the goals of the course, and the first unit. The workshop is followed by a three-credit fall course: Classroom Strategies for TAs. Despite its "strategies" title, which is residue of another era, the course is a blend of on-the-ground preparation for teaching and the principles that underlie the teaching of writing (Roen, et al.) and additional genre theory. The survey considered the workshop and the course as part of the teacher preparation.

Overall, the degree of satisfaction in the surveyed population was very high, with over 75% indicating they were satisfied or very satisfied; the responses to the usefulness of the pre-semester workshop were the same. The overall degree of satisfaction led Rupiper Taggart to conclude that using much of the framework and materials from the previous WPA would be effective.

Several trends emerged in the NDSU results that seemed to correlate with the UTA results, which is why we focus on them throughout this report. The NDSU TAs reported as most valuable not having to develop all of their own teaching materials, being offered materials to use and developing them collaboratively, as well as "casual discussions about class issues, problems, developments." The "casual discussions" point is important because it was the item from the entire survey that received the greatest percentage of "very useful" responses (77.8%), and, as you will see in the next section, the UTA TAs agreed. As we suspected going into the study, this emphasis on the practical and immediate emerges as a trend in the surveys. After these teaching materials, the TAs emphasized that others in their cohorts were most important in their development as teachers and as support. Valuing cohorts also emerged under the "assignment/resource usefulness category," as 33.3% claimed a question-and-answer session with experienced TAs was very useful, and 44.4% claimed it was useful.

In response to the kinds of challenges for which they felt most ill-prepared in the first year of teaching, the answers were overwhelmingly grading and responding, with teacher *ethos* issues coming in second. Grading breaks down into several issues for this group: "Grading and providing feedback to students" (Respondent 2); "time management" (Respondent 2); "How to balance the time between grading papers and my own school work" (Respondent 3); "grading" (Respondent 4); "Knowing strategies to use with students when they get upset about the grade they got" (Respondent 6); and "Evaluation and feedback. Developing a rubric" (Respondent 9). The one piece of information that seems slightly counterintuitive is that TAs put end-of-semester assessment very low on the usefulness scale (44.4% "minimally useful"). In theory, assessment should help people to become more efficient respondents to student writing, because readers are exposed to a larger pool of student writing for comparison, and they engage with other teachers in discussing strengths and weaknesses in student work. However, in terms of preparing them to grade that first semester, end-of-semester assessment comes too late. In a future study, Rupiper Taggart plans to survey teachers in the program about how and whether assessment ultimately helps them to improve as grader/responders, even if it comes late for the first make-or-break semester.

Teacher *ethos* also breaks down into several issues in the NDSU results, as can be seen in a few individual responses: ". . . how to put my foot down on students who hassled me" (Respondent 1); "Knowing strategies to use with students when they get upset about the grade they got or try to bend policies pertaining to late work or attendance" (Respondent 6); and "How to deal with sexist students, who felt like they could take advantage of young, women TA's" (Respondent 7). In each of these situations listed by the surveyed graduate instructors, the issues center on gaining the power and control to hold a line or not be manipulated by students.

Results of the UTA Study

UTA's teacher preparation program differs in some respects from NDSU's program. At UTA, TAs take two three-hour graduate teacher preparation courses: the first, taken the summer before TAs teach their first course, prepares them to teach first-semester composition. That course is team-taught by two instructors, and, like the NDSU course, begins to ground students in composition theory while also addressing how the theory informs practical aspects of teaching. The course also addresses the specific goals of the program, including learning outcomes and the goals of all major assignments for the course. The second course, taken during the fall semester, prepares TAs to teach second-semester composition and focuses more specifically on argument theory. As during the summer course, TAs discuss the learning outcomes for the program and course. New TAs also attend a weekly one-hour practicum during their first year. The survey asked TAs for information about the three-hour summer course and the weekly practicum, not about the fall course because that one is taught by a different faculty member.

The UTA survey results were similar to the NDSU findings. First, the TAs reported that their peers are their most important resources. Respondent 7 wrote, "GTA summer 'bootcamp' is an important experience . . . because it helps forge bonds between new GTAs." Another wrote, "I rely on other, more experienced GTAs for help" (Respondent 4). Because faculty perceptions had been that UTA TAs were not a close group, Lowry was surprised at how highly the TAs reported valuing each other. The TAs reported that they forge strong relationships within their cohorts that often continue for the rest of their graduate work at UTA. After reviewing the survey data, Lowry felt strongly that the TA preparation should provide increased opportunities for TAs to get to know each other and to support each other as teachers and scholars.

Second, TAs wanted more preparation for the nuts-and-bolts work of teaching, including developing an assignment, creating lessons to help students complete the assignment, presenting those materials to students, and evaluating student work. Indeed, 92% of respondents said that casual discussions of teaching were "useful" or "very useful." As at NDSU, UTA TAs said that they were most ill-prepared for grading and responding to student papers. Scholarship in the field confirms that new TAs often want to focus on the practical, sometimes at the expense of theory, in order to allay their fears about entering the classroom for the first time as instructors (Bellanger and Gruber; Bly; Fischer; Latterell; Guerra and Bawarshi; Payne and Enos; Stancliff and Daly Goggin). Many of the UTA TAs expressed similar sentiments. One TA wrote, "Some of the reading for the class was too theoretical; I needed more practical advice and in-class interaction with veteran first-year English teachers" (Respondent 6). Another commented, "Although I enjoyed the theory, I thought it was too much at the expense of the hands-on activities and classroom practices" (Respondent 13).

After reflecting on the teacher preparation courses in which she had participated, Lowry felt that she and the other instructors had not been explicit enough about how the theoretical readings provided a foundation for the practical aspects of instructors' interactions with their students. She also found that the TAs' concerns about their preparation for practical issues directly related to their third main concern: they were not ready to assume the authority that comes with being a classroom teacher. As Bellanger and Gruber note, new TAs are often too overwhelmed by their new role to be able to find answers in composition theory. Indeed, one TA wrote, "Everything is overwhelming. I think just having people tell me that the students will learn something helped a great deal" (Respondent 20). Another wrote that she was most ill-prepared for "questions about authority, creating *ethos*, classroom management" (Respondent 8). The issue of instructor *ethos* relates specifically to grading and classroom management because both require instructors to be explicit with students about their behavior and performance; inexperienced instructors are often scared to assume the authority of teacher and uncertain about the standards to which they should hold their students. And TAs, of course, can find help addressing both concerns from their peers and mentors.

Both Lowry and Rupiper Taggart relied heavily on survey data to revise their teacher preparation programs; the implications sections that follow discuss both how the survey findings correlate with scholarship in the field and how the findings informed revisions to our courses.

Implications for WPA Transitions

For both Lowry and Rupiper Taggart, the survey had intended and unintended positive consequences. Most obviously, it helped us identify and continue the best practices of the previous Directors' programs while being respectful of Brooks', Wick's, and Wood's visions for the courses and workshops and the TAs' experiences as students and instructors.

Since Lowry had team taught two TA courses, and because over 50% of the TAs surveyed provided responses, she found the feedback particularly valuable. The survey results allowed her to pinpoint particular aspects of the preparation that were working well or required immediate revision. She also clearly saw that that the gaps in the UTA courses she had participated in corresponded almost exactly with the places where the NDSU TAs—and other TAs in the field—reported that they struggled with the most: grading, classroom management, and developing a teacherly *ethos*.

An additional area of revision was to provide more scaffolding for TAs as they developed their syllabi and assignment sequences. Before the survey, TAs received sample essay prompts for all three major essays and process materials for one of the three. Since the survey, Lowry has worked each year with a curriculum committee of experienced TAs to develop course materials for the first-semester composition course, and each year instructors note that they appreciate the support and would like to receive even more comprehensive teaching materials.[6] For 2010-2011, the curriculum committee created all three major essay prompts, along with process materials for each assignment. They also selected readings and developed response journal and discussion questions.

Another positive insight for Lowry was that although reviews of the course in which she had participated were not as glowing as reviews of her predecessors' course (TAs taking the course in 2005 or before were more likely to say that they were "very satisfied" with their preparation, while

TAs in the course in 2006 or 2007 were more likely to say that they were "satisfied"), the overall feedback was more positive than she had anticipated. Lowry, who had worried that it would be nearly impossible to fill her predecessor's shoes, felt affirmed by the knowledge that the new TAs reported that many aspects of their preparation were beneficial. Thus, the survey can help manage a director's perceptions the way good formative assessment tools often do: If we don't ask the learners in our varied classes how things are going, we may overreact to the problems we perceive to exist.

Rupiper Taggart, too, found the whole process deeply informative. The combination of receiving rich materials from the former WPA, her own experience and involvement in the program broadly, and the specific feedback of the survey respondents—NDSU's and UTA's—offered her a few specific focal points for change and emphasis in the first year. Being able to keep much of the previous professional development program in place and supplement with support for specific areas (in this case, grading and classroom management/teacher *ethos*) was far more manageable than creating an entire curriculum for the new teachers. It also left more time and energy to write a strong version of the first-year course the TAs would teach in tandem with her, including an additional multimodal assignment that others have also since adopted.[7]

The final primary benefit was seeing how strongly the TAs valued building course materials together. Rupiper Taggart's tendency as a teacher is to try to plan a class almost completely before the semester begins. This survey helped put that tendency in check and ensure that there was some room for discussing class decisions together. In the spirit of pedagogical scaffolding (Hammond; Hogan and Pressley), Rupiper Taggart developed the first unit completely, the second unit partially, and, although they still used the already written final assignment, the TAs largely developed their own class plans for the final unit.

Deepening Rupiper Taggart's understanding of the data is feedback acquired from all instructors teaching in the first-year writing program (including long-term, benefitted lecturers and faculty members) during the assessment session at the end of each semester. During that session, in addition to scoring portfolios, Rupiper Taggart surveys all instructors about their experience of the program and solicits suggestions for future professional development (e.g., "What's one thing you still struggle to teach well in 120 that the First-year English Committee can help you develop through a future workshop?"). The assessment survey is different from the survey instrument used for this study, evolving each semester to address programmatic issues. Interestingly, in 2009-2010, one or two new teachers indicated in the assessment survey that they still would like even more experi-

WPA 34.2 (Spring 2011)

ence building teaching materials in their first semester, so Rupiper Taggart has a sense that she may need to pull the scaffold back a little bit further (Rupiper Taggart). She will do this by pushing the date forward when she asks the new teachers to develop class plans for the immediate semester and present them for feedback to the cohort.

Upon reflection, we also see ways that all WPAs can prepare for transitions so that teacher preparation and other program dimensions are seamless in positive ways while also productively transformative. All of us can think about building material repositories held not on our hard drives or in our privately owned spaces. Program wikis, shared course management sites, and departmental files of materials are a beginning for long-term shared knowledge. Additionally, we can consider how to maintain contact with alumni of our programs for post-assessments and surveys.

IMPLICATIONS FOR BUILDING COHORTS

TAs from both UTA and NDSU reported that their peers' feedback was invaluable, and best practices in the field confirm the importance of community building among TAs. In "Training the Workforce: An Overview of GTA Education Curricula," Catherine Latterell argues for the importance of "multiplying the places and the people TAs interact with as they develop their own teaching practices and philosophies"(21). As a result, both Lowry and Rupiper Taggart worked both to strengthen and maintain camaraderie and contact among TAs.

One way to foster cohorts is through class observations. Cohort observations knit graduate instructor communities, as Cooper and Kehl suggest in their 1991 discussion of peer coaching. Since the surveyed NDSU TAs valued peer classroom observation (55.6% of TAs found it very useful while 44.4% found it useful), Rupiper Taggart maintained the classroom observations her predecessor had assigned as part of the teacher preparation course. Students in the class observed each other and one person outside the class (usually another, more advanced graduate student). The UTA TAs felt just as strongly about the importance of peer classroom observation (41.7% found it very useful, and 41.7% found it useful), so Lowry also began requiring new TAs to observe experienced TAs' summer composition classes. The new TAs found the observation to be particularly beneficial because it gave them the opportunity to observe a peer's teacherly presence and pedagogy, as well as students' responses to the instructor and class activities. Finally, observing another teacher often leads to assignment sharing.

Additionally, getting more advanced TAs involved in the new teacher preparation program deepens and strengthens cohorts. At the suggestion of one of the UTA TAs, Lowry asked experienced TAs to lead workshops during the summer training on topics such as developing syllabi; creating and teaching mini-lessons; addressing the needs of ESL, ELL and generation 1.5 students; and integrating technology into composition courses. Rupiper Taggart also added a panel of experienced TAs to the pre-semester workshop and invited experienced TAs who had particular expertise to present at the program-wide workshop (a practice her predecessor also used but Rupiper Taggart hadn't maximized in her first year) on topics such as online annotation programs. She had another experienced TA run the technology set-up session.

Both Lowry and Rupiper Taggart are also able to involve advanced TAs in program administration. At UTA, an experienced graduate student is selected biennially to serve a two-year term as the program's Assistant Director; in recent years, Lowry has also hired additional Assistant Directors for one-semester terms. The UTA TAs indicated in the survey that they wanted more mentoring from experienced TAs (83.3% were very or somewhat interested in attending workshops led by experienced TAs, and 95.9% were very or somewhat interested in formal mentorship relationships among new and experienced TAs). The Assistant Directors help fulfill that need by leading program workshops on best practices, working with fellow TAs to select winners of undergraduate essay contests, serving on a curriculum development committee with Lowry and other TAs, and talking informally with their peers about teaching challenges and successes.

For fall 2010, Rupiper Taggart also developed a field experience opportunity for an advanced graduate student to serve as an assistant WPA to the first-year program. When two people applied, she proposed they both work with the writing program, one semester each with the first-year and upper-division portions of the program. The field experience has real implications for cohort building because the students in these positions lead portions of the pre-semester workshop, conduct observations of their peers each semester (providing in many cases lengthier feedback than Rupiper Taggart has had time to do), and develop and lead brown bag sessions on topics in their strength and interest areas. The Assistant Directors also invite others to present at the brown bags, as they see innovative and best practices when they visit classes. The Assistant Directors' activities at UTA and NDSU bolster connections among teachers, increase the visibility of advanced TAs, and build a broader cohort beyond a single year of entering students.

In future semesters, we might structure some of the observations even more like Cooper and Kehl's peer coaching, to include attention to a particular teaching method just taught in the course. This method pushes observations beyond the more casual reflective learning in the present model. However, we believe the non-evaluative and reflective nature of our present model balances learning and cohort building with the constraints of our students' workloads, and we would be hesitant to take on the entire system of Cooper and Kehl's peer coaching, as a result.

Implications for Grading

The surveys clearly indicated that our TAs felt they needed more hands-on, practical support in terms of responding to and grading students' writing. Both Lowry and Rupiper Taggart instituted regular workshops in which new TAs discussed grading criteria, responded to and graded sample student documents, and then discussed the comments they would make and the grades they would assign.[8] The workshops allowed instructors to discuss the pros and cons of various writing prompts or assignments and different methods for responding to documents and provided a shared sense of the "norm" for grades in our FYC programs. In addition, both WPAs began reviewing new TAs' graded work, looking at their feedback and grades to make sure that instructors were "on the right track" in terms of grading and responding. The TAs seemed to appreciate the support, and we found that reviewing sets or instances of graded writing allowed us to identify TAs who were struggling to develop grading practices that were internally consistent and that made sense to students. Equally importantly, it allowed us to emphasize and refine the teaching that happens through response, identifying overly strident responses as well as overly generous ones.

We also found that our support for instructors' grading practices has become an important part of our ongoing professional support for instructors. Lowry required all instructors to attend at least two grading workshops during spring 2009. During the workshops, instructors discussed the goals for the assignment and grading criteria; then they responded to student writing, assigned a grade, and discussed their findings with the group. Rupiper Taggart, too, expanded the professional development opportunities she offers to include more focus on responding and grading, making grading the focus of her fall 2009 workshop for all writing instructors, and responding the focus in 2010. In 2009, she provided a sample rhetorical analysis and had small groups do holistic grading, rubric grading, and grading with rubrics with number values. The entire group then discussed the merits of the various grading approaches and normed their grading on the rhetorical analysis. In 2010, though she planned to have everyone grade and respond to a common document, conversation emerged so quickly and energetically that the group never got to the activity, suggesting how much people have to say and how much they have thought about responding. The workshops in both programs provided productive forums for discussion about program norms and best practices for responding and grading.

IMPLICATIONS FOR DEVELOPING TEACHERLY *Ethos*

Probably one of the most difficult things about supporting new composition instructors can be helping them "feel" like instructors. Lowry and Rupiper Taggart found this issue to be the most amorphous, in part because instructors' gender, race, age, and sexual orientation, as well as their personalities and past professional experiences, affect their teacherly *ethos* as much as particular aspects of their teacher education. Indeed, much scholarship in composition studies and in the academy focuses on how instructors' subject positions affect students' reception of them (see Freedman and Holmes; the "Position" section of Vandenberg, et al.)

In order to address this issue, Rupiper Taggart asked TAs to write weekly, ungraded reflections on their experiences as teachers. As McKinney and Chiseri-Strater argue, TA reflection journals are positive tools for helping TAs explore the relationship between theory and practice and to define their personas in the classroom. Rupiper Taggart's prompts often asked TAs how the course readings informed their responses to the issues that arose in the classroom, and she and the TAs discussed the responses in class. The discussions gave Rupiper Taggart the opportunity to see how TAs were dealing with *ethos* and to help the TAs support each other as they addressed problems that arose. In addition, the second time she taught the course, based in part on this need for classroom management and *ethos* development and inspired by cases she worked on at the WPA Workshop,[9] Rupiper Taggart developed case study problems regarding classroom management and responding to disruptive students for the TAs to solve.

Lowry knew that UTA TAs' concerns about lack of guidance in terms of classroom management issues were valid, and she worked to provide more support for instructors. During the summer course, TAs read articles by other TAs about embodiment in the classroom (Eichhorn, et al.), and they reflected on and discussed the kind of teaching personas they wanted to present in the classroom. Experienced TAs spoke about their own classroom personalities, including a nuts-and-bolts discussion about how each instructor's course policies and calendar support her classroom *ethos*. The preparation course also included a section that focused entirely on classroom management, including a presentation from the Director of Student Conduct about university policies for addressing issues such as plagiarism and disruptive conduct. Finally, Lowry included regular discussions of classroom management as part of the fall weekly practicum for new TAs. As a result, TAs were provided with much more comprehensive support, both for thinking through their own identities as teachers and for addressing the inevitable problems that arise in any classroom.

In sum, Lowry and Rupiper Taggart used the survey data to identify and fill gaps in their respective teacher preparation programs. Our specific programmatic changes included:

- fostering cohorts by involving experienced TAs in the teacher preparation program; requiring TAs to conduct peer observations in which they observe each others' teaching and provide feedback, and even instituting an Assistant Director Field Experience option;
- supporting grading practices by instituting regular grade norming sessions and workshops (both for new TAs and all instructors) and by reviewing and commenting on essays graded by new TAs; and
- helping each new TA develop a strong classroom *ethos* by asking them to reflect regularly on their classroom personas and providing additional support regarding issues relative to classroom management, plagiarism, and disruptive students. This support includes case studies, role-playing, and explicit instructions regarding department and university procedures for addressing problems in the classroom.

We also continue to use surveys to gather information from TAs and adjuncts during large and small programmatic transitions, as well as part of program assessment efforts, and we learn a great deal from them. We have not, however, given the same end-of-course surveys to the TAs in the two cohorts that have followed since the initial survey. The cohorts in both UTA's and NDSU's programs are relatively small (between five and eleven new TAs per year), and we felt that TAs might be concerned that their responses would not be truly "anonymous" because of the small cohort size if we repeated the survey too soon. We do, however, continue to conduct informal interviews with new and experienced TAs to determine whether parts or all of the teacher preparation programs are working, and we plan to survey our three newest cohorts after completion of the 2010-2011 academic year.

FUTURE DIRECTIONS

The teacher preparation course is a singular challenge because the list of things that should/could/must be accomplished seems limitless, and time is often a fundamental constraint. These teachers aren't preparing for some distant moment but for next semester or next week. And yet there's perhaps no more generative time to define the scope of such a course than during a period of transition.

Our collaboration reveals several valuable lessons. The first is just how useful a survey of instructors can be. It is vital that, as much as possible, all major stakeholders be included in these surveys so that their input is solicited and their voices are heard. The second is our determination that teacher preparation should emphasize community building among instructors and should help instructors feel comfortable with grading and responding to student essays, classroom management, and developing a teacher's *ethos*, though any practical advice should be grounded in theory. Finally, we are reminded that cross-program collaboration provides an invaluable outsider's perspective on this process.

Beyond the specific tactics and suggestions we devised for our programs, many of which seemed applicable in both of our locations so are likely to be useful more broadly, we see other non-pedagogical implications of our study. As Bellanger and Gruber note, the composition teacher preparation course serves as an important reflection of the goals, strengths, and weaknesses of the program as a whole. Administrators must revisit those goals, strengths, and weaknesses each year as they guide each class of new teachers through the program's syllabi, assignment sequences, grading and responding practices, etc.

As well, each new cohort's contributions shape administrators' ideas about the program. Bellanger and Gruber suggest that one goal of the teacher preparation course should be for TAs to develop the skills to critique first-year composition courses, the teacher preparation course itself, and program goals. Even as we acculturate TAs into our programs, we also invite their critiques of the preparation course—and, by implication, the program as a whole—when we ask them to provide feedback on their experiences of the teacher preparation course. Because this course may serve as the intellectual heart of the writing program, any changes in the program have to be reflected in the course, and changing the course has reverberations for the program, the department, and the field.

There are important future directions for this research, and we are excited to know that others are addressing the gap. For instance, Shelley Reid at George Mason University is studying graduate teaching assistants' attitudes about teaching composition, and her studies include both surveys and interviews with respondents. Her research, completed in collaboration with WPAs from other institutions, will help us better understand how novice and expert teachers' processes differ and how effective reflective practitioners develop their skills and knowledge over time.

With the job market in a 30-year slump, graduate students must be strong instructors to land jobs. The quality of their professional development matters for them, the students in their classes, and the status of our graduate programs. These compelling reasons suggest that teacher preparation should not end when the course is over; rather, TAs' professional development as teachers continues until they graduate. Similarly, we should not stop rethinking teacher education and professional development.

NOTES

1. This survey study was deemed exempt by the IRB Office at NDSU for both sites (Protocol #HS08220, April 2008).

2. We are sensitive to this problematic term, which suggests that these teachers assist someone, when they really assist only in the sense that they help departments teach hundreds of sections of writing each year for very little pay. However, we recognize that TA is the commonly used moniker for graduate students who teach. Therefore, we retain the term so others might easily find our discussion of TA teacher preparation.

3. Thanks to *WPA* editorial board members and reviewers for their helpful suggestions for revision.

4. Lowry also had the invaluable opportunity to collaborate with Tim Morris, her team teacher, when developing the survey, reviewing the survey results, and revising the teacher development course.

5. For any future use of the surveys, the primary question that we would alter was Question #9, working for increased specificity. Question 9 read, "For the following assignments or resources, please indicate the degree of usefulness to your teacher training on a scale from 1 to 5. The question was then followed by a list of pedagogical resources and practices. This question complicated the data. Many of the TAs had not experienced some of the items in the question (because the former courses were not static from semester to semester) but might have been able to suggest the potential usefulness of each strategy. It may be useful to combine questions 9 and 10 dealing with the actual and potential usefulness of TA course content. One possibility would be to build a branching question that starts by asking the respondent to identify whether or not she or he experienced that approach or resource, e.g., "Did you participate in the assessment session?" If yes, the branching would lead to a question about the degree to which that approach or resource was useful. If no, the branching question would ask whether he or she sees potential usefulness in the approach or resource.

6. Because UTA's common reading text is taught in first-semester composition, instructors must revise their courses each year to accommodate a new

text. New TAs are required to use or adapt the provided materials; adjuncts and experienced TAs are given the materials but provided much more latitude when developing their courses.

7. A playlist profile assignment was inspired by a talk given by John Logie at the Social Media Conference at NDSU in 2008. In that presentation, Logie suggested we should consider crafting playlist assignments to tap into students' experiences of web authoring and media convergence. Rupiper Taggart had taught leadership profile assignments in the past and blended the two for a first-year writing course featuring music as a central theme.

8. Thanks to Kelly Kinney at SUNY Binghamton for providing the idea for these workshops.

9. Thanks to Chris Anson and Carol Rutz, who developed the materials and ran this workshop.

Works Cited

Angelo, Thomas A., and K. Patricia Cross. *Classroom Assessment Techniques: A Handbook for College Teachers.* 2nd ed. San Francisco: Jossey-Bass, 1993. Print.

Boardman, Kathleen A. "A Usable Past: Functions of Stories among New TAs." *Writing Program Administration* 18.1-2 (Fall/Winter 1994): 29-36. Print.

Bellanger, Kelly, and Sibylle Gruber. "Unraveling Generative Tensions in the Composition Practicum." Dobrin 113-140.

Bettencourt, Patrick J. "Voicing Experience." Good and Warshauer 10-18.

Blumberg, Phyllis. *Developing Learner-Centered Teaching: A Practical Guide for Faculty.* San Francisco: Jossey-Bass, 2009. Print.

Bly, Brian. "Uneasy Transitions: The Graduate Teaching Assistant in the Composition Program." Good and Warshauer 2-9.

Brookfield, Stephen D. *Becoming a Critically Reflective Teacher.* San Francisco: Jossey Bass, 1995. Print.

Cooper, Allene, and D. G. Kehl. "Development of Composition Instruction through Peer Coaching." *Writing Program Administration* 14.3 (1991): 27-40. Print.

Dean, Deborah. *Genre Theory: Teaching, Writing, and Being.* Urbana: NCTE, 2008. Print.

Dobrin, Sidney I., ed. *Don't Call It That: The Composition Practicum.* Urbana: NCTE, 2005. Print.

Ebest, Sally Barr. "Mentoring: Past, Present, and Future." Pytlik and Liggett 211-21.

Eichhorn, Jill, Sara Farris, Karen Hayes, Adriana Hernandez, Susan Jarratt, Karen Powers-Stubbs, and Marian Sciachitano. "A Symposium on Feminist Experiences in the Composition Classroom." *College Composition and Communication* 43 (1992): 297-322. Print.

Fischer, Ruth Overman. "Theory in a TA Composition Pedagogy Course: Not If, but How." Dobrin 200-213.

Freedman, Diane, and Martha Stoddard Holmes. *The Teacher's Body: Embodiment, Authority, and Identity in the Academy.* Albany: SUNY P, 2003. Print.

Good, Tina LaVonne, and Leanne B. Warshauer. *In Our Own Voice: Graduate Students Teach Writing.* New York: Longman, 2008. Print.

Guerra, Juan C., and Anis Bawarshi. "Managing Transitions: Reorienting Perceptions in a Practicum Course." Dobrin 43-66. Print.

Hammond, Jennifer, ed. *Scaffolding: Teaching and Learning in Language and Literacy Education.* Newtown: Primary English Teaching Association, 2001. *ERIC Full Text.* Web. 15 Apr. 2010.

Hogan, Kathleen, and Michael Pressley, eds. *Scaffolding Student Learning: Instructional Approaches and Issues.* Cambridge: Brookline Books, 1999. Print.

Huba, Mary E., and Jann E. Freed. *Learner-centered Assessment on College Campuses: Shifting the Focus from Teaching to Learning.* Boston: Allyn and Bacon, 2000. Print.

Latterell, Catherine G. "Training the Workforce: An Overview of GTA Education Curricula." *Writing Program Administration* 19.3 (1996): 7-23. Print.

Logie, John. "My Spaces and My Faces: On the Emerging Rhetorics of Social Networks." Social Media Conference. North Dakota State University. March 2008. Keynote Address.

Martin, Wanda, and Charles Paine. "Mentors, Models, and Agents of Change: Veteran TAs Preparing Teachers of Writing." Pytlik and Liggett 222-32. Print.

McKinney, Jackie Grutsch, and Elizabeth Chiseri-Strater. "Inventing a Teacherly Self: Positioning Journals in the TA Seminar." *Writing Program Administration* 27 (2003): 59-74. Print.

Merrill, M. David. "First Principles of Instruction." *Educational Technology Research and Development,* 50.3 (2002): 43-59. Web. 24 March 2010.

Payne, Darin, and Theresa Enos. "TA Education as Dialogic Response: Furthering the Intellectual Work of the Profession through WPA." Pytlik and Liggett 50-62.

Pytlik, Betty P., and Sarah Liggett, eds. *Preparing College Teachers of Writing: Histories, Theories, Programs, Practices.* New York: Oxford UP, 2002. 50-62. Print.

Reid, Shelley. "What and How TAs Learn about Teaching Composition: Report from Year One of a Three-Year Study." CCCC, New Orleans. 4 Apr 2008. Address.

Roen, Duane, Lauren Yena, Veronica Pantoja, Eric Waggoner, and Susan K. Miller, eds. *Strategies for Teaching First-year Composition.* Urbana: NCTE, 2002. Print.

Rupiper Taggart, Amy. First-year English Committee Assessment Report: 2009-10. Fargo, ND: North Dakota State University. July 2010. Print.

Stancliff, Michael, and Maureen Daly Goggin. "What's Theorizing Got to Do with It? Teaching Theory as Resourceful Conflict and Reflection in TA Training Programs." *Writing Program Administration* 30.3 (2007): 11-28. Print.

Van Bennekom, Fred. "Statistical Confidence in a Survey: How Many Is Enough?" GreatBrook, n.d. Web 15 June 2008. http://www.greatbrook.com/survey_statistical_confidence.htm

Vandenberg, Peter, Sue Hum, and Jennifer Clary-Lemon, eds. *Relations, Locations, Positions: Composition Theory for Writing Teachers*. Urbana: NCTE, 2006. Print.

Weiser, Irwin. "Surveying New Teaching Assistants: Who They Are, What They Know, and What They Want to Know." *Writing Program Administration*: 14.1-2 (1990): 63-73. Print.

Winslow, Rosemary Gates. "The GTA Writing Portfolio: An Impact Study of Learning by Writing." Dobrin 315-336. Print.

Yancey, Kathleen Blake. "The Professionalization of TA Development Programs: A Heuristic for Curriculum Design." Pytlik and Liggett 63-74. Print.

Appendix: TA Survey Questions with Results

1. Please indicate the year you were trained.

2. To what degree were you satisfied with your teacher training at this institution?

>   1 very satisfied
>
>   2 satisfied
>
>   3 neutral
>
>   4 not very satisfied
>
>   5 not at all satisfied

3. What were the most valuable aspects of the training, the things we should absolutely keep?

4. What were the least valuable aspects of the training?

5. For what kinds of challenges did you feel most ill-prepared in the first year of training?

6. Which resources have you used the most from your TA training (workshops or course)?

7. Were there particular pieces of knowledge that should have come earlier in the training or later to meet your needs in a more timely fashion? If so, which?

8. [NDSU-specific question] To what degree did you find the joint pre-semester workshop with all teachers of 110/120 useful?

>   1 very useful
>
>   2 useful
>
>   3 minimally useful
>
>   4 not at all useful
>
>   5 N/A

8. [UTA-specific question] If you have been trained to teach in another program before this one, what was your experience going through training a second time? What advice do you have for us about how we can make the transition from one program to another a smooth one?

9. [NDSU-specific question] For the following assignments and resources, please indicate the degree of usefulness to your teacher training on a scale of 1 (most useful) to 5 (not applicable).

	1 very useful	2 useful	3 minimally useful	4 not at all useful	5 N/A
Completing all of the student writing assignments	0.0%	33.3%	22.2%	0.0%	44.4%
Learning portfolio	0.0%	22.2%	33.3%	11.1%	33.3%
Pre-professional portfolio	11.1%	55.6%	0.0%	11.1%	22.2%
K-log	0.0%	0.0%	11.1%	0.0%	88.9%
Deep vs. surface web handout	22.2%	22.2%	33.3%	0.0%	22.2%
NDSU campus resources training (media carts, library databases, instrumented classrooms, cluster reservations)	22.2%	44.4%	11.1%	11.1%	11.1%
Strategies book	33.3%	44.4%	11.1%	0.0%	11.1%
Misunderstanding the Assignment book	0.0%	0.0%	11.1%	0.0%	88.9%
How to connect course goals and assignments	33.3%	33.3%	11.1%	11.1%	11.1%
PowerPoint video training	0.0%	33.3%	11.1%	0.0%	55.6%
Readings on new literacy	11.1%	44.4%	33.3%	0.0%	11.1%
Casual discussion of ongoing classroom challenges	77.8%	11.1%	11.1%	0.0%	0.0%
Observing each others' classes	55.6%	44.4%	0.0%	0.0%	0.0%
Instruction on how to use textual models to teach genres	33.3%	33.3%	11.1%	0.0%	22.2%

	1 very useful	2 useful	3 minimally useful	4 not at all useful	5 N/A
Grading norming session (reading and grading samples as a group)	55.6%	11.1%	22.2%	0.0%	11.1%
End of semester assessment sessions	0.0%	22.2%	44.4%	22.2%	11.1%
Reports in pre-semester workshop of assessment results from spring	0.0%	33.3%	33.3%	22.2%	11.1%
Other (write in item)					

#9 [UTA-specific question] For the following assignments and resources, please indicate the degree of usefulness to your teacher training on a scale of 1 (most useful) to 5 (not applicable).

	1 very useful	2 useful	3 minimally useful	4 not at all useful	5 N/A
UTA campus resources tour and training (Smart Classroom, library workshops, Writing Center tour)	25.0%	29.2%	20.8%	12.5%	12.5%
Teacher's Guide to First-Year English	41.7%	41.7%	16.7%	0.0%	0.0%
Readings on composition theory and pedagogy	39.1%	30.4%	21.7%	8.7%	0.0%
Completing a student paper assignment	37.5%	29.2%	20.8%	12.5%	0.0%
Class discussion	47.8%	39.1%	8.7%	4.3%	0.0%
Teaching a reading mini-lesson to fellow TAs and receiving feedback	65.2%	17.4%	13%	4.2%	0.0%
Teaching a writing mini-lesson to fellow TAs and receiving feedback	70.8%	20.8%	4.2%	4.2%	0.0%
Addressing the needs of ESL students lesson	16.7%	20.8%	33.3%	20.8%	8.3%

	1 very useful	2 useful	3 minimally useful	4 not at all useful	5 N/A
Using blogs in the composition classroom lesson	8.3%	37.5%	16.7%	16.7%	20.8%
Handling disruptive students lesson	16.7%	33.3%	20.8%	16.7%	20.5%
Grading norming session (reading and grading samples as group)	45.8%	37.5%	8.3%	8.3%	0.0%
Teaching the OneBook (common reading text) lesson	41.7%	16.7%	16.7%	4.2%	20.8%
Resource notebook	16.7%	16.7%	45.8%	16.7%	4.2%
Question and answer session with experienced TAs	25.0%	45.8%	16.7%	8.3%	4.2%
Casual discussion of ongoing teaching challenges	45.8%	45.8%	8.3%	0.0%	0.0%
Handling plagiarism lesson	12.5%	54.2%	20.8%	4.2%	8.3%
Teaching portfolio	12.5%	37.5%	25%	8.3%	16.7%
Observing a peer's class	41.7%	41.7%	16.7%	0.0%	0.0%
Responding and grading lesson	37.5%	37.5%	16.7%	4.2%	4.2%
Facilitating peer review lesson	26.1%	47.8%	17.4%	0%	8.7%
Developing 1302 syllabus lesson	41.7%	33.3%	8.3%	4.2%	12.5%
Creating and evaluating essay exams lesson	33.3%	25.0%	20.8%	4.2%	16.7%
Feedback on set of graded essays	25.0%	54.2%	4.2%	8.3%	8.3%
Dealing with disruptive students lesson	16.7%	20.8%	37.5%	8.3%	16.7%

10. [NDSU-specific question] How useful would the following resources be, if used in the teacher training, from 1 (most) to 5 (least?)

	1 most potentially useful	2 potentially useful	3 neutral	4 minimally useful	5 not useful
Teach a segment to classmates/fellow TAs and get feedback	33.3%	44.4%	11.1%	11.1%	0.0%
Handling plagiarism lesson	55.6%	44.4%	0.0%	0.0%	0.0%
Efficient grading and responding lesson	55.6%	22.2%	22.2%	0.0%	0.0%
Conference modeling	11.1%	55.6%	33.3%	0.0%	0.0%
Conference lesson	22.2%	33.3%	33.3%	11.1%	0.0%
Managing collaboration lesson	33.3%	55.6%	11.1%	0.0%	0.0%
Grading collaboration lesson	44.4%	44.4%	11.1%	0.0%	0.0%
How to develop a unit	75.0%	12.5%	12.5%	0.0%	0.0%
Scaffolding assignments	44.4%	44.4%	11.1%	0.0%	0.0%
What is formative assessment and how to use it (minute papers, unit reflections, etc.)	44.4%	33.3%	22.2%	0.0%	0.0%
Addressing the needs of ESL students lesson	22.2%	66.7%	0.0%	11.1%	0.0%
Handling disruptive students lesson	44.4%	33.3%	11.1%	11.1%	0.0%
Using blogs in the composition classroom lesson	0.0%	55.6%	11.1%	33.3%	0.0%
Question and answer session with experienced GTAs	33.3%	44.4%	11.1%	11.1%	0.0%

10. [UTA-specific question] How useful would the following resources be, if used in the teacher training, from 1 (most) to 5 (not applicable)?

	1 very useful	2 useful	3 minimally useful	4 not at all useful	5 N/A
Teach a segment to classmates/ fellow TAs and get feedback	69.6%	21.7%	8.7%	0.0%	0.0%
Efficient grading and responding lesson	62.5%	37.5%	0.0%	0.0%	0.0%
Conference modeling	8.3%	54.2%	29.2%	0.0%	8.3%
Conference lesson	4.2%	62.5%	25.0%	0.0%	8.3%
Managing collaboration lesson	16.7%	45.8%	25.0%	4.2%	8.3%
Grading collaboration lesson	13.0%	47.8%	30.4%	0.0%	8.7%
How to develop a unit	43.5%	43.5%	8.7%	0.0%	4.3%
Sequencing assignments	37.5%	50.0%	12.5%	0.0%	0.0%
What is formative assessment and how to use it (minute papers, unit reflections, etc.)	25.0%	62.5%	8.3%	0.0%	4.2%
Classroom management	41.7%	37.5%	12.5%	4.2%	4.2%
Workshops led by experienced TAs	54.2%	29.2%	12.5%	0.0%	4.2%
Formal mentorship relationship between new and experienced TAs	66.7%	29.2%	4.2%	0.0%	0.0%

WPAs Respond to "A Symposium on Fostering Teacher Quality"

Response to "A Symposium on Fostering Teacher Quality"

Sue Doe

The symposium on fostering teacher quality caused me to recall a moment at the beginning of the semester when I was trapped in a groundswell of students in the stairwell of my building, the location where most of the teaching of writing, foreign languages, and other humanities occurs on our campus. This moment occurred during the first week of classes and the halls were teeming with students, so much so that the hallways had become impassable and I found myself in human gridlock, stuck about halfway up three flights of stairs. If someone were to fall, I realized, it would set off a domino effect like the ones we've seen in videos of malfunctioning escalators. As we moved one step at a time, I grew angry. Why were we crowded this way? Why was the important teaching of the university relegated to these cramped quarters? How much expansion to enrollment was going on at the expense of teaching and learning? And what was the effect of this growth on students who were no doubt internalizing a message about the crowded and confused state of the humanities? This feeling was exacerbated, I realized, by the fact that I had just come from the brand new multi-million dollar Behavioral Sciences building just fifty yards to the south of my building, a location where minutes before I had basked, albeit briefly, in the sunlight and open space of New Construction.

However, this perception of material inequity was challenged as I read the essays in the Fostering Teacher Quality Symposium which address how to develop and reward teachers and teaching quality, particularly in the context of teaching that is performed off the tenure track. These essays admonish us to commit to professionalism. The WPAs here suggest that even if we find ourselves in a crowded stairwell, we must still push forward rather than falter, and they offer practical suggestions. Specifically, Moneyhun shows us how the annual review of contingent faculty can be transformed from "uneasy transaction" (161) to a deepening of expertise; Brunk-Chavez connects self-directed faculty development of contingent faculty to useful assessment; Ashe argues for ongoing reform and data capture (assessment) as a central feature of good teaching. The models reported here reinforce what fourth symposium author, Beason, describes as the essential role of "place" or "rootedness" (150) to the development and support of the affective dimension of faculty effectiveness. What are these practical suggestions and how do they contribute to the affective? Here's my sense of how these ideas contribute to this important line of thinking.

Moneyhun's transformation of the annual performance review to "a natural part of the rhythm of the year" (165) shows how closely tied faculty development and a rising sense of professional teaching agency can be. A central component of Moneyhun's model is the involvement of instructors in creating the terms of their own appraisal, even as the WPA provides leadership that pushes instructors to reach disciplinary and institutional objectives. Called upon to participate in the development of their own performance indicators, and subsequently held accountable for them, the contingent faculty in Moneyhun's program were "to a person, amazingly patient and generous," and "began to take advantage of the opportunities… offered to professionalize with reflective teaching practices" (165). Moneyhun's example suggests what is possible when both collaboration and leadership are directed toward setting expectations, measuring performance, and negotiating priorities. This model gives attention to the affective dimension of teaching without sacrifice of high expectation.

Brunk-Chavez, like Moneyhun, argues for practices that help develop "a program community" that focuses on supporting "the faculty member as teacher, professional, and person" (153). Brunk-Chavez suggests that while such professional development is the norm for graduate students, it is less commonly provided for experienced instructors, who nonetheless profit from the experience. Using the notion of "embracing our expertise," (154) contingent faculty in Brunk-Chavez's program not only participate in faculty development but lead it. Such practices, Brunk-Chavez argues, improve the quality of instruction and specifically the teaching of writing. With Brunk-Chavez, we see the importance of the affective addressed through non-tenure-track leadership in professional development, which in turn leads to proactive cultures of teaching.

The notion of culture is addressed even more fully by Ashe's strategies for building a culture of teaching. Her call for measures of teacher quality, after material conditions of the workplace have been addressed, is absolutely essential. She points out that effective teaching is not necessarily popular teaching, and argues for measures of teaching quality that go beyond the current semester to demonstrate "learning that students carry on to later and more challenging courses" (158). She also argues for annual review processes that provide space not just for information about new courses but for improvements to existing ones. Her point is that an attitude of continuous revision to teaching practices, based on a culture that treats assessment as positive, ongoing reform, is quite simply, "what good teachers do" (159). Her article reminds me of the important 1995 *Change* magazine article by Barr and Taggart that shifted the discussion in higher education from the content of teaching to evidence of learning. Ashe's article suggests that contingent faculty can be part of such change.

Taken together, these three writers—Moneyhun, Brunk-Chavez, and Ashe—suggest strategies for building the essential "sense of place" that Beason argues is needed by all faculty yet is frequently absent in the lives of contingent faculty. Beason asks, "How do we develop the affective components of teaching?" and these essays suggest several concrete steps. As Beason points out, "places are human constructs" that lead people to "feel satisfied, accepted, and attached to significant people and events in their lives" (150). Each WPA in this symposium offers a meaningful approach that demonstrates a commitment to teachers and the quality of their teaching. As such, these WPAs are building nothing less than a sense of place through the development of professional teaching identity and culture, and these approaches are theoretically informed and locally responsive. They treat teaching as high calling and instructors as professional practitioners and partners. They argue for the formation of programmatic bonds derived in a shared local space and through a clarification of values.

Perhaps most importantly, these essays suggest what can happen when we take hold of the potential of our writing programs in their current forms. By this, I mean that these WPAs have embraced what *is*, over some eidolon of what *was* or what *ought to be*. Their articles carve out a new discursive space of self-respect and practical accountability and away from the language of scarcity, sacrifice, and defeat. They suggest that we have choices when we stand in the crowded stairwells of our crumbing old buildings and compare our situation to the clean spare spaces across campus. One option, they suggest, is to take a deep breath and move forward. With responsible leadership like theirs, which integrates a professionalized contingent faculty into measures of teaching quality, we can improve teaching conditions while also showcasing improvements to the teaching and learning of writing. In the process, our writing programs might become more visible models of the relevance and success of the teaching mission even as it is conducted largely off the tenure track.

WORKS CITED

Ashe, Diana. "Fostering Cultures of Great Teaching." *WPA: Writing Program Administration* 34 (2010): 149-52. Print.

Barr, Robert B., and John Tagg. "From Teaching to Learning: A New Paradigm for Undergraduate Education." *Change: The Magazine for Higher Learning* 27.6 (November/December 1995): 12-25. Print.

Beason, Larry. "Fostering Quality through Sense of Place." *WPA: Writing Program Administration* 34 (2010): 149-52. Print.

Brunk-Chavez, Beth. "Embracing Our Expertise through Faculty and Instructional Development." *WPA: Writing Program Administration* 34 (2010): 152-55. Print.

Moneyhun, Clyde. "Performance Evaluation as Faculty Development." *WPA: Writing Program Administration* 34 (2010): 161-65. Print.

Fostering Teacher Quality through Cultures of Professionalism

Claire Coleman Lamonica

Each of the four articles published in the "Symposium on Fostering Teacher Quality" has important points to make about the ways in which WPAs can foster teacher quality and, in turn, improve student learning. In a way, however, reading the four individual texts is like looking at the pieces of a puzzle without seeing the whole picture. We have to assemble the pieces before we can tell if anything is missing. Providing writing instructors with a strong sense of place (Larry Beason), encouraging them to engage in ongoing professional development (Beth Brunk-Chavez), involving them in educative[1] evaluation processes (Clyde Moneyhun), and fostering "cultures of great teaching" (Diana Ashe) can each have a profound impact on teacher quality and retention. But I would suggest that to have the most profound impact on student learning, our writing programs need to be infused with a culture of professionalism that not only includes, but extends these.

The cultures of professionalism to which I refer are clearly broader than Ashe's "cultures of great teaching." Ashe is advocating primarily for evaluation processes that include "multiple points of evaluation" (160) and "encourage the habits that create 'superstar' teachers" (159). These are excellent ideas, and certainly one highly-desirable result of effective faculty evaluation, as Moneyhun points out, is professional development, or, more accurately, the "professionalization" (165) of teaching. But a culture of professionalism must be more than a system of evaluation, even one as well considered and comprehensive as those described by Ashe and Moneyhun.

As Ashe points out, a good place to start developing a culture of great teaching or, I might add, a culture of professionalism, is with a consideration of "findings [such as those offered in] *Teaching as Leadership* [that] encourage us to think about how our departments and programs can influence and encourage the habits that create 'superstar' teachers" (159.) Ashe is careful to note that the "characteristics [offered in the report]... emerge from K-12 schools" (159), but in fact that they are not so very different from the findings of a more relevant study reported in *What the Best College Teachers Do,* by Ken Bain.

Bain bases his findings on fifteen years of research into the "practices and thinking of the best [college] teachers, those people who have remarkable success in helping their students achieve exceptional learning results" (3). Because Bain's investigation *begins* with student achievement as the standard for identifying "the best;" because it focuses on college, not K-12 teachers; and because it includes teachers from a wide variety of institutions (including both two and four-year schools) and academic disciplines (including not just STEM disciplines, but also the arts and the humanities), it addresses most of Ashe's concerns about the studies she cites in her article while also extending the findings of those studies.

Bain's book is organized around seven broad questions: What do [the best college teachers] know about how we learn? How do they prepare to teach? What do they expect of their students? How do they conduct class? How do they treat their students? How do they evaluate their students and themselves? Because the answers to these questions are offered in rich, thoughtful, highly contextualized prose, they are not easily summarized. They do, however, largely support and extend Farr's findings (as discussed by Ashe) while echoing Carrell and West's concerns about the "value and accuracy" of using student evaluations "as a measurement of teaching quality for academic promotion and tenure decisions" (qtd. in Ashe 157), particularly when student evaluations are the only—or even the primary—measure taken into account.

In short, Bain notes that (and I provide these synopses reluctantly, for they reduce Bain's rich findings to exactly the kind of mundane sound bites that can only fail to do them justice) "the best college teachers" understand that learning is a developmental process of constructing, extending, and revising "mental models" (27); prepare to teach by asking themselves important questions about what students need to learn, how best to support student learning, how to best assess student learning, and how to most effectively assess their own teaching; expect that all students can and will learn; create in their classrooms the kind of "natural critical learning environments"[2] (99) that promote and support student learning; treat their stu-

119

dents with respect; and regularly assess both their students' learning and their own teaching in a variety of appropriate ways, both formative and summative.

Ideally, a writing program that embodies a culture of professionalism would build on Bain's findings in a number of ways. First, it would recognize that even the most thoughtful teacher evaluation process, while a necessary component of any successful program, is not sufficient for ensuring quality teaching. Quality teaching is most likely to become a hallmark of a program in which instructors are, first and foremost, prepared to teach. That means providing those "unstable cadre[s] of graduate student and part-time contingent faculty" (Smagorinsky 3, qtd. in "Symposium") with professional development opportunities that help them construct both disciplinary and pedagogical knowledge.

Both Brunk-Chavez and Moneyhun identify rationales for and approaches to this challenge, chief among them being the inclusion of instructors themselves in the design and implementation of professional development programming. This approach mirrors the National Writing Project's highly effective model of "teachers teaching teachers," in which teachers are provided opportunities to develop their own expertise and share that expertise with each other, resulting in demonstrable gains in student learning (About NWP).

At the same time, we must understand that there is no "quick fix" to the issue of faculty development. Students' mental models are not the only ones that change slowly. Thus, in a culture of professionalism, "professional development," like "teacher evaluation," cannot be relegated to once or twice-yearly events. It must be woven into the fabric of the program, ideally in ways that are natural outgrowths of the work writing instructors are already doing.

We also need to recognize that even highly-evolved, well-integrated systems of professional development and teacher evaluation alone are insufficient for creating a culture of professionalism. Such a culture also needs to address, as Beason notes, the affective domain of teacher work/life. Certainly, supporting instructors in their quest to develop a "sense of place" grounded in their own classrooms and programs is a start, but even more prosaically, we need to take what we might call the Abraham Maslow approach to professionalism.[3]

If we work backward, through Maslow's hierarchy of needs, we discover that writing instructors are unlikely to even feel the need for a sense of professionalism unless they have already established a sense of belonging (Beason's "sense of place"), which is likely rooted in a sense of security (contracts for periods as long as we can make them), and which grows from the fulfillment of basic human needs.

When I was a WPA, creating a culture of professionalism occasionally involved making sure that graduate students new to the US had access to basic household furnishings or coats warm enough to ward off winter winds. In my current role as a faculty developer, we devote part of our annual New Faculty Orientation to a session called "Connecting with the Community," during which community leaders answer new faculty members' questions about where and how to access community resources for themselves and their families. In other words, we don't expect either graduate students or new faculty members to be truly focused on developing a sense of professionalism without also providing access to resources that meet their more basic needs.

In short, creating a culture of professionalism is about creating a community of caring professionals who share high standards for themselves and their students, work collaboratively to help each other reach those standards, and continually evaluate and re-evaluate their own progress as developing professionals in light of those standards. If we can do that, there is a growing body of evidence[4] that these cultures will have a positive impact on student learning.

NOTES

1. "Educative" assessment, introduced by Grant Wiggins in *Educative Assessment: Designing Assessments to Inform and Improve Student Performance*, focuses on measuring learning through engagement in authentic tasks. Its central components, as described by Wiggins, are criteria and standards, forward-looking assessment, and self-assessment. To these, L. Dee Fink, author of *Creating Significant Learning Experiences*, adds FID-eLity, feedback that is frequent, immediate, discriminating, and loving. Typically, the goal of educative assessment is improved student learning. Educative approaches to faculty evaluation would focus on providing criteria and standards for authentic, professional work (as described by Moneyhun, not only teaching, but also research and service) in an effort to encourage professionalism, improve teacher performance, and, ultimately, enhance student learning.

2. "Natural critical learning environments," as described by Ken Bain in *What the Best College Teachers Do* include "five essential elements" (100): "an intriguing question or problem" (100); "guidance in helping the students understand the significance of the question" (100); the engagement of students in "some higher-order intellectual activity" (102); support for students as they work to answer the question (103); and students who are left with an additional question or questions (103).

3. In "A Theory of Human Motivation," originally published in 1943 in *Psychological Review*, Abraham Maslow identified what has come to be called his "hierarchy of needs" (Maslow). His theory posits that, along the road to becoming a fully "self-actualized" human being, we must first find ways to meet a variety of more immediate needs, including physiological, safety, love and belonging, and esteem.

4. This "growing body of evidence" includes not only the Farr article cited by Ashe and data from the National Writing Project at http://www.nwp.org/cs/public/print/doc/results.csp, but also a presentation at the January, 2011 AAC&U Conference in San Francisco to which Bill Condon, Washington State University, contributed. The title of the session was "Faculty Development Within Cross-Curricular Initiatives: What Are the Effects on Student Learning?" Gudrun Willett et al.

WORKS CITED

"About NWP." *The National Writing Project*. Web. 25 Feb. 2011.

Bain, Ken. *What the Best College Teachers Do*. Cambridge: Harvard UP, 2004. Print.

Fink, L.Dee. *Creating Significant Learning Experiences*. San Francisco: Jossey-Bass, 2003. Print.

Maslow, A. "A Theory of Human Motivation." Web. 25 Feb. 2011. http://psych-classics.yorku.ca/Maslow/motivation.

Wiggins, Grant. *Educative Assessment: Designing Assessments to Inform and Improve Student Performance*. San Francisco: Jossey-Bass, 1998. Print.

Response to "A Symposium on Fostering Teacher Quality"

Mike Palmquist

As I've considered my response to the symposium, I've found myself returning again and again to the notion of place—and of those among us who feel out of place. Larry Beason's essay, "Fostering Quality through Sense of Place," resonates not only with my experiences as a WPA and, more recently, as the director of an institute that focuses in part on professional development of faculty, but also with my work with the National Council of Teachers of English on its recently published Position Statement on the Status and Working Conditions of Contingent Faculty.[1] These experiences have helped me appreciate the importance of place in its many meanings: as a location in space (as someone who comes to work each day, for example, in a particular institution); as a position within a particular program or department (full-time or part-time, tenure-line or contingent); as a member of a community, with all of its social relationships, affinities, and hierarchies; and as a location for our scholarly interests and professional activities. Within the context of professional development, place offers a useful set of metaphors for considering where we are as we begin a program, where we might be as we move through it, and why we might resist or embrace a program's messages about teaching and learning, professional growth, and our role within our institution and the larger field of composition studies.

Citing work dating to the 1970s, Beason argues, "Place attachment, or a feeling of rootedness, is a powerful human need that helps people connect and 'be themselves.' It results in emotional ties to places that 'involve a sense of shared interests and values…bringing a sense of belonging and order to one's sociospatial world' (Cuba and Hummon 113)" (150). Beason's focus on the affective dimensions of place reminded me of observations recently offered by Lisa Meloncon and Peter England in an article included in the March 2011 special issue of *College English* on contingent faculty, which Sue Doe and I edited. As editors, we were intrigued by their use of non-place, a concept developed by Auge' (O'Beirne). Meloncon and England present non-place as "a disconnect between individuals and their interaction with their surroundings" (404).

While Meloncon and England refer specifically to instructors in contingent positions within the field of technical and professional communication—and more generally to the implications of their location within an area of study that is not fully recognized by the academy—their observations apply well to the conditions under which many of our colleagues in composition studies find themselves. With more than 70 percent of composition courses taught by faculty members in contingent positions (2007 ADE Ad Hoc Committee on Staffing), any discussions of professional development must take into account the conditions—that is the places, or in far too many cases, the non-places, in which so many composition faculty members find themselves.

As we consider professional development initiatives for faculty members working in contingent positions, we must ask whether our colleagues feel rooted in our programs and our discipline. Perhaps more important, we must ask how we might create the conditions in which the sense of "rootedness" that Beason calls for might develop.

Some of these conditions are addressed by the other members of the symposium. Beth Brunk-Chavez offers a promising approach in her description of "a high quality faculty and program community," something she also refers to as a "writing program community" (153). Her argument for the value of exploring the relationships among professional development, teacher assessment, and curriculum design suggests (in a move that echoes recent applications of activity theory within composition studies) the conditions under which shared work can lead to a stronger sense of community—and, I would argue, following one of the key recommendations in the NCTE position statement, a sense of shared ownership—in local institutional and larger disciplinary communities.

Similarly, Diana Ashe's discussion makes clear the importance of full-time, long-term teaching positions as a precondition for the development of measures of teaching quality that are "reliable, fair, and consistent." She calls attention to the need for faculty members to find a place within local institutional communities (156). Her argument that "[i]mprovements in labor practices should go hand-in-hand with improvements in our understanding and assessment of teacher quality" highlights the critical relationship between professional development, working conditions, and investment in the community (157).

Clyde Moneyhun, in turn, offers a thoughtful and useful description of the kind of assessment process that Ashe calls for, one in which all members of the composition faculty share in creating, refining, and enacting a writing program community. In his observation that this kind of assessment process should be consistent with (we might say "rooted in") institutional practices and codes, Moneyhun calls attention to the importance of local context and history. Equally important, his argument for an open process that leads to dialogue about improvements in teaching and learning points to a process that, in his words, is not simply an evaluation process, but is also "a valuable opportunity for fostering faculty development" (165).

The symposium offers strong evidence for the importance of predicating professional development on equitable working conditions, shared governance, and long-term security of employment. My recent immersion—admittedly from a position of privilege—in work related to the status and working conditions of faculty in contingent positions convinces me of the importance of informing our professional development efforts with an understanding of the implications of our increasing reliance on instructors who work in contingent positions. Professional development initiatives must begin with an understanding of the places in which so many members of our discipline find themselves and of the places where we hope to go, together, as a profession. This understanding should also inform our efforts to develop places—local and national, physical and digital, social and disciplinary—where we can work together as communities that advance our teaching and learning.

NOTE

1. The statement was developed by the NCTE College Section Working Group on the Status and Working Conditions of Contingent Faculty, endorsed by the College Section Steering Committee in 2009, and adopted in 2010 by the Executive Committee. The working group was made up of Sue Doe, James McDonald, Beatrice Mendez Newman, Mike Palmquist (chair), Robert Samuels, and Eileen Schell. It can be found at http://www.ncte.org/positions/statements/contingent_faculty.

WORKS CITED

ADE Ad Hoc Committee on Staffing. "Education in the Balance: A Report on the Academic Workforce in English." Modern Language Association. MLA, 10 Dec. 2008. Web. 28 Feb. 2011.

Ashe, Diana. "Fostering Cultures of Great Teaching." *WPA: Writing Program Administration* 34 (2010): 155-61. Print.

Beason, Larry. "Fostering Quality through Sense of Place." *WPA: Writing Program Administration* 34 (2010): 149-52. Print.

Brunk-Chavez, Beth. "Embracing Our Expertise through Faculty and Instructional Development." *WPA: Writing Program Administration* 34 (2010): 152-55. Print.

Committee on Economic Status. "2008–09 Report on the Economic Status of the Profession, 2008–09." American Association of University Professors. AAUP, 14 Apr. 2009. Web. 28 Feb. 2011.

Cuba, Lee, and David M. Hummon. "A Place to Call Home: Identification with Dwelling, Community, and Region." *Sociological Quarterly* 34 (1993): 111-31. Print.

Meloncon, Lisa, and Peter England. "The Current Status of Contingent Faculty in Professional and Technical Communication." *College English* 73.4 (2011): 396-408. Print.

Moneyhun, Clyde. "Performance Evaluation as Faculty Development." *WPA: Writing Program Administration* 34 (2010): 161-65. Print.

O'Beirne, Emer. "Mapping the Non-Lieu in Marc Augé's Writings." *Forum for Modern Language Studies* 42.1 (2006): 38-50. Print.

Crabgrass and Gumbo: Interviews with 2011 WPA Conference Local Hosts about the Place of Writing Programs at their Home Institutions

Shirley K Rose, Irwin Peckham, and James C. McDonald

At its March 2010 meeting, the Editorial Board of *WPA: Writing Program Administration* decided to begin devoting space in the spring issues of the journal to a feature related to writing programs in the area where the summer conference would be held. In these interviews with the local hosts of the 2011 WPA Summer Conference in Baton Rouge, Louisiana, Irvin Peckham at Louisiana State University in Baton Rouge and James C. McDonald at University of Louisiana at Lafayette, I explore the ways they see the writing programs at their universities reflecting their institutional and regional cultures. —SKR

November 15, 2011: Conversation with Professor Irvin Peckham, Louisiana State University, Local Co-Host for the 2011 Summer Conference of the Council of Writing Program Administrators in Baton Rouge, Louisiana

SKR: Thanks for taking the time to talk with me, Irv. What I want to do in this conversation is to explore the ways the writing program there at LSU reflects the place where it is. With all of us coming to Baton Rouge this summer for the conference, it seems like a way to help us all start thinking about the conference and also to be thinking about the ways that in fact our own writing programs are placed. They do reflect the places where they are. That's what I had in mind as I developed these questions, so let's just see where this conversation takes us.

Let me begin by asking you about some basic demographic information about writing programs at LSU. What are the various writing programs, how are they organized, who leads them, and does the organization reflect the larger institution?

IP: There are basically three programs. The required writing program includes the basic writing program, a first and second year writing program—that's your ordinary required writing program, with a writing program director and with an associate writing program director, and now we have a graduate assistant who is an assistant director. Probably one of the most notable things about the required writing program is that it has historically resisted the use of adjuncts or part-time teachers and I think that's a long-time thing. That might go back to the 1970s or 1980s when they insisted on hiring fulltime renewable Instructors. They created a model for evaluating Instructors and giving them something that is *de facto* tenure. That's the primary one.

About five years ago we developed a communicating across the curriculum program that Lilly[1] came in to get going and she did a marvelous job, but last year she resigned. The Director of Communicating Across the Curriculum is charged with spreading writing and communication systems with a strong focus on multi-media in the different programs across the campus. The emphasis on multi-media took hold pretty solidly. Sarah Liggett is now directing it.

The third part is the creative writing program. That's a historically important part of LSU's English department. It's been an important part of our identity, and I can't speak as authoritatively as others in the department, but it goes back to the creation of the *Southern Review*[2] and the various luminaries, like Cleanth Brooks and Robert Penn Warren, who were brought in. Huey Long brought them here. He had an emphasis on bringing in big names—mostly literary writers—to start the creative writing program. The Director of the Creative Writing is basically the sub-chair of the department and right now Jim Wilcox is the director.

SKR: When was it that the creative writing program got its start?

IP: Early 1940s.

SKR: That's a long time in higher education.

IP: The luminaries' names are all over the halls. They're famous. Try to think of literary scholars of the South and they were here. That heritage has still been with us. I would say that the creative writing program reflects the larger institution. It's a large part of our heritage and is a large part of our identity. So Southern literature is a very big part of our program. It's grounded in Southern culture. There's an immense pride in our Southern culture. It maybe helps us to raise our heads above the kind of press that that we get as Louisianans who have somebody like Bobby Jindal[3] leading them.

Within the culture of the creative writing program there is an external program that's part of the creative writing program—it's the Readers and Writers at LSU. It's an organization that links the creative writing program with the community. It's a very important community program. It was actually started by three or four people, one of whom is my neighbor right now. Louise and Charles Prosser were instrumental in starting it about twenty years ago. Readers and Writers brings in very big names; they ask various readers and writers to read their work and then they ask them questions. It's definitely a very well recognized community organization.

SKR: How do students and teachers in your writing programs reflect the local culture and economy?

IP: Who comes to LSU is in many ways determined by the economic situation of LSU. The one important thing to remember is that essentially there is free tuition for students with a high school 2.5 GPA. This is the TOPS[4] program. It was initiated maybe twenty-years ago by a wealthy oil-man who then moved to Texas; I can't remember his exact name.[5] He left a good part of his fortune to generate income so that the tuition for all our students from the lower social class or working classes could attend the LSU for free. Our legislature got a hold of that and maybe about ten years after the original program was started they argued against this discrimination against the wealthy people so they expanded that program so that no matter what your income level if you had a certain grade point you would be able to go to LSU essentially for free.

The legislature then takes the local taxes and a portion of or certain amount of state income to fuel that TOPS program. So that's an important part of LSU's culture. It's our economy—we are trying to of course keep these students in Louisiana; that's part of the idea, but the other part was to offer free education.

It would be hard to explain all the dynamics of the difference between private schools and public schools here. This has been historically a socially and a racially segregated community and that segregation feeds into social class-racial segregation. That is, the black people are most of the poor people and most people in prison are African American. All of the private schools are largely white while public schools are largely black and there's a kind of *de facto* method of trying to make sure that the wealthier whites do not lose this kind of financing that other people are entitled to, if you see what I mean. And so the large number of the tax dollars in Louisiana definitely are going to a private school system because that's where all the kids of people who are state legislators go to school. So that's certainly in many ways a reflection of local culture. I wouldn't call it a positive reflection.

The positive part of the local culture is just basically southern culture. You recognize that as a professor when you come from the north as I did. The local culture is very friendly. People are generally very polite. Kids are very polite. They're much more polite here than you see in other parts of the country, and it's "Yes, Sir" or "Yes, Ma'am" everything--they're taught to do that. It's kind of unique. It hits you in the face as soon as you come here.

The teachers mostly grew up here. The students grew up here. They just absolutely love the South. You tell graduate students that they actually have to look someplace north of Tennessee for the job and they just look at you like you're crazy. They do not want to leave the South. It's very extended-family-oriented—more so than you would see in another part of the country, certainly than in California.

I can't really give you the demographic figures, yet I'd guess that maybe 15% of our LSU students are African American. We have an extraordinarily prevalent Cajun culture—not as much as at the University of Louisiana Lafayette, but Cajun culture is very important here. It's the Anglo-French that came down I believe from Nova Scotia—I think that might have been in the 1850s and 1860s, but it might have been earlier than that—and they settled on the western side of the Mississippi, south of Lafayette pretty much in the swamp lands and became fishermen and swamp farmers, so this is a very strong French culture. There's a French culture and then there's a French Cajun culture and on the other side of the Mississippi there's a Spanish culture still very much intact. Baton Rouge is actually an area where you're sitting right in middle of Native American culture, the French culture, and Cajun culture, the Spanish-American culture and the African American—brought by the Africans who were brought here as slaves from Africa. But a little bit to the south from here towards New Orleans you get the Caribbean black culture and many were free blacks. I didn't know anything about the free black culture before I came here, but it's been an important part in the Louisiana culture that centers in the New Orleans area but that comes up to the Baton Rouge area as well. It's a very rich and diverse culture. Of course there's the Anglo culture, but that doesn't count. If you go about maybe thirty maybe forty or fifty miles north of Baton Rouge and then the north part of Louisiana there is considered Anglo culture.

SKR: Are most of the LSU students from Baton Rouge?

IP: No, No—they come from across the state. We do get a lot of Baton Rouge students, without question. If people from Baton Rouge are going to go to college then many are going to go to Louisiana State if they can. But we definitely get kids from across the state. Out of state is about 20%.

SKR: How is this diversity reflected in your writing programs, or is it?

IP: I don't think it's reflected in the writing program. It's just what you see. If you're a teacher you respond to individual students as individual students. I think most people are very happy with the diversity. It seems like a rich diversity. I think most of us are fairly clear we'd like to see a much larger African American population in our classes. Since I've been here, which is ten years, that's increased significantly.I remember when I first taught a first-year writing class here there might've only been one or two African Americans. I'm teaching one now, and out of twenty-two, I might have six or seven. That's quite a change. Now one of the problems is that we have a historically black college—one of the important historically black colleges—in northern Baton Rouge, so that draws an awful lot of the African American students. The college is called Southern University.[6] That's largely all black. There are a few Anglos that go up there.

SKR: I was reading about LSU's "Flagship Agenda," and it's my under-standing LSU is the premier research university in Louisiana. This is on the University's website, and the Agenda is introduced with this paragraph:

> Since its beginnings in 1860 LSU's history has been a story of growth and transformation. As the flagship institution for the state LSU has long been recognized for a rich intellectual environment and distinc-tive educational programs that are rooted in the unique culture, his-tory, and geography of Louisiana.[7]

So in what ways do you see the writing programs at LSU being rooted in the unique culture, history, and geography of Louisiana?

IP: Well, that really reads to me like an act of rhetoric, not a reality. It says nothing. Certainly not about the writing program. But at LSU you will see a lot of programs that are concerned with water, swampland, forestry, coastal erosion—things of that sort. We're very heavy into that and of course into oil. The portion of the Engineering Department that is devoted to a petroleum engineering is heavily subsidized and an important part of the institution. Nobody's actually offered me $1 million so I'm not really into that very much but you can definitely sense that people know here that

Louisiana politics work in the way that the culture works: the dominance of the oil industry seeps through everything—has its fingers every place.

SKR: Is there very much influence from Middle East oil interests?

IP: No. I would say you don't sense that at all. It's the people who work here, who have jobs here. Probably one of the best ways to describe the oil influence is that we have a Shrimp and Petroleum Festival and—yeah, the Shrimp and Petroleum Festival—it's down in Morgan City in the southernmost part of Louisiana. It's a very important fishing area. That juxtapositioning of the shrimp and the petroleum for a festival, that pretty much says it all. The people who live there work part of the season as fishermen and women, part of the season in the oil industry. When the season is out, they're out on the platforms or going out into the Gulf working in the oil industry. So those two things are just linked. Now they're linked in another way, with the last oil spill.[8]

SKR: Well, talk a little about how the oil spill has affected the university and the writing program. I would expect that there would be of course expertise from the Petroleum Engineering Department and elsewhere as far as the ideas about how to deal with the oil spill and so forth.

IP: With respect to the writing program, I haven't really seen any particular effect. There were certainly a lot of teachers who used those topics and, as a matter of fact, our semester assessment at the end of the semester was based on the topic of the oil spill. There are a lot of people who make hay out of topical issues in an all fields and there were a lot of grants of course that came out. The same thing with Katrina—Hurricane Katrina—there were all sorts of grants. Tragedy is a huge employment market supported by grants. None of us in the field of writing really tried to get into that that I know of although there are other people, say for instance in folk studies, who applied for grants to go down and get the stories of people in the wake of Katrina. And there were people interested in film in the department who were interested so they went down to make documentaries in New Orleans. They also got grants as well.

SKR: I'm interested in different ways that things that are happening locally get felt in the institutional culture. You said that writing people have not really gone after any of the tragedy-based grants.

IP: In creative writing maybe, but those of us in rhetoric and composition—there are five—I don't think any of us applied for grants. One of my friends makes TV documentaries and another one of my friends in creative writing thought she should keep collected stories of people and tell them. You know there's another issue about the flagship agenda. I think it reflects Mark Emmert's[9] idea of the flagship agenda. Emmert started it and I think he probably tried to get it going about 1999 and 2000. He's since left and is now the head of NCAA. The flagship agenda was Emmert's agenda to bring LSU up in its national ranking. We were not in the first-tier then and Emmert was talking about how we were going to be one of the top fifty state universities in the nation. I think we have now reached the top tier, but the purpose was to try to haul LSU up to a top ranking and by the way, that's what led to the dismissal of all the Instructors. You probably heard all about it when I first came here. We had to release many of our instructors, from about seventy-five down to thirty-eight. As I interpret it, that whole notion of a flagship agenda could be related to an insecurity about Louisiana—rural Louisiana—and our perceived lack of culture. The flagship agenda may be a way to push us into mainstream America. I may have expressed it badly, but you get the drift.

SKR: Tell me about the issue with the instructors. I don't quite understand the cause and effect.

IP: Emmert was using as his benchmark or his way of marking progress the rankings by the National Research Council. One of the important indicators of the National Research Council ratings is the ratio of tenured faculty to untenured faculty or tenure-track and non-tenure-track faculty. We had a very high ratio because we didn't hire adjuncts. When you're a university and you hire a high ratio of part-time teachers in your first-year writing program you're going to have a lower ratio of instructors to professors because part-time teachers don't count; but the instructors who are hired as full-time employees of the university do count. So the consequence was that we had that high ratio. Also, the provost before Emmert came in had tried to raise our rankings in *US News and World Report*. In *US News & World Report* they use an opposite kind of ranking; they use the use class sizes in ranking. So actually the year that I came here we were in the middle of hiring massive numbers of instructors. I had to hire in my first year eighteen new instructors in order to lower the class size from twenty-two down to nineteen. Emmert came in with his program and reversed that process because he was no longer looking at *US News and World Report*; he was looking at the National Research Council, which had a different criterion. So the order just came down to us in the department that we had to go from seventy-five full-time instructors to thirty-eight within three years.

SKR: That really helps to see these effects on the writing program of something happening at the institutional level. You think that was motivated by his feeling that LSU as a university in Louisiana—in the South—already had some things against it because of perceptions about the South? Top fifty is pretty ambitious.

IP: I'll say. Emmert definitely was aiming at the top tier—more than the top tier—the top tier of the top tier. Emmert kept saying this and he pointed out which ones the top tier schools were and he wanted us to be in that group. And then he left and became the President of the Washington State University system. He's been there and he's now just left there and is at the NCAA.

SKR: Do you want to talk about Katrina?

IP: Okay. That had a momentary and a radical effect on the writing program on and the university because we just had an immense increase in population with the refugees from the New Orleans area and from the area to the south. I don't know the number but the increase was close to 150,000 and there was a radical increase in the number of students who came in. Let's see, Katrina happened in the end of August and the spillover started in September—about the third week of September—and we suddenly had a huge influx of new students coming in from the various universities in the southern portion of Louisiana. So basically that increase caused a radical adjustment of the writing program. We created classes like mad. It was basically mildly controlled chaos. We made a lot of new sections and then hired additional people and teachers would take overloads of ten people. A lot of students actually did end up staying so it took the student population maybe a couple of years past that to settle down and still Baton Rouge did increase its population by maybe over 100,000 people.

SKR: And that's been a permanent increase?

IP: Yes that's been a permanent increase. I would say, culturally, there were still quite a lot of complaints about increasing crime because the theory is that a lot of the people who came to Baton Rouge were the dispossessed in New Orleans and so on. There were a lot of quite wealthy people who came as well. I think there was quite a conversation about increased criminal element for a couple of years as well. But on top of that, there was a huge increase in the tax base, so actually the city enjoyed quite an increase in income for maybe three or four years, actually just up until the last economic crisis.

SKR: Are there ways that that had any kind of long term impact on the writing program in terms of curriculum?

IP: No. I wouldn't say so. As I think of the curriculum, I would say a curriculum has a kind of base to it that is not going to be swayed or pushed in another direction as a consequence of a sudden natural disaster. Certainly people wrote about the issue but that didn't change the nature of the writing program.

SKR I can't expect you to know what happened with the New Orleans colleges and universities, but what's your sense of the differences in how they have been affected long-term?

IP: Well, it was a much longer effect. They were really struggling for, I would say, maybe three more years than we were. It really affected our program in the sense of a different kind of population, an increased population that we weren't prepared for maybe for two or three years. But for the New Orleans area, there are probably still schools that are still reeling and I'm talking about colleges. I think they just had a very difficult time adjusting due to a difference in population and a significantly different culture.

SKR: I have another question that's about the flagship agenda. The flagship agenda states its desired outcomes as these: "As a national flagship institution, LSU will advance knowledge and intellectual inquiry by promoting groundbreaking research; produce enlightened citizens by fostering critical thinking, ethical reflection, historical understanding, and cultural appreciation; enhance Louisiana by converting scientific and technological discoveries into new products and processes, by preparing an informed and creative labor force, and by applying university resources to solve economic, environmental, and educational challenges."

My question is, what part do the writing programs play in achieving those outcomes?

IP: In the first place, that whole paragraph is like somebody raising a flag and everybody saluting. It's just a mouthful—everybody believes those things. I can't take it too seriously. I think that we in our writing program—at least while I was working in it—I can't say how the new WPA is going to imagine the writing program—but we were just trying to help kids do well in their undergraduate courses. We were paying attention to what kind of writing assignments they would meet. We did a lot of work looking at those writing assignments and we were trying to imagine instruction to help them get through their undergraduate year, so that feeds into the "enlightened citizens" or "critical thinking," "ethical reflection," and "historical understanding" agendas. I think we had a more pragmatic goal.

SKR: You mentioned this earlier, but I want to go over it again. You were WPA at University of Nebraska Omaha before you went to Baton Rouge.

IP: I went back to graduate school when I was forty years old and I went back to UC San Diego. I took my first job as a WPA at Nebraska and I think I did that for three or four years. I should also mention I was at Wisconsin and also at a Canadian university. University of Wisconsin Madison—I went there for undergraduate and a Master's.

SKR: Are there ways—comparing different places and schools and their writing programs—are there ways that you see that those other programs reflected their places or that showed their differences?

IP: I wouldn't say geographical or cultural; I would say the nature of institution, actually. It was a metropolitan institution at the University of Nebraska Omaha and it catered to a lot of nontraditional students, a lot of working-class students as opposed to middle-class students and upper-middle-class students. So there was a more pragmatic focus—or a more recognizable pragmatic focus—a larger recognition of the role of technical and professional writing in the programs than at LSU. As a matter of fact, to a certain extent, because of the *Southern Review* heritage at LSU, there's a--let's call it cultural snobbishness—about technical and professional writing here that was not the case at Nebraska.

There was a link between the kind of writing program that we were running in Nebraska and professional writing, with the purpose that the kids who came through our writing programs would actually be able to take many of the jobs available in technical and professional writing in Nebraska. And there was also a much larger emphasis on teacher education and teachers coming into the English department and therefore the writing program. We had a Master's program that we liked—we liked having teachers come into our program and work on a Master's with the certain knowledge that it was going to take several years for them to complete their degrees. We felt they were a very rich part of our environment in the English department. I would say the opposite is true at LSU—there's a negative attitude--and it's part of that literary culture—a negative attitude towards these part-time students. We really don't accept the people who are not full-time graduate students in our program. We don't accept people unless they get fellowships or scholarships to be in the graduate program because we don't want to create a two-tiered program, but it might be something else as well. By two-tiered program, I mean there was one social group of people who had fellowships and the other social group who don't have fellowships. There is a large-scale resistance to that that is a cultural construction. You know I can't help but think in terms of the kind of elitism that goes with the scholar as opposed to the worker. Some people just don't want the teachers to come into the English department. On the other hand, that prejudice is changing. Certainly the chair of the department doesn't think that way at all. He is very much in favor of trying to open up the program to Master's students who take a course during the summer and a course during the year while they are teaching, And there are a good many of the rest of us to do that, particularly the younger teachers, who are forging stronger connections with the Department of Education.

SKR: Do you think that those differences—the differences you are noting between an English department that does see or is very aware of the roles that English Education is playing and the role technical writing and professional writing are playing versus one where it might be there but is ignored, it's not mentioned—do you think those who think that way in the English department reflect the larger institutional contexts as well?. There's a whole history that those attitudes come out of.

IP: Yes, it's the difference between a research institution and a metropolitan university. It's certainly not surprising. I would say I do think that the literary heritage of LSU makes it a little more resistant to a newer way of looking. It's very powerful.

SKR: I have a metaphor for the writing program at ASU: the ocotillo. They're just amazing. When they're thriving, they're stunning and when they're not, they're pretty grotesque looking. I see some features of the ASU writing program that I think are grotesque that I think are the outcome of lack of resources. Do you have a metaphor for LSU writing programs?

IP: I had an image. The plant that came to mind is crabgrass.

SKR: Tell me about that.

IP: It spreads on its own and it's hard to get rid of. It's a creeper. It's great to hold the dirt.

SKR: It protects against erosion. It's fast growing.

IP: If you've got it, you'd better like it. I have a big lawn to take care of here so I know it intimately.

SKR: Say some more about how that's like a writing program.

IP: Well, it's the tendrils. It goes throughout the university. The writing program occurs in the required writing program. But the notion about writing and how we teach writing—it goes out like the creeper as the students go into their other classes. If we do a good job, that's a good growth. It's how you teach writing and the notion or illusion of carryover. The transfer factor has everything to do with what students feel about it and how they reflect on it and how it comes back; it has everything to do with how they move forward through the university. It's just there. That's the wrong notion. What I'm trying to get at is the plant doesn't exist in the classroom only. It moves out. It stays low. That's the secret.

SKR: You can't get it with the mower.

IP: No. Absolutely not.

SKR: Great metaphor. I have just a couple more questions. When we come to Baton Rouge this summer, what place on campus should we visit? Other than the writing programs offices themselves, what places should we visit in order to understand how the institutional context has shaped LSU Writing Programs and why?

IP: You're not actually going to come to campus. You're going to be at a downtown hotel. We would love to have people come to campus because it really is a lovely campus.

SKR: If people wanted to get away on Saturday afternoon and come to campus, what should they see?

IP: I would say walk around in the area of the quad and in walking around, the most notable feature of the campus are the live oaks. They're absolutely beautiful. They're all over. Just try walking in these areas, particularly in the quad, which is in the central part of the campus by the union. That's where there are some gorgeous areas. There's another beautiful area if you go to the south end of the quad where there's a sculpture garden, with another quite huge display of live oaks. If anything distinguishes the campus, it's the live oaks.

The buildings themselves have the atmosphere that Huey Long[10] wanted to create. He wanted to create LSU to be the Stanford of the South so he sought an architecture for the main buildings of the campus that would reflect Stanford. It's as if Stanford had been brought here.

SKR: Why did he choose Stanford?

IP: I couldn't tell you that.

SKR: Why Stanford of the South and not Harvard of the South?

IP: I think it's more agrarian. More country. You know, Harvard would reflect too much of elitist Eastern culture. Huey Long was a populist. There wouldn't have been any way he would emulate Harvard or Yale. If you've been to Stanford, it has that rolling kind of Salinas feel to it—the golden hills, the spread-out buildings. We don't have the golden hills—we have the swamps—but we have that kind of spread-out building. That's the really remarkable feature or feeling of the campus.

The feeling of the campus is south. It's a very southern campus. The foliage is southern, the buildings look southern. It has an old genteel quality to it. I don't know that there are particular buildings—oh yes, people should come into Allen Hall, where the English Department is located. Not because the Department of English is anything extraordinary, but in Allen Hall, particularly on the first floor, are murals that were painted on the walls during the WPA[11] [Works Projects Administration] in the 1930s and 1940s by unemployed artists. They were painted over in the 1960s. People didn't even know they were there. About ten or fifteen years ago some paint came off and somebody saw them and totally restored them very, very carefully. It's a very folk-artist kind of painting. Very working-class painting representing the people who actually work with their hands. Those are kind of remarkable. They're fun to see.

Unfortunately, the stadium dominates. It kind of soars like the Empire State building. Ninety thousand people can fit in that stadium. So if people want to get the culture of LSU they should also go to one of those football games because it's a big deal here. The Library… we have a really strong online library; the physical reality of the library is not so much. Just walk around. The old library—it's a rare books library—is very beautiful and it's right by the Department of English.

SKR: What else would you like for other WPAs around the country to know and understand about LSU Writing Programs?

IP: It's focused on academic writing and on helping students try to manipulate their way through very difficult writing situations in their undergraduate courses. We don't have any question about that. We developed a program by looking at a large swath of writing tasks in other disciplines and really developed our program as a consequence of that research. One of the consequences of that investigation was a serious appreciation of the kinds of writing tasks that people in other departments were giving to their students. Many of the people were sophisticated and serious about their assignments and they wanted their students to write—particularly in the Engineering and Agricultural departments.

The other thing that we think is a model is the way in which we don't hire part-time teachers. Unfortunately, we still have the two-tiered classification of the non-tenured and the tenure-track teachers, but nevertheless we have moved in the right direction. The social network within the English department, are just all people who've lived here a long time and it's more of a social group rather than a professional group, or a tiered group. The friends I play with in my band, which is called the Musicians of Mass Destruction, are mostly people who work in the writing programs. And finally, we have institutionalized the culture of assessment in a productive way such that the way we assess writing always comes back and feeds into how we are seeing our students' writing and what's working and what's not working and how we consequently adapt instruction.

SKR: I'm looking forward to being in Baton Rouge this summer. Thanks in advance for being a local host for the WPA Workshop and Conference and thanks you so much, Irv, for talking with me about the writing programs at LSU.

IP: My pleasure, Shirley.

November 15, 2010: Interview with James C. McDonald, English Department Chair at University of Louisiana Lafayette, and Local Co-Host for the 2011 WPA Summer Conference in Baton Rouge.

SKR: Thanks for taking the time to talk with me, Jim. Let's start with basic demographic information about writing programs at the University of Louisiana at Lafayette. What are your writing programs, how are they organized, who leads them, and how does their organization reflect the larger institution?

JCM: We have a first year writing program of four courses: English 101 and 102, which is the usual sequence; English 115, which is the honors course for which students have to qualify; and English 90. We have a small developmental English course—that's English 90—that students with ACT scores below 18 get slotted into unless a writing sample shows they should be in English 101. In addition, we have an advanced writing courses, English 370 Academic Writing, and a technical writing class, English 365. We have an extensive creative writing program with an Introduction to Creative Writing class at sophomore level, in which students write in three genres and additional sophomore level classes, one in each genre. We have some senior level creative writing classes at the 400 level in which there are likely to be some graduate students.

We have Clancy Ratliff as the Director of First Year Writing, and she has an assistant director, Garnet Branch, who specifically helps the adjunct teachers and now included in that are the dual enrollment classes. Clancy also has an assistant director who is a graduate student, and the writing center director also reports to her, and she reports to me. For the technical writing and advanced composition we have two separate faculty committees which are in charge, and for the Creative Writing Program we have a director.

We are in the midst of changing our advanced composition program. We'd been trying to make some changes and hadn't been successful for various bureaucratic reasons. When I became Head I asked the chair of the Advanced Composition Committee if I could sit down with the committee and have them tell me what their dream program would be. They came up with a program very much like Brigham Young University's, with writing in the disciplines—writing in the humanities, writing in the arts, writing in the social sciences—and they looked at who's required to take our advanced comp class right now and they are developing separate classes in each of these courses. They're just beginning. They gave me a written proposal recently and we're going to take it to the Curriculum Committee and at same time get started talking with the deans and department heads in those disciplines that would be affected. We can have some kind of collaborative arrangement and they can have input into these classes and take some responsibility for what we're teaching and take advantage of that. I'm hoping that we might be able to use that as the basis for a writing across the curriculum program that we've never really been able to get going.

SKR: You mentioned that the developmental writing program was getting small. Has ULL made an effort to raise the admission requirements?

JCM: Oh yes. Definitely.

SKR: Is that part of what's shaping the developmental writing program?

JCM: In a big way. The history of all Louisiana universities was that they were all open admissions, including LSU, and that goes back to Huey Long. As a result, Louisiana did not have a community college system. But a number of universities lobbied for years to be able to establish admissions standards. LSU was the first to do that in 1989, I believe. Southwest Louisiana Community College opened in the late 1990s, and in the year 2000 ULL ended open admissions and put in admissions requirements and a number of universities around the state did that at the same time. Now we have a community college system set up so that all state universities have admissions requirements and we now have pressures to increase admissions requirements. As a result, while we used to have a large English 90 program that had its own director, and we were offering maybe twenty or more sections in the fall, now we have maybe four or five. It just isn't a big enough program to have a director anymore. In its time, it was considered a model program, particularly in the 1970s and we were trying to work with some of the things Mina Shaughnessy was doing. That really was part of the Huey Long tradition, that everything in the universities was open rather than having admissions requirements, and as a result, Louisiana was late getting into the community college movement. LSU had a couple of two- or three-year campuses and New Orleans had Delgado Community College. There were five two-year campuses in the whole state until the late 1990s.

SKR: Some of the first community colleges in the country were started in the 1960s weren't they?

JCM: Yes. I remember that when I was going into college, in Southern Illinois they were opening up community colleges. Louisiana wasn't a part of that because we were already admitting all high school graduates into universities and everybody had to have extensive developmental programs. We may have had at one time a two-level developmental writing program. I know LSU had a two-level developmental program. We had two classes for math. Some community colleges still have some students who have to take two courses. That wasn't unusual then, though, for state universities to do that.

SKR: You mentioned that the First Year Composition has a director and assistant director and a Writing Center director, but that the 300-level classes have a committee, not a director. Why is that? Does that reflect department culture?

JCM: Part of it was that the President we had for thirty-four years resisted creation of administrative positions even at the department level so it took a while to negotiate getting any released time for additional department-level administrators. The administration always prided itself on keeping administrative costs well below the average—we're at 62% of the average university's expenditure on administration. For that reason, we haven't had administrative releases for a single director of advanced composition courses.

We actually had someone who for many years was in charge of technical writing and I'm not sure if she had released time for that. We had an advanced technical writing class at that time and had a very active internship and then she died and we weren't able to hire someone to take over technical writing in that way and as a result the program just dwindled to having just one course and occasionally we could find someone to set up an internship for somebody with a strong desire. We had a program we were proud of in the 1980s and 1990s, but it was driven by one person who really was dedicated to that. We're talking about, with the advance composition course proposals, making a request to create a director for advanced comp, and it would include technical writing. If we're going to have it, it would include a whole range of writing in the disciplines classes and there will be a need for administrative oversight for that. The course history has been that people can do pretty much whatever they want to do in that class. That has tightened up and the committee has created more structure for that class. Our accrediting agency has required assessment that has encouraged standardizing. The history has been you could teach it from many different approaches, so it didn't seem to need much administrative oversight. The university has moved into greater assessment—we're just about to receive our report from our ten-year SACS [12] visit next month. In the last few years, SACS has pushed us into more assessment and I think the institutional culture and English 360 in particular has been affected by that.

We did make a change in the First-Year program a few years ago that's probably worth mentioning. The second semester class, English 102, used to be a writing about literature class, and the research paper would always be in the first semester. There wasn't much of an emphasis on research in the second semester, so we decided to make the second semester class a research writing and argumentation class and really see that the big research papers that students read and write in first year would be the culmination of the second semester class. That was not popular with our literature and creative writing graduate students who enjoyed teaching literature in the 102 class and now they found they couldn't do that. It was an important move for us to make and a lot of the newer faculty in literature as well as rhetoric were behind making this move but it brought out some of the tensions between literature and composition and we've made extensive use of the WPA Outcomes Statement in designing those two classes. [13]

SKR: Tell me something about the teachers and students in the program and whether and in what ways they reflect the local culture and economy.

JCM: This institution has an interesting history in that way. We were the first university in the South to desegregate. Thurgood Marshall [14] was one of the attorneys, though not the lead attorney. I did a little research on this. University of Louisiana at Lafayette opposed the students who were trying to get in. We lost the initial court case and lost the appeal and at that point decided to accept African American students into the university in fall of

1954. It was not like what happened at University of Alabama and the University of Mississippi in the next decade. That meant we have always had a substantial African American student population—25% at one point. Since we put in admissions requirements, that's down to 20% and we're trying to be more aggressive in recruiting African American students.

At the same time we're the Cajun university. Cajun is a distinct ethnic group. They're descendents of French Canadians who were kicked out of Canada after the French and Indian War and were a belligerent group who couldn't fit in back in France or in the Caribbean and eventually many of them ended up settling in southwestern Louisiana, which didn't have much of a white population. It had a Native American population. Unlike in New Orleans, there was a lot of land that could be had. This was more of a French-speaking part of the country than an English-speaking part until the first generation or two after World War II and there was a real effort to change that. Students who in the 1960s went to public school would be punished if they spoke French on campus and that hurt the French language. Now we've put a French immersion program into the public schools to try to strengthen the French. We still have a lot of French radio programs in the French and Cajun music and Zydeco music in French. A lot of that is in the French language so it's very much a part of the art and music

French, along with English, is the state language of Louisiana. That's not just because of the Cajuns but also because of the Creoles coming out of the Caribbean culture who are represented by a lot of the blacks as well as the French immigrants to New Orleans. Cajun French is one dialect; in fact, Cajun English is too. The dominance of that ethnic group has shaped the character of the university. There are only two universities in Acadiana, ULL and McNeese State University in Lake Charles.

SKR: What does it mean to be a Cajun university?

JCM: It means we have a very significant folklore program as well as the French department. It's one of the reasons Marcia[15] and I did the Zydeco book.[16] There's a lot of pride in the local culture and we had a desire to educate ourselves about it and keep it going and pass that culture down to the next generation.

Of course Mardi Gras is a big celebration. We get three days off for Mardi Gras. Cajuns don't celebrate Mardi Gras in the same way that New Orleans does. It's the small towns around Lafayette that celebrate it. There aren't kings and queens, but people ride on horseback out to the farms after drinking all morning. They descend down onto farms that are prepared to greet them. They perform tricks and the farmers throw chickens into the fields, then people from the parade run down the chickens and the chickens are sent back into town for the gumbo. The town has a party going on and a Cajun band is pulled around in a wagon that's pulled around all day from one farm to another. It's a more democratic kind of Mardi Gras. There's no royalty, although we have that in the Lafayette parade and the Lake Charles parade with kings and queens and courts, which are more like New Orleans parades.

We have a Lagniappe Day—Cajun French for "something a little extra for free." They used to give students a Lagniappe Day holiday in spring semester on a Wednesday just for no reason. That's gone—we couldn't manage that holiday with other state holidays. But there's still a celebration where we have crawfish races among other things that take advantage of the culture. The history department has a Saturday celebration where they sponsor a big boudin[17] cook-off.

Also, many of the Cajun musicians around here are people who have majored in French or English in folklore and are developing their French skills but also are really exploring the traditions of Cajun culture. Of course that makes our Louisiana literature class an important class as well. We've tried to bring nonfiction readings about Louisiana culture into the writing class.

SKR: So in part the Zydeco book is designed as a reader for composition classes?

JCM: As a reader in a writing class but also in Louisiana folklore classes as a set of readings.

SKR: Is it used in ULL composition classes?

JCM: Used to be, but eventually fell out of use after ten years. The textbook I did for Pearson called *The Reader* has several Louisiana readings in it and that's being used in a number of classes. It has readings about Mardi Gras and readings about Katrina. I think that has some popularity in our program because it has ten readings or so that people in Louisiana can particularly connect to.

SKR: The University of Louisiana at Lafayette started out as Southwest Louisiana Industrial Institute in 1900, the beginning of the twentieth century. Are there ways that you see ULL at the beginning of the twenty-first century reflecting those origins?

JCM: I'm not sure that I do. Eventually they dropped the "Industrial" from the name. Within fifteen years it was just SLI, then in 1960 it took the name of the University of Southwestern Louisiana. Then we dropped the "Southwestern" ten years ago and it became University of Louisiana at Lafayette. Those name changes represent a desire to move away from the origins in some ways, although the "Southwestern" remains important even though not in our name. We see ourselves serving the culture and promoting the culture and literature and it also goes on in the sciences with the interest in the wetlands. Many of our students in technical writing end up working for the Wetlands Institute, so we see ourselves as serving the region and representing the region in that way.

But there's also been a desire for us to move away from being a regional institute to being not the flagship but the number two research institution in the state. That was the reason for changing the name and getting rid of the "Southwestern" and becoming University of Louisiana at Lafayette. There was a big push starting in the 1970s when the President who was here for thirty-four years[18] took over and wanted to make this a PhD-granting university and to move up to Research II. Now they're hoping to move up to Research I and to represent ourselves as a university that represents the whole state. So that meant moving away from "industrial institute" origins, where there were courses on knitting and things like that in the 1900s.

SKR: We heard a lot about college and universities in New Orleans that were obviously affected by Hurricane Katrina. It also affected colleges and universities that were further inland. What are some of the differences in the ways ULL was affected and what are some specific ways it affected the writing programs?

JCM: Katrina struck the weekend after our first classes. We ended up adding eight hundred and some students in the aftermath of Katrina from New Orleans universities and colleges who were displaced. I would say—I'm guessing—two hundred of them went into first year comp classes. Only about half lasted the first semester. A lot weren't able to focus on college or realized this wasn't where they wanted to be. They wanted to be at Tulane or at UNO. At the same time we had our own students from New Orleans, many of whom had their family coming to them living for a few days in their dorm rooms and apartments. The university had to be in business of helping their parents and other family members find places to live. While we were closed in anticipation of Katrina for one day, we didn't have any bad weather. We had to close later when Rita came through. McNeese State University in Lake Charles—Rita closed down that university for a whole month and we got a whole new group of evacuees right when Katrina evacuees were moving into more permanent places. It made a permanent increase in the Lafayette population and it also meant an increase that continued in our enrollment. The New Orleans schools all reopened in January, but to much smaller student enrollments. They laid off a number of faculty. Some of them had to cut numerous programs and that re-defined their universities.[19]

In fact, Tulane eliminated all its PhD programs after Katrina and decided to focus on its undergraduate mission more. Many universities also got more involved with service learning where students were part of rebuilding New Orleans. It had a huge effect on New Orleans schools and they're still recovering from that, but they have not reached the numbers that they were pre-Katrina. The University of New Orleans dropped their basketball program for example. The University of New Orleans, among others, has compiled an archive of stories, many of them from their students, so in many ways that has changed the mission and character of those universities.

Our university's desire to be the number two university was helped by Katrina and Rita because we didn't have to shut down programs and we've been able to withstand the last two years of budget cuts that other universities couldn't. Part of that was due to fiscal conservatism of our previous president. We've been able to add some programs or add to programs, even as other departments were cutting. That was a big difference for us.

SKR: How were writing programs affected?

JCM: Obviously there was a lot of writing about Katrina and after that a lot of people were tired of talking about Katrina. Melissa Nicolas is writing a book about this. We opened one or two sections of 101 entirely of students who were evacuated from New Orleans, starting one or two weeks late. Melissa ended up interviewing that teacher and all of those students and some other students. She has continued to work on that.

The hurricane changed the way Louisianans think about themselves and the state. There's a lot more nervousness about safety and the future and whatever you build, will it remain, and there's less complacency about surviving hurricanes and it's affected us financially. Insurance rates have gone way up. It's harder to get mortgages south of Interstate 10. Probably the BP spill and budget cuts and recession have all combined to make Louisianans less sure about themselves and the future.

SKR: Let me ask about the other big disaster, this time man-made, when the Gulf region was hit with the BP Oil Spill. I know ULL has a department of petroleum engineering. Besides being a source of expertise for responding to the spill how has the spill affected the university? Has ULL's connection to oil shaped the writing programs at all?

JCM: A lot of that is yet to be played out. There were predictions of great job losses because of the BP spill. At first, because of the damage to fishing and later because of the moratorium on deep sea oil drilling. But the immediate loss of jobs wasn't nearly as great as people expected partly because BP was hiring a lot of the people who were laid off or whose businesses were hurt to do the cleanup. A lot of the companies hunkered down and tried to see if they could avoid layoffs and they seemed to have done that to some extent. I'm not sure what the lingering effects will be.

I know in my first-year writing class the spill comes up a lot in discussions about various economic issues and environmental issues. Discussion comes back to the spill. It highlighted a longstanding tension in Louisiana where we have a lot of jobs dependent upon the environment in fishing and tourism. Louisiana is a big hunting state and big fishing state and at the same time we're dependent on the oil and gas and chemical industries that do damage to the environment and we as a state have allowed lax regulations to attract that industry here. So you didn't find a lot of the shrimp fishermen complaining a lot about BP because, well, they have family members who work for oil. So the moratorium was unpopular. I think Obama was more unpopular for declaring the moratorium than BP and Halliburton were unpopular for mismanaging, although they certainly took a hit in their popularity. But BP is putting a lot of grant money and some of that is not just to understand the environmental damage but to understand how it is affecting the culture. We have some English professors who are collaborating with folklore professors in other parts of the state to get grant money to get into cultural exploration of how BP has affected Louisiana. That, I think, will probably affect writing classes and we will have a lot of issues students can write about with what has happened with the hurricanes and with the wetlands and with the oil spills. It's a state that has suffered a lot of problems and that gives students a lot to write about and the BP spill will just become a bigger part of that.

SKR: How long have you been at ULL?

JCM: Since 1987.

SKR: That's a long time. How has working there and living in the region changed you?

JCM: It's changed my cholesterol! All the southwest Louisiana food is not the healthiest. I have a large Louisiana music CD collection and I'm very big on attending the Cultural Festivals down here. I've developed an amateur interest in Louisiana folklore and Louisiana music and culture that has gotten into my research in some ways. It's also a poor state and is always ranked in bottom five as far as income and employment and literacy rates and high school dropouts. It ranks lowest. The education system has been a matter of a lot of concern for decades. Education is not a top priority for a lot of people in this state. I think that's one of the reasons we have a very high percentage of nontraditional students and older students. Something like 25% of our student population is considered non-traditional—people who've worked in the oil fields and lost their jobs or been injured or for other reasons decided higher education was important for them later in life instead of just after coming out of high school. That means having older students in your classes and that changes your teaching. They're going to be more assertive and they're going to bring more knowledge of culture. They're going to bring different economic realities. That's changed my teaching in some ways.

It's a relaxed culture. It's not a culture that seems to produce a lot of Type A personalities. I like that. We don't make a lot of money in Louisiana universities. We took years to reach the southern average, as far as salaries go for higher ed, from being the bottom. We reached that and then they started cutting our budget. But I decided early on that I needed to attend the festivals—Acadian, Internationale, and Blackpot. I take advantage of all the music down here and consider that part of my salary. Otherwise I might as well be teaching in North Dakota or someplace like that if I'm not going to these places. So I hit the festivals and some of the clubs and a fair number of times do take advantage of the music out there. At my age it helps if the bands play earlier.

SKR: I mentioned my metaphor for the writing program I direct, which is the ocotillo. If you were going to choose a metaphor for one or more writing programs at ULL – a metaphor that was native—what would it be?

JCM: Well, the most popular metaphor down here is *gumbo* because every gumbo is unique. It all depends on what you put into the gumbo. We have gumbo parties down here when the weather is cold enough. Everybody has to bring something to put in the gumbo. It's different depending on who shows up and what they bring. People bring chicken or sausages or shrimp. It's always a different mix, and that makes it a nice kind of metaphor for multiculturalism. Everything in the gumbo doesn't get mashed up. It's adding to the flavor but also retaining its uniqueness.

The gumbo metaphor is a way to see how the university should work in the community. It has distinct flavors, but at the same time each individual needs to contribute something different to it. That's what we aim for if we think about our writing program as a community of teachers and students.

SKR: If I were to visit your campus in person, what place or places should I visit other than writing program offices and classrooms in order to understand how the ULL context shapes writing programs?

JCM: We'd definitely take you to the swamp we have in the middle of campus. There are several alligators there. There's a sign that says "Don't feed the alligators." The campus swamp has a bunch of cypress trees growing out of it and some Spanish moss and it's the symbol of the university and the culture and the natural environment around here. That would be one. It's also interesting that we have a fast food Lebanese restaurant on campus. Actually the Mediterranean and Eastern Mediterranean cultures are actually part of this culture. They're brought here for the oil industry, so it's not just French Francophone. The place is becoming more mixed. They actually have pretty good gyros, chicken shawarma, and things like that at that restaurant.

I think I'd have you take a look at some of the archives in the library—particularly the music archives. We have recordings of Cajun and Creole bands going back to the 1920s, 1930s and 1940s and Cajun storytelling as well, although in French. That gets into the university seeing itself as something that's supposed to preserve the culture and not just the high culture.

I'd maybe end up taking you to Eunice where they have a live radio program of Cajun music and other Louisiana music that's hosted by folklore scholar Barry Ancelet, who was Department Head of Modern Languages, who is a great storyteller himself and sees his program as a way to educate people about the culture around here.

SKR: Sounds like fun! Thanks so much for talking with me, Jim. I'm looking forward to seeing you in Baton Rouge this summer.

JCM: You're welcome.

NOTES

1. Lillian Bridwell Bowles.

2. The *Southern Review* literary magazine, first published at LSU by editors Robert Penn Warren and Cleanth Brooks from 1935 to 1942, has been published continuously at LSU since 1965. For Warren and Brooks' account of the early history of the magazine, see the *Southern Review* website at http://www.lsu.edu/thesouthernreview/history.html .

3. Piyush Amrit "Bobby" Jindal, current governor of Louisiana.

4. Taylor Opportunity Program for Students.

5. The late Pat Taylor, an LSU alumnus, was a New Orleans oilman, businessman and philanthropist.

6. Southern University and A&M College is a Historically Black 1890 land grant institution.

7. For the full statement of the Flagship Agenda, see http://www.lsu.edu/flagshipagenda/Flagship2010/index.shtml.

8.The Deep Water Horizon Oil Spill, also known as the Gulf Oil Spill and the British Petroleum Oil Disaster, began on April 20 and lasted until July 15, releasing nearly five million barrels of oil into the Gulf of Mexico.

9. Mark Emmert was Chancellor of LSU from 1999 until 2004, when he became the President of the University of Washington. Emmert became President of the National College Athletic Association in September 2010.

10. Huey Pierce Long, Jr. (August 30, 1893 – September 10, 1935), was the 40th Governor of Louisiana from 1928–1932 and U.S. Senator from 1932 to 1935.

11. WPA is the acronym for the Works Progress Administration, later named the Works Projects Administration, an agency created as part of FDR's New Deal to employ millions in building and creating public works, including art. Part of the mural is used as a banner on the Department of English website: http://uisw-cmsweb.prod.lsu.edu/ArtSci/english/#

12. Southern Association of Colleges and Schools (SACS) is the regional accrediting association for higher education in Louisiana.

13. Update March 2011 from JCM: The English faculty voted last month to offer concentrations in the English major, including concentrations in professional writing and in creative writing. We will need to do much more with internships

for the professional writing concentration. I'm also planning to talk soon with the department head of Communications about proposing an interdisciplinary professional writing minor, which would have a curriculum including journalism and other writing courses in Communications as well as the business college's business communication course.

14. Nominated to the Supreme Court by Lyndon Johnson in 1967, Thurgood Marshall (July 2, 1908 – January 24, 1993) was the first African American to serve on the United States Supreme Court. Prior to his service on the court, he was a lawyer, and is remembered for the victory in Brown vs. Board of Education, a decision that declared that state laws establishing separate public schools for black and white students were unconstitutional.

15. Marcia Gaudet.

16. *Mardi Gras, Gumbo, and Zydeco: Readings in Louisiana Culture*. University of Mississippi Press, 2003.

17. JCM's note: *Boudin* is grilled pork and rice dressing with various spices in a sausage casing, though there are variations with seafood, crawfish, alligator, or turkey instead of pork.

18. Dr. Ray P. Authement, President of ULL from 1974 to 2008.

19. JCM's note: The journal *Reflections: Writing, Service-Learning, and Community Literacy* devoted Volume 7.1-2 (Spring 2008) to a special issue, *Writing the Blues: Teaching in a Post-Katrina Environment*, and it is a fine source on what Louisiana writing programs went through after Katrina, especially in New Orleans.

Review Essay

What Is Real College Writing? Let the Disagreement Never End

Peter Elbow

Sullivan, Patrick, and Howard Tinberg. *What is "College-Level" Writing?* Urbana, IL: NCTE, 2006. 418 pages.

Sullivan, Patrick, Howard Tinberg, and Sheridan Blau. *What is "College-Level" Writing? Volume 2: Assignments, Readings, and Student Writing Samples.* Urbana, IL: NCTE, 2010. 329 pages.

Suppose I reviewed a book about breast cancer by saying, "They shouldn't have written about breast cancer. Their prestige will add to the neglect of some other form of cancer that badly needs attention." Surely people get to write books about topics they want to write about. If I write a review that complains about their neglect, *I'm* neglecting the traditional job of a review: "How well do they do the task they set out to do?" Yet if I think my complaint is important, I can resort to the baggy genre of "review essay" and try to complain as respectfully as I can. Thus the review essay that follows.

The task chosen by the editors and authors of these two NCTE volumes is a valid and complex one. They write to figure out what goes on and should go on in first-year composition courses and how that relates to what goes on in the teaching of writing in high school. One obviously useful goal of the enterprise is to help high school teachers know better how to prepare their students for college. In fact the first volume grew out of a conference that brought high school and college teachers of writing together. In a sense these essays are a kind of macro-version of that perennial conversation where a couple of high school English teachers ask a couple of college composition teachers over dinner: "Now tell us concretely: what *are* you really looking for in your first-year students? And what are you trying to achieve in your teaching? Help us prepare our high school students better." A virtue of the volumes is the mixture of high school teachers and college teachers (and students!) as authors.

I hasten to say that I found the writers doing a good and useful job with this task. They represent a huge variety of different minds going to work at it—richly, interestingly, intelligently, lucidly—and often in admirable detail. (For example, in *Volume 2* Tom Thompson and Andrea Gallagher team up to write "When a College Professor and a High School Teacher Read the Same Papers.") Ed White and Sheridan Blau have essays in both volumes—which might seem unfair—but they were central in producing the whole enterprise and I found their four essays remarkably interesting and useful—at times brilliant.

* * *

But frustration grew in me and I reflected back on it (thus demonstrating a meta-cognitive move that some authors called essential to college level writing).[1] My simpler and more obvious frustration is at the narrowness of the realm the volumes chose to investigate. I felt in the title a promise of breadth: "college writing." There's so *much* college writing—in all the different courses and different colleges. What a jungle. How nice it would be to get a bit of an understanding through an overview. But no. The two volumes focus on a very small slice of college writing—what goes on in first-year comp. Virtually none of the authors are from disciplines other than English.

I'm troubled at a decision to investigate what goes on or ought to go on in first-year composition without looking at all the rest of the writing that students will have to do in their continuing college courses. Surely one of the goals of our first-year course (not the only goal, I'd insist—see my "Reflections") is to prepare students for writing tasks in other disciplines. Plenty of faculty across the curriculum don't even consider writing in first-year composition courses as real writing.

But I had a larger and more complicated frustration. That little word "level" in the title (*What is College-Level Writing?*) was a signal that I missed at first. But it *preoccupied* most of the writers and led them to assume that their job was to figure out *levels* or *standards*. In other words, the impulse that informs both volumes is mostly *normative*. They investigate not so much what college writing *is* but what it *should be*. In a final section reflecting back on the essays in the two volumes, Ed White argues explicitly that college level writing is a certain *kind* of writing that might occur anywhere—not necessarily in college. "College writing goes on in many secondary schools, while much writing that takes place in a first-year college course would be unlikely to be called college level" (Sullivan, Tinberg, and Blau 295).

He makes explicit what most of the writers seemed merely to assume: that the goal is a search for a Platonic essence or small constellation of essences. "In order for readers to respond to this book, we need to seek for certain essences: What characteristics clearly must be present in writing for us to call it *college level?*" (Sullivan, Tinberg, and Blau 296). Jeanne Gunner provides a notable exception. She speaks eloquently against the pretense even of trying to *define* college writing:

> Writing . . . happens among real people in real places over time for a vast range of purposes. When people writing in college environments write, we see embodied instances of college writing. To attempt to define college writing outside this human social context is to invite its commodification . . . . (Sullivan and Tinberg 119)

Behind this normative emphasis I sense a fear of chaos. Life continually threatens to overwhelm us with chaos; the world around us is chaotic; and as teachers we continually feel the classroom threatening to fall apart. Many of the writers start out by almost throwing up their hands at the dizzying variety of writing that goes on in even in the small world of first-year composition courses. If you set out to write an essay for this volume, you would doubtless feel your nose being rubbed in the total nonagreement about standards in first-year composition courses around the land. One of the few references to writing in the other disciplines came when Muriel Harris remarked that an A paper for composition might well get an F in engineering (Sullivan and Tinberg 121–22).

How should we respond to this chaos of standardless writing? Perhaps it was natural that the writers—and the editors in planning the enterprise— decided to search for a "level," a *measure*. What writing *ought* to be called college level writing?—what writing deserves the name?—where is the line that will show how lots of this welter of writing isn't real college level writing—even though some teachers give it a passing or even good grade? What makes writing *good enough* to be called college work? If we can find a standard or essence there won't be so much chaos. And as Blau points out, there's a huge bureaucratic and financial force at work here: many state governments are refusing to *pay* for any course that is not "college work" (or perhaps pay for it only at the two-year college level).

This is one way to deal with chaos. But there's a different way that I began to yearn for more and more as I read: a more empirical approach— a methodological impulse that drives much science. Scientists don't try to reduce the chaos of nature by trying to show that some parts don't belong; rather they try to *map* and *understand* the chaos. Yes, they rule, for instance, that tomatoes don't deserve the name *fruit*, but there is nothing normative in this decision, nothing unworthy about tomatoes. They are looking for any potential logic hiding behind what looks like chaos. (I think of Mina Shaughnessy looking for the logic in all the chaos of punctuation she found in the hurried essays written on timed open-admission placement exams.)

Humans are so prone to *judge*. "Judge not lest ye be judged" said someone—but he didn't have tenure. "Most people are obviously far more anxious to express their approval and disapproval of things than to describe them" (Lewis 7). I've long sought relief from the normative addiction that drives education. Starting with my *Writing Without Teachers*, I began to advocate for what I called "movies of the reader's mind." Instead of asking readers—teachers or peers—to say what they think is good or bad about a text, let's hear them tell as accurate a story as they can of what actually went on in their minds as they were reading. Normative judgments of quality are deeply untrustworthy; stories of what went on in mind have the virtue of being *facts* even if they tell only about one reader. I was hungry for more *facts* and *maps* of college writing. The pretense of agreement about what is good and bad in a text is always undermined by the root fact that human readers differ: what succeeds with one may fail with another.

What if these two volumes succeed and leading figures in the profession actually come to agreement about what *real* college level writing is? (More likely it will be a committee set up by some arm of the government.) There were so many good definitions suggested: for example abstraction and complexity; response to a text based on genuinely understanding it; doing justice to points of view other than your own; questioning self and culture; audience awareness and reader-based prose; rhetorical self-consciousness; meta awareness of your thinking or writing process or of the goals you are shooting for. What if one definition or set of criteria wins? What about all the good kinds of writing that this agreement excludes? (I sense that the WPA Outcomes Statement and Common Core Standards are a bit less vulnerable to this charge.)

There was a moment in the first volume that showed the problem that comes from trying for a single standard or essence of college level writing. Sheridan Blau tells the story:

> . . . the college composition teachers were initially shocked but then wildly amused to hear an elementary school teacher modestly and hesitantly observe that the standard for college-level competency in writing as defined in the new intersegmental document described what she required of student writers in her 6th-grade class. . . . This

observation was then seconded by a number of upper elementary and middle school teachers . . . who claimed that they too expected students in their classes to learn and exhibit all of the same competencies apparently expected of entering college students . . . . (Sullivan and Tinberg 362)

This anecdote echoes the careful scientific work by Margaret Donaldson showing that Piaget was wrong in his single sequence stage-model of cognitive development. She showed that children at "lower levels" can do the "higher level thinking" if only the questions or tasks are set in a way that they can understand. Bruner was probably the most authoritative voice arguing that cognitive or intellectual development doesn't follow a linear path, as in Piaget, but rather move in an ascending spiral:

> We begin with the hypothesis that any subject can be taught effectively in some intellectually honest form to any child at any stage of development. (33)

And:

> A curriculum as it develops should revisit basic ideas repeatedly, building upon them until the student has grasped the full formal apparatus that goes with them. (13)

But after telling that story of how college level criteria refuse to distinguish college students from much younger less experienced children, Blau can't resist going on in the second volume to suggest yet another essence of true college writing (centering on the ability to to enter and take part in an intellectual or academic community). His definition is elegant, but do we really want to force everyone to agree on one? Every definition of true college writing will *exclude* some other kinds of excellent writing. And it might exclude some teachers. I question whether we want to be better at excluding or failing students because they don't meet a single standard—students who don't fit *one model* of what counts as good writing.

I understand the impulse behind the search for a level or standards. Some teachers do a poor job; some schools don't give a real education. The desire for standards drives "No Child Left Behind" exams. We don't want to leave children behind—especially if they are poor or victims of racist structures in our society. But surely the problems caused by NCLB (which I won't try to lay out) should alert us to problems with this way of dealing with chaos.

I can be clearest if I am blunt. I feel the need here to stick up for non-standards—for chaos. But note that this is *not* an argument against excellence. I'm fighting the unthinking assumption that says we don't get excellence without standards or the imposition of a level. A focus on standards leads too often to a sad kind of "excellence" that consists of "meeting all the criteria" and "not having any faults." How good, really, is all the writing that gets the highest score or the grade of A? How much of it would we actually read by choice?

My goal is *real* excellence (not an "essence," however). We seldom get it unless some standards or criteria are *not* met. Really excellent writing often has some genuine faults or problems. Insofar as these volumes are successful as a large scale symposium bent on figuring out what writing deserves the name college writing, it will function as a machine for saying to *more* students: "You are not doing college level work. You are remedial." I ask the question in all seriousness: How useful is that machine? What are the effects of succeeding? Will that lead us to more excellence? I think not.

* * *

At this point I want to stand back and look at this issue from a larger perspective—as it applies to higher education. Insofar as these essays might succeed in figuring out what real college level writing actually is—the essence—they would move US higher education closer to what we find in France and Britain (among other places). Those countries have clearer standards and more unified exams; more uniform barriers; a better mechanism for excluding students who don't meet the standard. In contrast, I want to argue for the deep tradition of permeability or even chaotic nonstandards across US higher education.

What I love about higher education here is that almost anyone can go to college somewhere—all because we lack unified agreed-upon standards. What is "basic writing" at one place is good writing somewhere else. Students who look marginal or worse as they find some college to go to often end up doing good work—sometimes during college but often only afterwards. We have a kind of tradition here of people doing important work even though they went to a "lousy" college. US higher education has a good record of leading to brilliance and innovation; and often not from folks who went to Harvard or Stanford. I'm not usually a chauvinist about my country, but I think that I see less of this innovative grassroots brilliance in England and France where they do a better job of telling more students that they aren't smart or good enough. (Note too, in those countries, how it seems harder to do work that's recognized if you're not in the central city, London or Paris. Single intellectual centers like these are a feature of tightly coupled systems; see below.)

When we set unified standards and invite only the "qualified" into higher education, we starve the system. Even though Ed White proposes a kind of single, Platonic definition of college writing, he also praises US higher education for its messiness: "The standardization implied by a single term *college level* is not only foreign to the diversity of US universities and colleges but actually runs counter to the great strength offered by this diversity" (Sullivan, Tinberg, and Blau 295).

Consider what kinds of people fail or drop out because of a unified standard:

- Many are simply refuseniks: kids or people who don't like to obey orders or do what some teacher tells them to do. The way schools function tends to make them all about obedience. Not everyone is good at obedience—and some of our smartest and most independent entrepreneurial young are not.
- Some people don't meet standards for a class or for college entrance because they don't like the standard. In the case of writing, they want to write poetry, personal venting, comic books, science fiction, computer games or some such thing. Sometimes these students are pursuing a good kind of writing, but a kind that got left out when folks agreed on a standard.
- And sometimes they insist on writing something that is clearly "inferior" or "worse"—a kind of writing that few would praise. Yet sometimes "bad" or "naive" or "uncritical" writing is enabling. By doing *that* writing, the writer is led eventually to sophistication and brilliance. When teachers emphasize working on the approved kind of writing, they tend to close off different pathways to good writing.
- Some are simply "slow." (Note that the word is used to mean "stupid.") It takes them longer. One more reason why it's good to have marginal colleges for students who are "behind." (As long, that is, as *they* want to go to college. It's a sadder story if they are in some college only because their parents or the culture makes them feel no choice.)

When was it that people started saying that we should run higher education like a business? I certainly never heard it in the early days of my career. I'm not sure US business has been a great success story, but surely US higher education long has been a huge success. As long as I can remember, people from all over the world have struggled to come here for higher education—even from countries where "standards are much higher." The presence of marginal colleges does nothing to impede the flourishing of elite colleges and outstanding universities.

At a recent conference I heard Suzie Null give a talk about loosely coupled and tightly coupled systems. Businesses tend to push for tightly coupled systems—systems that work through rules and conformity. But even in business, people are beginning to look at the advantages of loosely coupled systems. They are noticing that such systems are often more nimble and adaptable when conditions change (think GM). They allow for more creativity and innovation; they are more permeable; less hierarchical and thus "flatter" and more "grassroots" in bureaucratic structures. Loosely coupled systems work not by rules but by networks and culture and influence; instead of frowning on variation and nonconformity, they see it as a plus.

Schools and colleges tend to be loosely coupled systems. The contrast between US and British and French higher education is a contrast between loosely and tightly coupled systems. Loosely coupled systems are good at fostering creativity and diversity, and I sense the British and French systems less good at it. NCLB and all the testing have made US secondary education more tightly coupled than it used to be. We can all see the pressures on US higher education to push it in that direction.

Yes, I know the dangers in what I'm saying—the critique. I fear my line of thinking sounds merely elitist: I just want to get rid of standards so smart kooky kids from privileged families can be brilliantly creative. What about all the terrible schools, terrible teachers, and poor students and students of color not getting the advantages of a solid education?

But nonagreement on a single standard for good writing doesn't have to mean leaving children behind. The two volumes of essays I would like to see written would investigate how to make schooling less unfair with some *other* mechanism than system-wide exams and universal standards. There must be other ways. We might try paying teachers well and making the job of teaching attractive—so half of them don't quit after five years.

So my fear is that these two rich and interesting volumes are implicitly serving the interests of standardization: the business model of tightly coupled systems that will do a better job of excluding people who don't fit the system. I see secondary schools being undermined by the bulldozer pressure for testing, standards, shared criteria, and testing—and some of the essays give evidence for this. I fear that these two skilled volumes are trying to push higher education in the same direction.

NOTE

1. One more methodological reflection. In various essays, I have enthusiastically analyzed and celebrated what I call the "believing game." Many readers have read my enthusiasm as hostility to critical thinking or the doubting game—despite my repeated insistence that I value *it* just as deeply and all it accomplishes. But the doubting game doesn't lack support; indeed it enjoys a kind of cultural monopoly on our conception of good thinking itself. My goal has been simply

to show that the doubting game is not *sufficient* as a complete picture of human intelligence or intellectual work. I've been insisting that we need an additional and contrasting intellectual, cognitive, and psychological method in the form of the believing game.

I'm hoping that this review essay might help demonstrate that I am not so one-sided. For I'm insisting here on viewing these two volumes mostly through a doubting lens. I have full trust that they'll get plenty of believing by all the high school and college teachers who will read them and find them full of useful insights.

Works Cited

Bruner, Jerome. *The Process of Education*. New York: Vintage, 1960.

Donaldson, Margaret. *Children's Minds*. New York: Norton, 1978.

Elbow, Peter. "Reflections on Academic Discourse: How it Relates to Freshmen and Colleagues." *College English* 53.2 (1991): 135–55.

Lewis, C. S. *Studies in Words*. 2nd ed. Cambridge: Cambridge UP, 1967.

Shaughnessy, Mina. *Errors and Expectations: A Guide for the Teacher of Basic Writing*. New York: Oxford UP, 1977.

Review Essay

Reinventing Writing Assessment: How the Conversation Is Shifting

William Condon

Adler-Kassner, Linda, and Peggy O'Neill. *Reframing Writing Assessment to Improve Teaching and Learning.* Logan: Utah State UP, 2010. 207 pages.

Broad, Bob, Linda Adler-Kassner, Barry Alford, Jane Detweiler, Heide Estrem, Susanmarie Harrington, Maureen McBride, Eric Stalions, and Scott Weeden. *Organic Writing Assessment: Dynamic Criteria Mapping in Action.* Logan: Utah State UP, 2009. 167 pages.

Elliott, Norbert. *On a Scale: A Social History of Writing Assessment in America.* New York: Peter Lang, 2005. 408 pages.

Ericsson, Patricia Freitag, and Richard Haswell. *Machine Scoring of Student Essays: Truth and Consequences.* Logan, Utah: Utah State UP, 2006. 268 pages.

Huot, Brian and Peggy O'Neill, eds. *Assessing Writing: A Critical Sourcebook.* Boston: Bedford, 2009. 500 pages.

Huot, Brian. *(Re)Articulating Writing Assessment for Teaching and Learning.* Logan:Utah State UP, 2002. 216 pages.

Lynne, Patricia. *Coming To Terms: A Theory of Writing Assessment.* Logan: Utah State UP, 2004. 193 pages.

Neal, Michael R. *Writing Assessment and the Revolution in Digital Texts and Technologies.* New York: Teachers College P, 2011. 152 pages.

O'Neill, Peggy, Cindy Moore, and Brian Huot. *A Guide to College Writing Assessment.* Logan, UT: Utah State UP, 2009. 218 pages.

Paretti, Marie C. and Katrina M. Powell, eds. *Assessment of Writing*. Tallahassee: Association for Institutional Research, 2009. 218 pages.

Weigle, Sara Cushing. *Assessing Writing*. Cambridge: Cambridge UP, 2002. 268 pages.

Wilson, Maja. *Rethinking Rubrics in Writing Assessment*. Portsmouth: Heinemann, 2006. 111 pages.

Wolcott, Willa, with Sue M. Legg. *An Overview of Writing Assessment: Theory, Research, and Practice*. Urbana: NCTE, 1998. 206 pages.

The plethora of books written by scholars within the field of Rhetoric and Composition about writing assessment over the past ten years is a strong indication that the conversation about writing assessment has reached a kind of tipping point. Beginning in the 1970's, Edward M. White led a movement in the California university system for direct testing of writing—with the help, we must acknowledge, of insiders at the Educational Testing Service (Albert Serling and Paul Diederich most prominently) who had long been proponents of timed essay testing within their organization. White's group of faculty, who got more support from ETS than from their own system administrators (White, "The Opening"), represents perhaps the first meaningful engagement of the classroom context with the testing community since 1874, when Adams Sherman Hill was hired at Harvard to assess the writing of incoming students and to teach them expository writing. Almost from the beginning of writing assessment in the United States, as Norbert Elliot and as Peggy O'Neill, Cindy Moore, and Brian Huot document, teachers' voices were not welcome in the negotiations. In 1895, Wilson Farrand, of Newark Academy, put forth a plan for what would become the College English Examination Board (CEEB) in which secondary schools that were feeding students into the universities would collaborate in testing those students, the payoff being the kind of communication that would result in better faculty and curriculum development (Elliot 22-26). While the CEEB grew out of Farrand's proposal, there would be no collaboration with teachers: "teacher judgments about student preparation were found suspect. A test was assumed to be better at helping university admissions personnel make important, consequential decisions about students than judgments of secondary teachers" (O'Neill, et al. 17). Peter Sacks documents the continuing irony of the College Board's arrogant early position: studies overwhelmingly demonstrate that high school grades are better predictors of success in college than test scores of any kind (271). In fact, even in its formation, the CEEB held direct tests of writing

an attitude that the Board would maintain until the 1970's—
⁚ reports, in the face of their own experts who consistently
ˑhe direct test.

...᷍ breakthrough that White led in California was soon followed by
further developments of tests by other large agencies as well as by colleges
and universities themselves. My connection to writing assessment began in
1987 at the University of Michigan, which from 1978 forward conducted
its own timed writing test of incoming students in order to place students
at an appropriate point in the first-year writing curriculum (Bailey and Fosheim). Even at that point, however, the next stage of the conversation was
coming into view. Again, even from the beginnings at Harvard, few teachers were satisfied with the outcomes of a timed test of writing. Elliot quotes
Adams Sherman Hill, writing in 1878:

> Those of us who have been *doomed to read manuscript written in an
> examination room* (emphasis added)—whether at a grammar school,
> high school, or a college—have found the work of even good schol-
> ars disfigured by bad spelling, confusing punctuation, ungrammati-
> cal, obscure, ambiguous, or inelegant expressions. (qtd. in Elliot 341)

While Elliot describes the ways this dissatisfaction simmered at the College Board and, later, in its testing arm, the ETS, by the 1970's teachers
were beginning to take matters into their own hands. Since that time,
indirect tests—examinations that do not engage test-takers in writing—
have declined as placement instruments and even, in latter years, as college
entrance instruments. Direct tests were a good first step away from multiple
choice question tests, but the timed sample was itself of dubious quality.
There are simply not many instances in education or in life when a writer is
called upon to sit and in a limited time (ranging from twenty-five minutes
on the new SAT to an hour or two on most college-based tests) produce an
essay on a topic of which the writer has no prior or specialized knowledge.
In fact, I can think of only one such circumstance: the timed writing test.

Shouting "Validity!" as their battle cry, teachers began looking for ways
to examine students' writing abilities in a more natural context, using
more authentic samples. Thus was born the writing portfolio. Portfolios
gained fairly widespread use in classrooms during the 1970's, but in 1986,
Peter Elbow and Pat Belanoff reported on their program-wide use of writing portfolios for grading students in first-year writing courses at SUNY
Stonybrook, and the second phase of the conversation had begun. In the
writing portfolio, teachers had found an instrument with which to fight
back against the way both indirect and timed direct tests of writing under-
represented the construct *writing* (Hamp-Lyons and Condon). In other

words, since portfolios include writing that students do under normal conditions—which may vary from one student to the next and even for one student from one assignment to the next—portfolios represent more fully *how that writer writes*. For decades, developers of timed writing tests at ETS struggled to achieve acceptable reliability in scoring their samples, a struggle that Paul Diederich finally resolved in developing a holistic scoring system that engaged raters in applying standard, if limited criteria in assessing each sample, in double- (and, if necessary, triple-) readings of each sample. The challenge for proponents of portfolio-based writing assessment, then, was twofold: to advance the cause of validity while meeting the challenge of reliability.

During the decade of the 1990's, those challenges were met. Entry-level portfolios at Miami University and the University of Michigan and the Junior Writing Portfolio at Washington State University led the way by demonstrating that portfolio-based writing assessments were logistically possible, that portfolios could be scored as reliably as timed writings, that placements made on the basis of portfolios were more appropriate, and that portfolios engaged with and supported the curriculum in ways that timed writings cannot (see Hamp-Lyons and Condon; Willard-Traub, et al.; Daiker, et al.; Haswell). Writing teachers and a growing cadre of writing assessment experts within academe (White, Huot, Kathleen Yancey, Elbow, Belanoff, Richard Haswell, William Smith, Michael Williamson, Hamp-Lyons, and several others) had established the prominence of construct validity as a necessity for legitimate writing assessment, as well as the value of the multiple kinds of validity that scholars such as Samuel Messick, Lee J. Cronbach, and Pamela Moss were isolating and describing (consequential, predictive, face, concurrent, and other kinds). These experts from within the academy reasserted the value of traditional validity—that the test actually addresses the construct it sets out to assess—as the means for insisting on including actual writing in any test that purports to yield results that speak to the test-takers' writing ability(ies). In furthering the cause of authentic tests of writing, the field has followed the development of additional kinds of validity, which require that tests not only match the construct, but also offer evidence that their consequences provide educational benefits, that the predictions they make turn out to be accurate once the student is placed into a curriculum, as well as the basic assurances that the assessment is conducted in a manner that is fair to test takers. O'Neill, et al. point out that timed tests have difficulty meeting these descriptions of validity, especially since the American Psychological Association (APA), the American Educational Research Association (AERA), and the National Council on Measurement in Education (NCME) testing standards require a test to meet a unified standard of validity (27). Michael Neal puts the dilemma of timed essay testing this way:

> Many of the current writing assessment technologies are aligned with values of efficiency, uniformity, speed, and mechanization. Some of these technologies are so deeply entrenched in educational contexts that they seem nearly impossible to challenge, and yet there are voices that have and continue to speak into these contexts. [Large-scale testing agencies] have mistaken elevated uniformity and consistency for fairness, resulting in writing assessments that are inconsistent with many of the most fundamental values and best practices associated with the field. These current assessment models are bolstered by their strong connection to large-scale social, public perceptions of technological fixes and reductive views of literacy that tend to reduce language to surface feature, formulaic arrangement, diminished writing processes, and social dynamics of written communication, and often function outside a rhetorical context for writing. These assessments allow us to manage and compare mass populations of students and perhaps reduce the "burden" of classroom assessments, but they fall short of more desirable outcomes. (132)

And the situation is even more grave today, as David Nye points out: the "written component of the new SAT Verbal ... is the antithesis of nearly every current theory of composition and writing assessment and does not take into account the composing technologies students use in authentic environments" (qtd. in Neal 49). Timed direct tests of writing, at least on the commercial side of the enterprise, fall so far short of the demands of unified validity that they do not meet the most basic standards for responsible practice laid out by the APA, AERA, and NCME.

Well-designed portfolio-based writing assessments, because of the broader educational benefits they bestow on students and on teachers, can meet those standards. As a result, portfolio practice and the scholarship around that practice grew exponentially during the 1990's. By 1996, Robert Calfee and Pamela Perfumo reported that sixty percent of secondary English teachers used portfolios within their classrooms, while twenty percent used them across classes, and another ten percent were using portfolios in ways that reached beyond their school buildings. The practice of assessing students' writing—and beyond that, their overall learning—via a writing portfolio had clearly taken hold. Willa Wolcott and Sue M. Legg include a chapter on portfolios in a volume otherwise devoted to timed direct tests—but oriented to K-12 classroom teachers. That 1998 volume, *An Overview of Writing Assessment*, acts as a kind of threshold to the conversation this article describes. Wolcott and Legg describe the basics of writing assessment so that teachers can understand not only how direct testing happens, but also the limits of these tests. In addition, the book has a "how to" flavor, an implication at least that teachers could be active participants in and even designers of responsible writing assessments (White did much the same thing for college-level teachers in his 1999 work *Assigning, Responding, Evaluating,* which is now in its fourth edition, 2007).

From that jumping-off place, the conversation over the past decade has grown to the point that teachers of writing increasingly recognize the inadequacy of the old paradigms of writing assessment and demand not just connections between the classroom and the assessment enterprise, but a meaningful role in those assessments as well. Over the years since Wolcott and Legg, too many books for one review article have emerged, and while no one article can hope to include them all, I address the remainder of this article to identifying in the last decade of writing assessment trends, currents, and crosscurrents, sampling the range of scholarship coming out of academic research on writing assessment, and describing how this re-entry into the conversation may be changing the dialog, tipping the balance away from the psychometrics-dominant past and toward a view of writing assessment that prizes the traditional emphasis on responsible assessment (reliability, validity, sound practices) while insisting, at last (pace, Wilson Farrand!), that what happens in classrooms matters. In so doing, I note the ubiquity of the prefix "re-" in these books, and not only in their titles (Reframing, (Re)articulating, Rethinking, Revolution). I hope readers of this essay will forgive my following these authors' lead, as their trope reinforces the basic theme of this essay that current scholars are (ahem) reconstructing writing assessment to provide teachers with a greater voice.

Rehistoricizing Writing Assessment

Let us be as clear as possible. In the twentieth century, "assessment largely promoted reductive views of language in favor of … efficiency, mechanization, and cost effectiveness" (Neal 5). The ever-continuing descent of commercial writing assessment is driven by (1) cost-cutting in the testing industry resulting from a profit motive on the part of assessment companies that forces assessments to become less and less valid (because tests become shorter and shorter, thus severely restricting the construct being tested); and (2) a budget-cutting desire on the part of colleges and universities to offload the cost of placement onto students. Thus, we find COMPASS, E-rater, Criterion, and others that use tests so limited that they can be scored—not read, mind you, but scored—by computers. We see the new SAT, a cynical response to the California system's threat to discontinue using the SAT for admissions unless it included a direct test of writing. The resulting test is weighted so that two-thirds of a student's "writing" score is based on an indirect test of vocabulary and grammar, and one-third is based on a twenty-five-minute (!) written sample that, as Les Perelman has demonstrated, ties quality of writing so directly to essay length that the samples can be scored from across the room (Anson, et al.). And because many institutions adopt these tests for their own reasons of economy—these are cheap assessments that also allow the college to pass the costs on to the students—writing teachers are put into a difficult position. Writing assessment as a technology informs "many of the habits and notions we have developed in contemporary educational settings. The most detrimental effect of such assumptions is that educators have become (often unintentionally or against our better judgment) proponents of writing assessments that often are reductive and at odds with our best understanding of teaching and learning" (Neal 5). In effect, teachers in colleges that employ such tests for placement or other purposes are put in the position of endorsing those tests, whether the teachers were consulted about the adoption or not.

Yet the reasons that these new voices are beginning to have an effect beyond the academy lie in the very origins of the timed writing test. Indeed, timed writing, while inevitably limited in its generalizability and usefulness, is still being practiced in more responsible ways—at universities such as Washington State, Louisiana State, MIT, Hawaii, and others that provide sufficient time for writing; collect multiple samples; engage teachers in constructing the tasks, creating the criteria, and rating the samples; tie the prompts to local curriculum; and in various ways create a community around the assessment so that instead of obtaining only a ranking that allows for a placement, the assessments provide far more information about students' learning experiences than can be produced by the kinds of short, too-tightly controlled, de-contextualized samples favored by the commercial side of writing assessment (see, for example, Condon).

Hill's objections to the quality of the writing in those early Harvard essays, Farrand's call to engage assessment with instruction, these early voices were ignored in the frenzy to develop indirect tests that is described, in a larger context, by Stephen Jay Gould's *The Mismeasure of Man*. In our own field, Elliot's *On a Scale* is essential in understanding the history behind the state of affairs to which so many who teach writing object so strenuously. Elliot's volume is a detailed history of writing assessment as it emerged in the context of the College Board and its eventual testing arm, ETS. The account comes about as close to vivid drama as a thoroughly scholarly work can, as Elliot tells the story of the internal clashes between the ruling faction, which favored indirect tests because of the reliability of the scoring process, and the sequence of test development teams who promoted investment in essay tests and even, in the 1980's and 1990's, portfolio-based assessments. Elliot had unprecedented access to internal records at ETS, and the resulting account—a social history, as the subtitle notes—provides, for the first time, a fully contextualized history of writing assessment, especially but not solely as it came to be a large commercial enterprise. Still, Elliot's account begins and ends with teachers, teachers who find that rubrics help them communicate expectations to their students, demystify the grading process, and provide a common language for talking about writing in the classroom. Even while telling a story about an assessment juggernaut that consciously and consistently excluded teacher input, this volume addresses what teachers need to know about the assessment enterprise and how teachers can apply the better aspects of that enterprise in the service of students' learning. In doing so, Elliot closes the feedback loop that CEEB and ETS steadfastly refused to close. This book helps teachers understand the history behind the dominance of indirect and direct tests of writing. As teachers grasp the import of separating assessment from what happens in classrooms, they can become more informed advocates of engaging instruction with assessment.

Elliot leads the emphasis among academics to reframe the history of writing assessment, and *On a Scale* remains the most detailed account—though it focuses almost solely on the College Board and ETS. O'Neill, Moore, and Huot's *A Guide to College Writing Assessment* begins with a history of writing assessment in the US that is shorter, if broader than Elliot's, since the authors' account is not limited to the College Board. In roughly thirty pages, O'Neill et al. summarize Elliot's account and reach beyond it to tie that history to events outside ETS. In effect, they extend the history beyond the development of robust indirect tests of writing, which is the effective close of Elliot's history. Huot's chapter in this collection provides a view of "Writing Assessment as a Field of Study" that tells this history from a different point of view. Huot's principal aim in the chapter is to lay out a clearly defined field of research, but in the process he deals usefully with the history of writing assessment from the advent of holistic scoring forward. All these accounts are grounded in the history of the field, yet all reframe that history to open the field for the participation of teachers in classrooms—from K-12 through university—whose aim of engaging assessment with instruction essentially changes the prior orientation of assessment away from the classroom. These accounts recast the enterprise by expanding the borders to include the growing number of assessment experts who ply their trade within schools and universities.

169

This decade's worth of new books also recognizes the explosion of schol-arship about writing assessment within the academy. Indeed, the reassess-ment of assessment is largely happening inside colleges and universities and within schools. Several books provide a compilation of that emerging wisdom. These books—all three of them collections of essays by various leading scholars—fill at least two valuable roles: they establish a canon of key readings on important issues, and they provide an accessible knowl-edge base for graduate seminars (much as Victor Villanueva's *CrossTalk in Composition Theory* does for teachers of writing). Brian Huot and Peggy O'Neill's *Assessing Writing: A Critical Sourcebook* collects the canon, begin-ning with a section on "Foundations," where key articles begin with the transition from indirect to direct testing and move forward to Huot's land-mark 1996 *College Composition and Communication* essay, "Toward a New Theory of Writing Assessment." "Foundations" encompasses the decades of scholarship in what I have described above as the second phase of the conversation on writing assessment. Thus, it provides examinations of top-ics ranging from holistic and primary trait scoring, to validity and reliabil-ity, to the beginning of the portfolio movement and the first attempt to create a new history of writing assessment, including a reprint of Yancey's "Looking Back as We Look Forward: Historicizing Writing Assessment." While the "Foundations" section in some ways represents the more distant past of writing assessment, the articles here hold up both in their treat-ment of persistent issues of test validation and in their presentation of the changes in thinking during the roughly two decades that laid the founda-tion for and anticipated the present day of writing assessment. The second section, "Models," is a much-needed nod toward essentialism. Newcomers to the field need to see examples of the foundational principles in action, and here the editors have assembled a gallery of programs that changed the way writing assessment works: William Smith's expert rater system at Pitts-burgh; Richard Haswell and Susan Wyche-Smith on Washington State's Junior Portfolio; Russell Durst, Marjorie Roemer and Lucille Schultz on Cincinnati's program portfolios; Dan Royer and Roger Gilles' founding article on directed self-placement; and examples of writing assessment in the context of WAC. Finally, "Issues" provides a summary of problems the field continues to struggle with, from the notion of holistic scoring of port-folios, to portfolios and second-language writers, to issues of culture and other contexts that impinge on writing assessment. For now, this collec-tion represents our canon, both in the selection of essays and in the authors included in the volume. These are the voices that have brought us to our current state, from White and Elbow, to Williamson, Huot, and Yancey, to Bob Broad and Haswell. Perhaps the sole weakness of *Assessing Writing* is its treatment of the move toward using computers to score timed essays. Given the long battle Huot, in particular, has fought to keep the elements of responsible test development on the table, even as colleagues in the field call for discarding some of those elements (Lynne, Wilson), I was surprised that only one essay related to machine scoring is included in that collection.

This deficit is more than remedied, however, by Patricia Freitag Ericsson and Haswell's *Machine Scoring of Student Essays: Truth and Consequences*. This collection, which in some ways acts as a response to the industry-sponsored *Automated Essay Scoring: A Cross-disciplinary Perspective* (Shermis and Burstein, eds), provides examinations of the claims that commercial writing assessment makes about automated essay scoring, finding most of them disingenuous at best. *Machine Scoring* also provides practical tests of the leading systems, such as E-Rater and Criterion, both by scholars and in writing programs. Finally, the collection looks more broadly at what is lost, in terms of curriculum and the community that develops around local assessments, when an institution chooses to employ tests that are designed for computers to score. *Machine Scoring* promises to be an important resource for years to come because the political economy of the commercial testing industry dictates finding cheaper and cheaper ways of delivering rankings of test-takers for the purposes of deriving a course placement on a given campus and, as this initiative evolves, for evaluating faculty, courses, and even academic programs. That devolution of what writing assessment is— merely a ranking that leads to a placement—is the opening that teachers and scholars in the academy are exploiting in order to change the assessment landscape to engage a broader range of purposes and effects. In this way, the conversation about machine scoring can help counteract the reductive notions of writing assessment inherent in legislative efforts such as No Child Left Behind and government statements such as the Spellings Commission's report.

As that broader range becomes more apparent, the academic assessment community will inevitably expand, as indicated by *Assessment of Writing* (Paretti and Powell, eds.), the fourth volume of the Association for Institutional Research's series, Assessment in the Disciplines. This collection of essays provides models of writing assessment in a WAC context. As the sponsorship indicates, the book addresses an audience of institutional researchers, so each essay addresses essentially the same set of issues that are important to that audience. For example, most essays respond to the Spellings Commission report, and most also address concerns directly or indirectly related to accreditation. The collection is important within the Rhetoric and Composition community for a couple of major reasons. First, the inclusion of voices from our field indicates that the conversations about assessment are already reaching across disciplinary and institutional boundaries. Yancey, Terry Zawacki, O'Neill, Joseph Janangelo, Huot, Charles Moran, and Anne Herrington are familiar names that represent model programs within our discipline. These people and programs should be informing practice in institutional research, so their presence here is encouraging. Second, we see the emergence of potential partners in the fight to sustain more robust forms of writing assessment. Two essays in particular address writing in engineering, engaging the Accreditation Board for Engineering and Technology (ABET) standards in the process. ABET's writing requirements for students in engineering programs make them a natural partner in pushing for authentic assessments of many kinds and in resisting the increasingly reductive forms of writing assessment coming from the commercial assessment enterprise.

As a whole, then, these volumes provide resources that promote a deeper and broader understanding of the writing assessment landscape, especially as it exists within academe—in writing programs of several kinds, in accreditation efforts, in pushing back against reductive governmental initiatives and even more reductive forms of assessment coming from the commercial side of writing assessment. These collections demonstrate that in the past three decades, we have built a canon, a body of high-quality research and debate that supports our current efforts to promote better, more authentic, more useful and generalizable assessments, and that aids us in preparing the next generation of academics in the field.

Regrounding Writing Assessment

Another set of volumes builds on that substantial base of research by laying out assessment processes from a perspective that includes and promotes more robust forms of writing assessment, forms that move beyond ranking and placing and provide output that can help us engage assessment with instruction in order to improve both. Beginning with Wolcott and Legg's *An Overview of Writing Assessment* (1998), these volumes lay out the case that teachers need to understand the values represented in "the education and psychometric traditions" (O'Neill, et al. 54), without being trapped in their underlying assumptions. Writing assessment, these volumes argue, should rightfully exist within this larger framework of assessment, but it should also engage writing theory so that the constraints of the larger context can no longer exert a reductive pressure on *writing* assessment. The mistake of the early assessment community was to treat writing assessment the same as other kinds of assessment: sorting military enlistees into categories based on general aptitudes, for example. The stakes in making a transition to better instruments are high. We can neither withdraw from the field, as Patricia Lynne and Maja Wilson argue, nor can we be the sole assessors of writing, as Chris Gallagher favors. The key to our participation, as O'Neill, Moore, and Huot point out, is that "[b]ecause writing assessment is fundamentally about supporting current theories of language and learning and improving literacy and instruction, it should involve the same kind of thinking we use every day as scholars and teachers" (59).

While Wolcott and Legg arguably marked the threshold of this latest phase of the conversation, it was first and most clearly defined by Huot's 2002 work, *(Re)Articulating Writing Assessment for Teaching and Learning*. If we can say that White is the father of modern writing assessment, then Huot has surely become its godparent, at least. Huot's article "Toward a New Theory of Writing Assessment" (an updated version of which is chapter four in this volume) is the defining statement of the second phase of this new conversation, as I argued above, and his name is everywhere in this third phase. Assessment, Huot argues, is a field of study with its own set of methodologies. Assessment should be regarded as part of the research enterprise—it is, in fact, primary research. If writing assessment engages with writing theory, then the assessment practices that emerge will be consistent with the best that has been thought, researched, and written about writing as a construct, as a set of competencies, and as a social practice. This volume sets the expectation that teacherly readings need to be at the heart of writing assessment. Writing, Huot argues, cannot be learned without assessment (165), but assessment, following his argument, cannot be responsible without engaging the contexts for writing, in particular the classroom context. His chapters three and five most clearly contribute to this argument.

Jumping ahead, we can see how this argument engages assessment with learning in O'Neill, Moore, and Huot's *A Guide to College Writing Assessment*, cited above because of its succinct history of writing assessment in the twentieth century. The book's principal mission, however, is the *praxis* of writing assessment—putting theory into practice in placement, proficiency, program, and faculty assessments. These four activities are the bread and butter of writing programs of all kinds, from first-year composition to WAC and WID. If, as Huot asserted in *(Re)Articulating*, the most important element of writing assessment lies in working methodologies (165), then O'Neill, et al. present working methodologies for the most common kinds of assessment for writing programs, and the appendices provide "best practice" examples for scoring rubrics, classroom observations, portfolio-based assessments, surveys, and more. If assessment was once something we needed to do defensively—lest, as White warned, someone do it *to* us—then this book outlines the practice of proactive assessments, assessments conceived and run by the people inside writing programs, geared to inform us about our own students, programs, processes, and faculty.

In an allied book, Linda Adler-Kassner and O'Neill's *Reframing Writing Assessment to Improve Teaching and Learning*, the authors state, "Our position is that writing instructors and program directors know a lot about writing instruction and need to be centrally involved in discussions about writing assessment" (9). The twentieth century began with a conscious exclusion of writing teachers from the assessment process. Adler-Kassner and O'Neill's assertion, which echoes Huot's in *(Re)Articulation*, is fast becoming the anthem of twenty-first century writing assessment. Excluding us never made much sense, except in the political economy of twentieth-century assessment (see Neal, above), and this set of books acknowledges, first, the hard-won expertise of writing teachers and writing program administrators in the theory and practice of writing assessment and, second, the political contention that without the input of writing experts and without a thorough recognition of the contexts surrounding writing assessments, those assessments simply cannot be valid. Absurdly, the values composition teachers hold and the theoretical bases upon which they operate have rarely—and never really seriously—been part of commercial writing assessment. Noting that omission, Adler-Kassner and O'Neill argue that "not only can contemporary understandings of psychometric theory accommodate composition's frames but that they can also help us connect to the larger frames about education and assessment that operate in the public, which can help shift these larger frames so that they reinforce— or at least accommodate—composition's values, theories, and pedagogies" (71). I would put the issue this way: beginnings matter. The fields of composition and writing assessment began in a context that emphasized deficit and error (recall Hill's response to such writing, cited above). So, the public frame for what we call Composition Studies is that we tend to issues of correctness, that good writing is the same thing as error-free writing. Resolve the problems that result from severely limiting the construct and, these books claim, we can build our own perspective from which to influence and perhaps gain control of the more important conversation about writing, as well as the one about writing assessment.

Sandwiched between *(Re)Articulating* and *Reframing*, Sara Cushing Weigle's *Assessing Writing* (2002), published in the Cambridge Language Assessment Series, bears mention because together with *A Guide to College Writing Assessment*, it provides a thorough survey of writing assessment as conceived on a world-wide basis. Beyond the United States, writing assessment is just one piece of the larger sphere of language assessment, and in that context, those who teach writing are and have long been well acquainted with the educational and psychometric methodologies for testing writing within the framework of language assessment. For the international assessment community, Weigle's book summarizes current practice and introduces possibilities that go beyond the timed impromptu test. In doing so, she provides a clear, useful summary of the construct ("the nature of writing ability"), of assessment theory ("basic considerations in assessing writing" and "research in large-scale writing assessment"), of the processes of designing and scoring direct tests of writing, and most useful, of classroom writing assessments and portfolio-based writing assessments. Huot has consistently promoted the importance of assessment theory for writing teachers and administrators, bemoaning the fact that "the emphasis in assessment is on practice without adequate attention to theory" (O'Neill, et al. 35). In a body of work extending from *Validating Holistic Scoring* (1993) to *A Guide to College Writing Assessment*, he and his co-authors have insisted, with good reason, that a knowledge of sound writing assessment theory and practice can save us from the evermore reductive assessments that the for-profit assessors try to push upon us. Weigle's book contains just such a synthesis of traditional theories and methodologies of writing assessment, clearly and cogently presented. Taken together, Wolcott and Legg,; Weigle,; O'Neill et al., and Moore and Huot leave no excuse for anyone within the Rhetoric and Composition community to be uninformed about writing assessment.

Reintegrating Assessment with Instruction: Classrooms Matter

As the conversation has shifted to include the voices of teachers, scholars, and administrators of writing, one wonders what a reviewer in 2111 might write of the past century or so of writing assessment. Looking back from that distant vantage point, surely one shift would be the entry of the writing classroom into the writing assessment arena, but another would be the engagement of writing assessment within the writing classroom. Perhaps the work that marks the beginning of that sector of the conversation is Patricia Lynne's *Coming to Terms: A Theory of Writing Assessment* (2004). In one sense, Lynne's book expresses the discipline's frustration with commercial writing assessment. Tired of reductive assessment instruments and the misconceptions about students' learning that those instruments foment, and annoyed at the commercial firms' resistance to more valid forms of writing assessment—portfolios in particular, but other forms of authentic assessment as well—Lynne argues, basically, for boycotting the old testing order, which clearly is not engaged with what happens in classrooms.

Lynne argues that those in charge of constructing writing theory and of teaching writing must throw off the trappings of traditional writing assessments and develop their own models. That argument expresses a frustration that anyone in the field of Rhetoric and Composition has felt, but Lynne's call to reject *all* aspects of traditional writing assessment goes too far when she identifies concepts such as validity and reliability as hegemonic forces of the commercial enterprises that inevitably undermine attempts to establish better assessments. Lynne's call to resist the ever more reductive, ever less valid samples, scored ever more cheaply, is of course completely sensible and a much-needed addition to the past decade's conversation. However, the best tactic for making that argument is not to abandon aspects of responsible assessments that professional organizations within the academy universally accept, but to point out in how many ways the commercial assessments hide behind concepts such as validity, which they themselves violate or ignore outright. O'Neill, Moore, and Huot, citing the 1999 APA, AERA, and NCME Standards, point out that validity is a unified standard that "not only includes all notions of validity and reliability, it also demands that test consequences and implications for the local educational environment be considered" (27). Thus, while ACT may advance statistical correlations to make claims that COMPASS has concurrent or predictive validity, there is no way to demonstrate construct validity for an extremely reductive test such as COMPASS (which is simply an exercise in editing). O'Neill, et al. conclude, "[u]nless decisions based upon a test can demonstrate educational value for students, it is difficult to make a convincing argument for validity" (27). Instead of disregarding tenets of responsible testing, which Lynne promotes, it is more useful to use those tenets, which actually support the more robust forms of assessment that have emerged from the academy, to demonstrate that the commercial tests are unacceptable and irresponsible. Furthermore, deserting foundational concepts like reliability and validity robs us of the ability to compete on a level playing field with those older, more reductive forms of assessment.

As much as I sympathize with Lynne's displeasure over the way numbers have come to dominate writing assessment, I believe we have to acknowledge the place that statistics have in national conversations about writing, and our assessments need to speak back with numbers of our own. For the foreseeable future, if we cannot mount counterarguments grounded in our own responsibly designed assessments, then the commercial assessments will continue to dominate as they did in the twentieth century. This power shift in the conversation has only begun in this decade. We have attained a voice in a conversation from which we were previously excluded. Our presence in the conversation may—*may*—allow us, in time, to change the face of writing assessment. However, ignoring the widely accepted bases for responsible assessments will not advance our cause. Instead, Lynne's concept of "meaningfulness" as a condition of responsible assessment does help articulate for the public the same statements that Huot and others advance within the scholarly community: that the kinds of writing we assess need to be meaningful to the writers.

Meaningfulness helps the classroom talk back to the commercial assessments, to begin the process of change by helping the public understand the challenges students and teachers face in classrooms, to assert the authority that comes from our own expertise. Bob Broad has been an important voice in taking back control over important aspects of assessment and in framing discussions about standards in ways that are friendly to the writing classroom. Broad's *What We Really Value* (2003) begins a look at the ways the commercial assessment establishment has influenced the making of rubrics. While Elliot begins *On a Scale* with a sense of the hope a teacher like Katherine derived in 1913 from the newly published Hillegas scale, Broad points out that many widely disseminated rubrics, like the commercial assessments for which they guide scoring, have also become reductive. The ubiquitous "Six Traits" rubric, for example, emphasizes surface features of writing in four of its six traits, leaving only two traits for what the writer is trying to say, for what purpose, and to what audience, how the writing is organized, and other traits that have much more to do with the effectiveness of a piece of writing than surface features. Not that spelling, grammar, and mechanics do not matter, but even the most basic understanding of what constitutes good writing would not weight them as two-thirds of success. And the more robust, detailed, and locally generated rubrics that Broad endorses not only provide teachers with a useful tool for grading, but they also provide a far more useful support than "Six Traits" kinds of rubrics for curriculum development, for constructing assignments, for talking with students about their writing, and for responding to and grading student writing.

Broad, et al. extend and enrich that argument in *Organic Writing Assessment: Dynamic Criteria Mapping in Action*. Eight authors in this edited collection present their institutions' experience with Dynamic Criteria Mapping (DCM), complete with practical examples of applications of DCM and key documents—criteria maps and rubrics, of course, as well as surveys, training materials, etc. The collection is important for at least two reasons. First, it documents the ability of DCM to accommodate the additional complexity of local assessments. Authentic assessments are "messy" in a good way, and that messiness challenges the tight controls of more reductive assessment methodologies. The examples here demonstrate that DCM allows for local assessments tailored to local curriculum and to local programmatic and institutional needs, yet sufficiently rigorous as to yield outcomes that are comparable with other local assessments. In other words, DCM provides a practical alternative to "one size fits all" assessments. Second, the values expressed in these maps and rubrics come from the classrooms in these eight institutions and speak to the larger context of a national conversation about writing assessment—essentially reversing the direction of impetus of the past century or so, beginning with Hillegas's rubric, in which the national context dictated what happened in classrooms. Portfolio-based assessment implies that the reverse is possible; DCM shows a system for enacting that reversal.

Maja Wilson's *Rethinking Rubrics in Writing Assessment* tells something of the same story from the standpoint of a secondary English teacher. Wilson's core argument is that "our assessments should be based on the same assumptions as our pedagogy" (52). Wilson documents a struggle with rubrics—and here the notorious "Six Traits" rubric demonstrates its chokehold on secondary English teachers. Elliot's 2004 version of Katherine strives to help her students understand the rubrics being used to rate their writing, downloading rubrics and writing samples from the Internet. Wilson unveils the extreme limitations of that move, illustrating in her own practice how such materials limit the teaching of writing in ways that diminish writing itself to the small portion of the construct that six-trait rubrics and timed essay tests can reach. Instead, Wilson struggles to give up rubrics in favor of making writing meaningful to her students, trusting that engaging in meaningful writing will lead students to develop the skills needed to pass the state-mandated tests. Her work points out the basic discord between the state tests, which view writing as a discrete set of skills, and a sound writing curriculum that recognizes that writing is far more than a set of skills. From the classroom, Wilson talks back to large-scale testing, clarifying the ways that such testing mounts huge obstacles to learning to write in the fuller sense. Writing, as a full construct, cannot be captured on a rubric. Only a reductive sense of writing can be judged in that way. Given that fact, we have a responsibility to develop rubrics that are as robust and non-reductive as possible, following the DCM model.

As writing moves into electronic environments, the construct becomes more, not less complex, raising Broad's and Wilson's arguments to an even higher plane. E-mail, social networking spaces, websites, multimodal compositions, all these and more engage writers in more complex ways than mere words on paper. Michael Neal takes on this scenario of writing's future in *Writing Assessment and the Revolution in Digital Texts and Technologies*, a volume in Columbia University Teachers College's Language and Literacy series. Neal echoes Broad's view, in *What We Really Value*, that modern writing assessment has gone astray. As Broad writes, "Rather than seek to understand and carefully map out the swampy, rocky, densely forested terrain of writing assessment found lying before them, they [the large-scale commercial testing corporations] quickly moved to simplify and standardize it" (5) which, Neal observes, "they did by defining seven characteristics of writing that could be isolated and measured" (63). In describing writing assessment *as* a technology, Neal provides not so much a history as an overview of the ways that the current technology, constructed by agencies outside the teaching enterprise, reduces the construct *writing* to the point that teachers and learners of writing can no longer recognize the construct being tested *as* writing. Looking to the more recent past, Neal discusses paper-based and electronic portfolios as complicating that process, though he also provides descriptions of the ways commercially available eportfolio systems actually reduce the possibilities for students to exhibit electronic texts—an irony of epic proportions, and one that completely disqualifies such systems from being legitimate eportfolios in much the same way as reductive assessments like COMPASS cannot meet the validity standards to qualify as systems that test writing. Neal's solution is, in part, a common trope among writing teachers who work with new technologies: rather than wait for others to design the technologies for future writing assessment, teachers need to become involved in the design and construction of these spaces. That many in the profession are already participating in that way seems to have escaped Neal's attention, as he does not mention Texas Tech's ICON system, or the University of Georgia's EMMA; nor does he provide much information on the locally grown eportfolio systems coming out of Barbara Cambridge and Yancey's eportfolio initiatives or Trent Batson's Association for Authentic, Experiential, and Evidence-Based Learning. Still, Neal's volume provides a useful look at the ways new technologies—and in particular new genres of writing in electronic spaces—complicate the construct *writing* and, in turn, challenge existing models for assessing writing.

Overall, this decade of the conversation on writing assessment provides a great deal of encouragement and hope about the future. The commercial assessment industry is engaged in a race to the bottom as it promotes tests that are less and less valid—so much so that the general public is beginning to see the inadequacy of their tests, as evidenced by states such as Oregon and Washington, which have de-emphasized or eliminated such tests. Teachers, scholars, and administrators of writing can stop this devolution by affirming a common thread among the voices represented above: that "our assessments should be based on the same assumptions as our pedagogy" (Wilson 52; echoed in Huot; Neal; O'Neill, et al.; Adler-Kassner and O'Neill; and Broad). If we are at a tipping point in the conversation, we have arrived there by understanding more clearly what we are about when we teach writing. Beginning with Janet Emig's *Composing Processes of 12th Graders*, our field has pushed writing theory forward. Through the decades since, our understanding of the construct *writing* has grown more sophisticated, more complex, more substantiated, and more complete. As that theoretical framework has advanced, so have the assessments *we* have designed. Therefore, we now have a set of practical alternatives to what is happening on the commercial side. As late as 1943, John Stalnaker, writing for the CEEB, wrote,

> The type of test so highly valued by teachers of English, which requires the candidate to write a theme or essay, is not a worthwhile testing device. Whether or not the writing of essays as a means of teaching writing deserves the place it has in the secondary school curriculum may be equally questioned Eventually, it is hoped, sufficient evidence may be accumulated to outlaw forever the "write-a-theme-on"...type of examination. qtd. in O'Neill, et al. 20).

While we can join Stalnaker in his final wish, we do so for different reasons. In the years since Stalnaker, the fields of Rhetoric and Composition, WAC, Cognitive Psychology, and Education have advanced the importance of writing throughout school and university curricula, and of course no one today would question the need for students to write in order to improve their writing, or to evaluate their writing abilities. The CEEB tests, which in 1943 had devolved to indirect tests of grammar and usage, vocabulary, analogies, etc, were that era's race to the bottom—Stalnaker was responding to teachers' objections over the elimination of writing from the CEEB's tests. That the CEEB succeeded in 1943 shows how little regarded were the opinions of teachers. Today, our knowledge of the construct has grown so that no one can responsibly suggest that a writing assessment should not involve writing. Today's devolution toward less and less valid tests of writing ability—including machine scoring of students' writing—occurs in a different context. Today, we know that a major reason timed essay tests produce bad writing is that they ask students to write in circumstances that are not conducive to good writing. And we know that focusing on the deficits and errors in those low-validity, context-poor samples leads to curricula that are focused on deficit and error, and are therefore not sufficient to support students' efforts to become better writers. Thus, as this review of a decade of writing assessment scholarship reveals, we are ready with practical alternatives, assessment instruments that meet the unified standard of validity, that provide far more useful information than merely a ranking or a placement, and that are grounded in a much more advanced understanding of what writing is and of what is required to further the cause of improving writing instruction. Part of that progress is the need for better assessments, and the past decade is evidence that the conversation is tipping in that direction.

WORKS CITED

Anson, Chris, Les Perelman, Maya Poe, and Nancy Sommers. "Symposium: Assessment." *College Composition and Communication* 60.1 (2008): 113-164. Print.

Bailey, Richard W. and Robin Melanie Fosheim. *Literacy for Life: The Demand for Reading and Writing.* New York: MLA, 1983. Print.

Belanoff, Pat and Peter Elbow. "Using Portfolios to Increase Collaboration and Community in a Writing Program." *WPA:Writing Program Administration* 9 (Spring 1986): 27-39. Print.

Broad, Bob. *What We Really Value: Beyond Rubrics in Teaching and Assessing Writing.* Logan: Utah State UP, 2003. Print.

Calfee, Robert and Pamela Perfumo. *Writing Portfolios in the Classroom: Policy and Practice, Promise and Peril.* Mahwah: Erlbaum, 1996. Print.

Cambridge, Barbara, Susan Kahn, Daniel P. Tompkins, and Kathleen Blake Yancey, eds. *Electronic Portfolios: Emerging Practices in Student, Faculty, and Institutional Learning.* Washington, DC: American Association for Higher Education, 2001.Print.

Condon, William. "Looking Beyond Judging and Ranking: Writing Assessment as a Generative Practice." *Assessing Writing* 14.3 (2009): 141-156. Print.

Cronbach, Lee J. "Five Perspectives on Validity Argument." *Test Validity.* Ed. Howard Wainer and Henry Braun. Hillsdale: Erlbaum, 1988. 3-17. Print.

Daiker, Donald A., Jeffrey Sommers, Gail Stygall, and Laurel Black. *The Best of Miami's Portfolios.* Oxford: Miami U, 1990. Print.

Emig, Janet. *Composing Processes of Twelfth Graders.* Urbana: NCTE, 1971.

Gallagher, Chris W. "At the Precipice of Speech: English Studies, Science, and Policy (Ir)relevancy." *College Composition and Communication* 73 (2010): 1, 73-90. Print.

Gould, Stephen Jay. *The Mismeasure of Man.* New York: Norton, 1996. Print.

Hamp-Lyons, Liz and William Condon. *Assessing the Portfolio: Principles for Practice, Theory, and Research.* Cresskill: Hampton P, 2000. Print.

Haswell, Richard. "The Two-Tier Rating System: The Need for Ongoing Change." *Beyond Outcomes: Assessment and Instruction Within a University Writing Program.* Ed. Richard Haswell. Westport: Ablex, 2001, 39-52. Print.

Huot, Brian "Toward a New Theory of Writing Assessment." *CCC* 47 (1996); 549-66. Print.

Messick, Samuel. "Validity." *Educational Measurement.* Ed. R.L. Linn._3rd ed. New York: Macmillan, 1989. 13-103. Print.

Moss, Pamela. "Can There be Validity Without Reliability?" *Educational Researcher* 23.4 (1994): 5-12. Print.

Nye, David E. "Technological Prediction: A Promethean Problem." *Technological Visions: The Hopes and Fears that Shape New Technologies.* Ed. Marita Sturken, Douglas Thomas, and Sandra J. Ball-Rokeach. Philadelphia: Temple UP, 2004. 159-176. Print.

Sacks, Peter. *Standardized Minds: The High Price of America's Testing Culture and What We Can Do to Change It.* Cambridge: Perseus, 1999. Print.

Shermis, Mark and Jill Burstein, eds. *Automated Essay Scoring: A Cross-disciplinary Perspective.* London: Routledge, 2002. Print.

Smith, William L. "The Importance of Teacher Knowledge in College Composition Placement Testing." *Reading Empirical Research Studies: The Rhetoric of Research.* Ed. John R. Hayes. Norwood: Ablex, 1992. 289-316. Print.

Commission Appointed by Secretary of Education Margaret Spellings U.S. Department of Education. *A Test of Leadership: Charting the Future of U.S. Higher Education,* 2006. Web. http://www2.ed.gov/about/bdscomm/list/hied-future/reports.html

Villanueva, Victor, ed. *Cross-Talk in Comp Theory: A Reader.* 2nd ed. Urbana: NCTE, 2003. Print.

White, Edward M. *Assigning, Responding, Evaluating.* 4th ed. New York: Bedford, 2007. Print.

-----. "The Opening of the Modern Era of Writing Assessment: A Narrative." *College English* 63:3 (2001): 306-320. Print.

Willard-Traub, Margaret, Emily Decker, Rebecca Reed, and Jerome Johnston. "The Development of Large-Scale Portfolio Placement Assessment at the University of Michigan: 1992-1998." *Assessing Writing* 6.1 (1999): 41-84. Print.

Williamson, Michael M. and Brian Huot, eds. *Validating Holistic Scoring: Theoretical and Empirical Foundations.* Cresskill: Hampton P, 1993. Print.

Yancey, Kathleen Blake. "Looking Back as We Look Forward: Historicizing Writing Assessment." *CCC* 50 (1999): 483-503. Print.

Contributors to *WPA 34.2*

Pamela Bedore is an assistant professor of English and the writing coordinator for the Avery Point campus at the University of Connecticut, where she teaches courses in American literature, popular literature, and the teaching of writing. Her research interests include peer review, library-writing center collaborations, detective fiction, and science fiction. Recent publications have appeared in *Writing Lab Newsletter*, *Academic Exchange Quarterly*, and *Studies in Popular Culture*, and she is currently working on a study of nineteenth-century detective dime novels, tracing the ways in which these ephemeral texts contributed substantially to much later developments in detective fiction.

Bill Condon is Professor of English at Washington State University. He has been a Writing Program Administrator at a variety of institutions—the University of Oklahoma, Arkansas Tech University, the University of Michigan, and WSU. Co-author of *Writing the Information Superhighway* and *Assessing the Portfolio: Principles for Theory, Practice, and Research*, he has published about writing assessment, WAC, program evaluation, and computers and writing. His teaching interests include writing assessment; theory and practice of teaching college composition; and any courses in which he can apply the innovative uses of assessment and computer-enhanced pedagogy that he has encountered over the years.

Collin Lamont Craig teaches rhetoric and composition at Wake Forest University. His research explores African American traditions of identity formation, cultural rhetorics, and writing program administration. His broad project is to investigate how African American identity and ideology work as rhetorical production. He is also interested in how students of color construct their literate lives in higher education. Currently, he is researching how black college males develop critical literacies to assess microinstitutional infrastructures that position them as learners in the academy. Craig writes, works out, and listens to music by Erykah Badu, Mos Def, and Common in his spare time.

Sue Doe, Assistant Professor of English at Colorado State University (CSU), directs a campus-wide writing integration effort and studies faculty development and WAC. She taught off the tenure track for over two decades before going on the tenure-track at CSU and now conducts research about labor issues and rhetorics. She helped to author the new NCTE position statement on contingent labor working conditions (http://www.ncte.

org/positions/statements/contingent_faculty) and recently co-edited (with Mike Palmquist) the special issue of *College English* (March 2011) dedicated to contingent faculty issues. She represents NCTE on the Coalition of the Academic Workforce and serves on the Executive Committee of the MLA Part-Time Discussion Group.

Peter Elbow is Professor of English Emeritus at UMass Amherst. He directed the Writing Program there and at SUNY Stony Brook, and taught at M.I.T., Franconia College, and Evergreen State College. He has written widely on writing and teaching writing. CEE gave him the James Britton Award for his Everyone Can Write; NCTE gave him the James Squire Award for his "lasting intellectual contribution"; in 2007 CCCC gave him the Exemplar Award. Oxford will bring out his new book in the fall: *Vernacular Eloquence: What Speech Can Bring to Writing*.

Claire Coleman Lamonica is currently the associate director of the Center for Teaching, Learning & Technology at Illinois State University, where she previously served as associate director of writing programs (1998-2005) and coordinator of student teaching for the English Department (2005-06). She has been teaching writing and the teaching of writing at the secondary, community college, and university levels since 1975 and is the author or co-author of a dozen articles related to the teaching of writing. She appreciates the opportunity to re-join the Council's conversation about teacher preparation and development.

Margaret Lowry is Director of First-Year English at the University of Texas at Arlington. Lowry teaches undergraduate courses in composition, American literature, and Women's Studies, and graduate-level teacher preparation courses. Her current scholarly interests include the role of common reading texts in first-year composition and the work of Ruth Millett, a nationally syndicated columnist from 1938-1968.

Brian O'Sullivan is an Assistant Professor of English and Director of the Writing Center at St. Mary's College of Maryland. He teaches courses in basic writing, advanced composition, peer tutoring, parody and intertextuality, the rhetoric of politics, literary theory, and twentieth-century literature. His scholarly interests include the rhetoric of laughter, the relationship between literary modernism and the teaching of writing, and collaborative assessment.

Mike Palmquist is Associate Vice Provost for Learning and Teaching, Professor of English, and University Distinguished Teaching Scholar at

Colorado State University, where he directs the University's Institute for Learning and Teaching. His scholarly interests include writing across the curriculum, the effects of computer and network technologies on writing instruction, and new approaches to scholarly publishing.

Staci Perryman-Clark is Assistant Professor of English-Rhetoric and Writing Studies and Director of First-Year Writing at Western Michigan University, where she teaches graduate courses in methods for teaching college writing and composition theory. She is the 2008 recipient of the CCCC Scholars for the Dream award. She publishes on Afrocentric curriculum design, black women's intellectual traditions, and culturally relevant pedagogy.

Bradley Peters is Professor of English and coordinator of Writing Across the Curriculum at Northern Illinois University. He teaches courses in rhetoric and writing pedagogy. His recent publications have focused on assessment and medieval rhetoric. He is grateful to the high school colleagues with whom he consulted, including Deb Spears, Lynn Graczyk, David Carson, and Nancy Cleburn. He co-edits, with Joonna Trapp, the *Journal of the Assembly for Expanded Perspectives on Learning* (JAEPL).

Shirley K Rose is Professor of English and Director of Writing Programs at Arizona State University. She is a Past President of the Council of Writing Program Administrators. She regularly teaches graduate courses in writing program administration and has published numerous articles on writing pedagogy and on issues in archival research and practice. With Irwin Weiser, she has edited three collections on the intellectual work of writing program administration, including *The WPA as Researcher, The Writing Program Administrator as Theorist,* and *Going Public: What Writing Programs Learn from Engagement.* She and Professor Weiser will co-lead the 2011 WPA Summer Workshop in Baton Rouge.

Amy Rupiper Taggart is Associate Professor of English and Director of First-Year Writing at North Dakota State University. Her research focuses on issues in composition pedagogy, including community engagement practices, formative assessment, and student and teacher reflection. She recently co-authored *Research Matters* with Rebecca Moore Howard and is working on a second edition of the *Guide to Composition Pedagogies* with Kurt Schick and H. Brooke Hessler. Her article with Hessler on formative assessment and student reflection recently appeared in the *International Journal for the Scholarship of Teaching and Learning.*

Announcements

Call for Proposals – 2011 Graduate Research Network

The **Graduate Research Network (GRN)** invites proposals for its 2011 workshop, May 19, 2011, at the Computers and Writing Conference hosted by the University of Michigan. The C&W Graduate Research Network is an all-day pre-conference event, open to all registered conference participants at no charge. Roundtable discussions group those with similar interests and discussion leaders who facilitate discussion and offer suggestions for developing research projects and for finding suitable venues for publication. We encourage anyone interested or involved in graduate education and scholarship—students, professors, mentors, and interested others—to participate in this important event. The GRN welcomes those pursuing work at any stage, from those just beginning to consider ideas to those whose projects are ready to pursue publication. Participants are also invited to apply for travel funding through the CW/GRN Travel Grant Fund. Deadline for submissions is April 25, 2011. For more information or to submit a proposal, visit our Web site at http://class.georgiasouthern.edu/writling/GRN/2011/index.html or email jwalker@georgiasouthern.edu.

Brian Fallon Receives 2010 NCPTW Maxwell Leadership Award

Dr. Brian Fallon, Director of the Writing Studio at the Fashion Institute of Technology, has won the 2010 Ron Maxwell Award for Distinguished Leadership in Promoting the Collaborative Learning Practices of Peer Tutors in Writing. The award was presented November 6 in Baltimore, MD, at the 27th annual National Conference on Peer Tutoring in Writing (NCPTW) held jointly this year with the 10th conference of the International Writing Centers Association.

The award recognizes a professional within the NCPTW organization for dedication to and leadership in collaborative learning in writing centers, for aiding students in together taking on more responsibility for their learning, and, thus, for promoting the work of peer tutors. Its presentation also denotes extraordinary service to the evolution of the conference organization.

Fallon has been a leader in the organization since he was an undergraduate student. He has continued his contributions of hard work and sharp thinking throughout his graduate career and now into his professional work as an assistant professor. As one member of the award committee wrote, "he has been active in all three capacities we value—undergraduate, graduate, and director. He embodies our collaborative learning ideals and carries them forward. And what a model he is!"

BEDFORD/ST. MARTIN'S

you get more | bedfordstmartins.com

A writer's handbook—reimagined

writershelp.com

Writer's Help
A Bedford/St. Martin's
Online Handbook

Diana Hacker, Stephen A. Bernhardt, and **Nancy Sommers**

Writer's Help lives online because your students do. It responds to searches by students who may—or may not—know standard composition terminology. And students get reliable, class-tested advice from our best-selling Hacker handbooks. Informed by testing with 1,600 student writers, powered by a search engine that recognizes student language, and based on the content teachers trust, *Writer's Help* is a robust new handbook that closes the gap between *search* and *find*.

What do you need for class today?

We want to make sure you're the first to hear about the things we do to help teachers: resources for professional development and the classroom, workshops, and symposia.

Sign up for updates and we'll be sure to send you two of our latest:

A brand new sourcebook, *Writing and Community Engagement*, by Thomas Deans, Barbara Roswell, and Adrian J. Wurr

Our forthcoming report, *How Has Composition Changed?*, based on a comparative survey of over 3,000 writing teachers

SIGN UP FOR NEWS.

bedfordstmartins.com/englishupdates

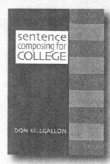

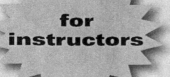

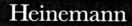

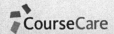

CPSIA information can be obtained at www.ICGtesting.com
259836BV00002B/2/P

9 781602 352315